P9-BYZ-585

NO LONGER PROPERTY OF
YAKIMA VALLEY LIBRARIES

STAR TREK

THE COLLECTIBLES

©2008 by Steve Kelley

Published by

krause publications
An Imprint of F+W Publications

700 East State Street • Iola, WI 54990-0001
715-445-2214 • 888-457-2873
www.krausebooks.com

Our toll-free number to place an order or obtain
a free catalog is (800) 258-0929.

All rights reserved. No portion of this publication may be reproduced
or transmitted in any form or by any means, electronic or mechanical,
including photocopy, recording, or any information storage and
retrieval system, without permission in writing from the publisher,
except by a reviewer who may quote brief passages in a critical article
or review to be printed in a magazine or newspaper, or electronically
transmitted on radio, television, or the Internet.

Library of Congress Control Number: 2008925111
ISBN-13: 978-0-89689-637-6
ISBN-10: 0-89689-637-4

Cover Design by Tom Nelson
Designed by Rachael Knier
Edited by Karen O'Brien, Mary Sieber, and Kristine Manty

Printed in China

STAR TREK

THE COLLECTIBLES

Steve Kelley

Acknowledgments

I want to thank my parents, Russell and Susan, for the many great years I had growing up and for helping me to become who I am today. I have so many wonderful childhood memories with many of those, of course, involving *Star Trek*. I can't begin to tell you how much your love and support all of these years has meant to me.

I want to thank my sister, Sharon, for all of those years growing up when you tolerated your younger brother being a Trekkie.

I want to thank my three wonderful kids, Stephen, Tarrah, and Jordan, for your love and support and for enjoying *Star Trek* with me.

I especially want to thank my wife, Alayne, for the idea that I should be the one to author the next collectibles book. Your love and encouragement, especially in those last few months as the deadlines came due, really helped me stay on task and finish.

Thanks also go to Peg Pearson and Joe Dukett for being such great friends and for help with those last-minute retakes.

Of course the book would not be as complete as it is without all of the expert help from my youngest son, Jordan, who, among other things, helped to locate some of my items for re-shooting and for just being an all around Trek expert in my absence when it was needed. Thanks Jordan.

I also want to thank all of the people at Krause Publications, who were involved in helping to make this book possible. I especially want to thank Paul Kennedy for giving me a chance, and Karen O'Brien and the rest of the KP staff for making my words and images look amazing in print.

My oldest son, Stephen, and daughter, Tarrah, "on set" in a full-size mock-up of the Enterprise bridge that I built in our basement in 1993.

My youngest son, Jordan, and Hobbs. Jordan is the most Trekkie of my children.

This is just part of the author's massive collection of everything Star Trek-related.

About the Foreword

In the very early process of creating this book, I was asked who was going to write the foreword. I attempted to reach former *Star Trek* cast members to see if I could convince one of them to write it. Then, during the process of my constant efforts to continue to add items to my collection, I came across an auction on eBay for a bottle of Dilithium Crystals taken from a large cluster used in the show. It was being sold from the private collection of the James "Scotty" Doohan family (please see page 190).

What makes this particular collectible extra special is the fact that I was able to actually communicate with the seller, Chris Doohan. It was then I realized that of all the possibilities of who could write the foreword, having the son of *Star Trek's* "Scotty" write it would be the ultimate honor.

Here is a picture of James Doohan with twin sons, Montgomery (Monty), left, and Chris as extras on the set of *Star Trek: The Motion Picture.*

I was excited to get a reply to my e-mail asking if Chris would be willing to write a foreword, and was absolutely thrilled when I read: "Steve, I would be happy to write a foreword for your book. Just give me details such as content and length of foreword. Chris"

And the rest, as they say, is history. The amazing behind-the-scenes story that Chris wrote for the foreword has become one of my favorite parts of this book.

Thanks again, Chris!

Chris Doohan, his daughter, Brittany, and his dad, James Doohan, who was best known to *Star Trek* fans as "Scotty" (Montgomery Scott).

Chris Doohan, his dad, James Doohan, and an unidentified woman.

Foreword

As the son of James Doohan, "Scotty" from the original *Star Trek* series, I have first-hand knowledge of how *Star Trek* and its vision of a better future has changed the world. The series, which was created by a true visionary, Gene Roddenberry, has uplifted our vision of what might be possible and gave us a positive vision of what the future may hold.

As a kid, I grew up with Tribbles and *Star Trek* uniforms scattered around the house but had no idea that they would become as valuable as they are today. The ingenious devices that seemed like science fiction back in the late 1960s are now common devices that we use in our everyday lives. The communicator that Captain Kirk used to hail Scotty is now a common cell phone. The tricorder that we all wished we had back then is now a hand-held computer or PDA.

Many of the props and collectibles from this iconic franchise are prized by Trekkers and Trekkies alike, and are even sought after by non-science fiction fans for their investment potential. From the pricey original props like phasers and uniforms, to scripts, autographs, Dilithium Crystals, and ship models, there seems to be something for every fan and every budget. With few exceptions, *Star Trek* memorabilia has become one of most valued and most sought-after entertainment collectibles in the world, and with the ongoing franchise still producing movies and conventions, the series' prolific history shows no signs of slowing down.

A little story: When my twin brother and I were 6 or 7 years old, my dad took us to the "Trouble with Tribbles" sound stage. He was called on set, so he put us in the shuttlecraft to play and "stay out of trouble." Well, we played for a little while, but being the inquisitive twin boys that we were, we had to wander. We opened the shuttlecraft door and escaped. We knew what studio my dad was in, so we avoided it at all costs. If my dad knew we were out and about, he would have been really angry. We entered one of the studios and started playing in the ship's hallways and even sat in the captain's chair on the bridge. We then decided to snoop around to see what was in the nooks and crannies. One of the rooms had these strange-looking cabinets that were very high (for a 7-year-old) and angled. Of course, we had to see what was in them. My brother got on my shoulders and slid it open. Just then, about 200 (or more) Tribbles fell on our heads. It scared the heck out of us! Not only because it freaked us out, but because we knew that we would be in a heaping load of Tribble trouble if my dad found out. We ran as fast as we could back to the shuttle and closed the door behind us. Not long after that, my dad arrived to find his angelic twins still in the safe little shuttlecraft where we were no Tribble at all.

Well, my father gave us both a few Tribbles and even a Dilithium Crystal or two. If I had known the future value of these amazing collectibles, I would have treasured them and kept them locked up for safekeeping. Instead, we gave our Tribbles haircuts and scribbled endlessly with crayon on all my father's scripts.

Chris Doohan

Contents

Values Given Within this Book

The two prices or values for each item listed in *Star Trek: The Collectibles* are based on the following:

A two-tier pricing system is based on the averages of "mint to near mint out-of-the-box/packaging" and "mint to near mint in-the-box/packaging."

Using these two prices, a collector, buyer or seller can then determine the worth of a collectible that may fall in between the mint out of package and mint in package, or below the mint out of package. For example, the pricing for a Mego Cheron is priced at $100 mint to near mint out of the package and $200 for mint to near mint in the package.

A carded Cheron that is mint in the carded package will keep its value of $100, but if in this example the card and blister are not mint, with, say, the bubble having a crack and the card with some damage, that figure would be valued based on the two-tier pricing at or around $150. The figure is easily worth the $100 mint but loose value, yet the in-package value loses half of its $200 for being in non-mint condition.

If the Cheron is loose but not mint, with say some black dye leakage on the white fabric outfit and is also missing its black and white boots, then that figure's value based on the two-tier pricing would be at or around $50, about half of its mint to near-mint loose out of the carded package condition price.

Cheron, series one Alien, Mego, 1975. A complete listing for this figure is on P. 17.

If the figure was loose with little to no black dye leakage and included the boots, but the outfit was not bright and clean, then the figure's value based on the two-tier pricing would be around $75.

The book as a whole is organized alphabetically by items, and each section is listed alphabetically by company/manufacturers that made them.

Star Trek Lives

"Space...the final frontier. These are the voyages of the Starship Enterprise. Its five-year mission: to explore strange new worlds, to seek out new life and new civilizations, to boldly go where no man has gone before!"

With these now-famous words during its opening credits, *Star Trek* debuted on NBC television on Sept. 8, 1966.

Growing up in a small town in Plainfield, NH, I spent many hours of my childhood watching *Star Trek* with my dad. Back in the late 1960s and early 1970s, black and white TVs were still pretty common and we relied on an antenna, as many people did, that sat on the roof of our house and brought in a few channels. I would come home from school and sit down at 3 p.m. to watch this awesome new show and as soon as my dad walked in the door from work at about 3:20 p.m., I was asking if he could climb up on the roof and turn the antennae to try and get the channel in better. As soon as he turned it enough, he sat down with me and we would finish watching the show. Over the years, things changed: our TV got bigger and was color and we were able to get more stations a bit better, but one thing that didn't change was my dad and I always trying to make time to watch *Star Trek* together.

Amazingly, the adventures of Captain James T. Kirk, First Officer Mr. Spock, Dr. Leonard "Bones" McCoy and the rest of the Enterprise crew never really became a ratings success during its original three-year run.

After making it through two seasons, *Star Trek* was cancelled due to lackluster ratings. But, unprecedented in the history of television, cancellation was averted thanks to a huge fan letter-writing campaign that caused network executives to reverse their decision and renew *Star Trek* for a third season. Unfortunately, NBC put the show on at a time later at night when fewer people watched and it was sadly cancelled again after its third season and the last episode, "Turnabout Intruder," aired on June 3, 1969.

But thanks to that letter-writing campaign, just enough *Star Trek* episodes aired in the third season to allow it to be marketed into syndication, where it flourished and became a ratings phenomenon. Thanks to local television stations that began airing it in more viewer-friendly time slots, it became popular in reruns and a new fan following developed. When the first Star Trek convention was held, the promoters expected only a few hundred fans to attend—they were shocked when thousands arrived.

With its growing popularity, an animated *Star Trek* series produced by Filmation was announced to air on NBC. The animated Saturday-morning series ran for two seasons, and twenty-two half-hour episodes aired from 1973 to 1974. Most of the original *Star Trek* cast performed the voices of their characters, and many original series' writers also came on board. Their efforts won *Star Trek* its first Emmy award on May 15, 1975.

Gene Roddenberry, using the growing popularity of his creation, began marketing to studio execs a possible new *Star Trek* series called *Star Trek: Phase Two*, picking up where the first series left off, with another five-year mission. Paramount agreed based on the fact it wanted to launch a new television network and have *Star Trek* be its anchor show. Then two things happened: First, on May 25, 1977, a movie called *Star Wars* premiered, becoming one of the highest-grossing films of all time. Second, as *Phase Two* pre-production finished and work was scheduled to begin on the feature-length pilot, "In Thy Image," the studio's network deal fell through. With every television and movie studio wanting to create their own *Star Wars*, Paramount chose to turn the pilot into a full-length feature film, *Star Trek: The Motion Picture*. Gene Roddenberry, thrilled with the prospect of his creation becoming a major motion picture, quickly went to work on a new script for the big screen.

On Dec. 7th 1979, *Star Trek: The Motion Picture* premiered and did well enough for Paramount to green light a sequel. With the release and more mainstream success of *Star Trek II: The Wrath of Khan*, the *Star Trek* movie franchise and many future television spin-offs were assured, including *Star Trek: The Next Generation*, *Star Trek: Deep Space Nine*, *Star Trek: Voyager*, and *Star Trek: Enterprise*.

Star Trek has made an indelible impression on popular culture—no small achievement for a science fiction show. Perhaps more impressive is the sheer quantity of merchandise licenses the franchise has generated in forty years.

The pictures in this book are all taken from my own large and cherished collection. I can remember as a kid each summer when my family would go to Kennebunkport, ME, for vacation. I was excited not only to go to the beach, but also because we would take a drive further north to Portland to the big mall. It was there that I obtained many of my first *Star Trek* items that began my collection. I would save up my money from after Christmas until vacation so I could buy as many cool items as I could afford. Some of the items I found were beach towels, flashlight phasers, Mego action figures, kites, books and more.

I also have fond memories of many Christmas mornings and birthdays when I would unwrap a present or two and happily find some incredible toy to add to my collection. Even back then, I was always careful with opening the packages. The Mego action figures, for example, had such great packaging and artwork that I wanted to keep them looking as great as they did the day I purchased them. I would carefully open the blister bubble on one side so as to not rip the package, which not only allowed me to remove the figure while keeping the package as a display item, but also allowed me to then carefully place the figure back in the package for protection and to display it on shelves in my bedroom looking just like it was still in the store.

Since they have a Trekkie for a dad, my own children have fond memories of also watching *Star Trek* on TV and going to the movies over the years with their grandfather and me. My oldest son, Stephen, remembers having a blue *The Next Generation* lunch box and making a *Star Trek* video with some of his friends at his 9th birthday party. My daughter, Tarrah, remembers

the good and the not so good like when I took over part of the house with my growing collection and she would have to walk her friends by this massive "museum" to get to her room on the other end.

Stephen and Tarrah are both moving on to college and work and sadly we don't get as much time right now to do a lot together, but my youngest son, Jordan, and I still share a lot of *Star Trek* from time to time and he especially enjoys the ships and space battles, but he says one of the main reasons he loves *Star Trek* is because his dad loves it and it's something we get to do together.

It is this younger generation that will carry on the *Star Trek* torch, whether it's a casual fan like Stephen and Tarrah or the more diehard fan like Jordan.

I hope you enjoy this book as much as I enjoyed creating it.

Live Long and Prosper.
Steve Kelley

Action Figures

MEGO, 1974

Mego was the first company to make Star Trek action figures, and its innovations set the standard for all action figures that have followed.

The first series or "wave" of 8" carded Mego figures were released in 1974. These figures were fully articulated and included cloth replicas of their respective uniforms with miniature accessories. Most of the figures display excellent likenesses of the TV characters they represented. The Captain Kirk and Spock versions are considered the most accurate.

Some figures were rushed to market with little attention to detail in their likenesses, and other figures were obvious resculpts of current offerings in the Mego toy line. For example, The Gorn was nothing more than a Klingon body complete with red phaser and communicator, but with a lizard head molded in brown from Mego's World's Greatest Super Heroes line.

In total, fourteen figures were made in three different series or waves, and released between 1974 and 1978.

The first series can actually be broken down into two versions; "five face" and "six face." The first release consisted of five members of the Enterprise crew and the Klingon. The "five face" cards were the first of the 8" figures to be released. They are called "five face" cards because the front and back of each card displays unique artwork of each of the first five character's heads against a blue background. Uhura was released soon after, and the "six face" carded figures became the more common and easier to find figures in the Mego line. The back of the "six face" cards features advertisements for two other Mego toys: the Enterprise playset, and the Communicators.

The second and third waves were the "Aliens" series. The Romulan is considered the rarest and so commands the highest prices. The Palitoy (UK) Alien versions are extremely rare and display different artwork from the U.S. versions.

It is worth noting that after demand dropped in the late 1970s, and as part of a special deal with Sears, Mego released a special Sears exclusive series of some of the first wave figures in 1979. The

easiest way to distinguish these figures from earlier releases is that the back of the card is blank. These are very hard to find and sometimes sell for double the value of a standard carded figure.

The field equipment accessories for the Enterprise crew figures were molded in blue plastic. The Klingon field equipment accessories were made of red plastic, which was also used for the Gorn and Romulan. All the belts were made of black plastic. The Uhura figure was never released in the UK by Palitoy.

MEGO, 1975

The first series of Star Trek figures, also called Type 1, have a 1974 date stamped on each body, but the series debuted in the 1975 Mego catalog.

Each of the Enterprise crew uniforms are detailed with a black neckband, one, two, or three gold foil rank stripes on each arm depending on rank, and a silver foil insignia on the chest. Though the gray backing for the silver foil was glued on to the shirt's fabric, the thin outer silver foil piece will usually come loose or fall off altogether over time, especially if the figure is loose and in played-with condition.

The Type 1 bodies used for male figures have black boots molded into the lower legs as a cost-saving design. The upper bodies are not as muscled, and the upper and lower bodies are strung together with elastic and held in place with metal rivets. The Klingon figure uses a standard bootless leg style Type 1 body.

The Type 2 body version of the Mego male figures is noticeably more muscular. Plastic pins replace metal rivets in the joints, and the upper and lower bodies are now strung together using a rubber band attachment with hooks. The crew member Type 2 bodies still have black boots molded into the lower legs, but some of the new Alien figures use a bootless design as the Type 1 Klingon figure has. Some of the bootless Type 2 bodies were molded in different colors depending on the character. (The smaller version of the Type 2 body used for the Alien Talos was also used for Mego's World's Greatest Super Heroes Teen Titans line-up.) Uhura's brown female body was the only female produced for the Mego Star Trek line.

Note: The British company Palitoy Bradgate (UK) was one of Mego's international partners and also produced Star Trek figures. The only real difference from the Mego version cards is the "Palitoy"

Loose WGSH Lizard, left, and Gorn, right, for comparison, Mego, 1975.

logo name added for a trademark. No currently accurate pricing is available for these, but you could easily estimate that since these are more rare, they will have a slightly higher value than the U.S. versions.

Note: Though the Uhura figure was released as the sixth and final figure in the first series, its item number suggests that it was meant to be the fourth in the series. Mego also seems to have skipped over number 6 as there is no carded figure produced with Item No. 51200/6 (possibly hinting to an unproduced seventh first series figure). The Klingon figure, along with the other five first series figures, were later made available through the Sears catalog and were shipped loose in catalog mailer boxes. The Klingon in the mailer box was issued Item No. 51200/6 which is interesting considering that all carded Klingons had the item number 51200/7.

The Sears catalog mailer box versions were available near the end of their run in 1978 and each loose figure came bagged in clear mailer bags and then packed in the plain white mailer boxes. The white catalog mailer boxes were sized so that the figure fit snuggly inside. The item number of the figure was stamped on the outside of the box along with other identifying production and manufacturer information.

Captain Kirk, First Series five face, Mego, 1975.

FIRST SERIES (FIVE FACE)

Capt. Kirk, No. 51200/1, yellow command shirt and black-cuffed pants. Accessories: Black belt with blue Communicator and Phaser.

    $150   **$250**

Mr. Spock, No. 51200/2, blue science division shirt and black-cuffed pants. Accessories: Black belt with blue Communicator, Phaser, and Tricorder.

    $150   **$250**

Dr. McCoy (Bones), No. 51200/3, blue science division shirt and black-cuffed pants. Accessories: Black belt with blue Communicator, Phaser, and Tricorder.

    $175   **$275**

Mr. Scott (Scotty), No. 51200/5, red engineering shirt and black-cuffed pants. Accessories: Black belt with blue Communicator and Phaser.

    $200   **$350**

Klingon, No. 51200/7, maroon and brown shirt with brown tights. Accessories: Black knee-high boots, black belt with red Communicator and Phaser.

    $175   **$275**

Mr. Spock, First Series five face, Mego, 1975.

The card back from Mego's First Series five face cards displays the first five characters the company released in 1975.

FIRST SERIES (SIX FACE)

Captain Kirk, First Series six face, Mego, 1975.

Capt. Kirk, No. 51200/1, yellow command shirt and black-cuffed pants. Accessories: Black belt with blue Communicator and Phaser.

Note: Capt. Kirk Six Face blister cards can be found with Capt. Kirk's name in either white or pink lettering.

$75 $150

The card back from Mego's more common First Series six face cards displays the Mego's Enterprise playset and Communicator toys, 1975.

Mr. Spock, First Series six face, Mego, 1975.

Dr. McCoy, First Series six face, Mego, 1975.

Mr. Spock, No. 51200/2, blue science division shirt and black-cuffed pants. Accessories: Black belt with blue Communicator, Phaser, and Tricorder.

Note: Mr. Spock Six Face blister cards can be found with Mr. Spock's name in either white or blue lettering.

$75   **$150**

Dr. McCoy (Bones), No. 51200/3, blue science division shirt and black-cuffed pants. Accessories: Black belt with blue Communicator, Phaser, and Tricorder.

Note: Dr. McCoy Six Face blister cards can be found with Dr. McCoy's name in either white or green lettering.

$75   **$150**

Mr. Scott (Scottie), First Series six face, Mego, 1975.

Lt. Uhura, First Series six face, Mego, 1975.

Klingon, First Series six face, Mego, 1975.

Mr. Scott (Scottie; note the different spelling), No. 51200/5, red engineering shirt and black-cuffed pants. Accessories: Black belt with blue Communicator and Phaser.

Note: Mr. Scott Six Face blister cards can be found with Mr. Scott's name in either white or blue lettering.

$100   **$175**

Lt. Uhura, No. 51200/4, red outfit, brown tights and black knee-high boots. Accessories: Black knee-high boots and blue Tricorder.

Note: Lt. Uhura Six Face blister cards can be found with Lt. Uhura's name in either white or purple lettering.

$75   **$150**

Klingon, No. 51200/7, maroon and brown shirt and brown tights. Accessories: Black knee-high boots, black belt with red Communicator and Phaser.

Note: Klingon Six Face blister cards can be found with the Klingon name in either white or yellow lettering.

$75   **$150**

SECOND SERIES: ALIEN SERIES ONE

The first Alien series was available with a black space background over an alien landscape on the front and referred to as a "10-back card." These blister cards displayed the faces of the first 10 figures on the back. Later, they were re-released on the rarer "14-back cards." These cards displayed a blue space background over the alien landscape and displayed the faces of the added Andorian, Mugato, Talos, and Romulan figures from the second Alien series.

The 10-back Alien cards also displayed eight of Mego's other Star Trek toys. Most interesting is the Tribble, a toy that sadly never went into production.

The 14-back cards had less room to display the other toys in Mego's Star Trek line-up.

Note: All four second series Alien figures, Cheron, The Gorn, The Keeper, and Neptunian were also available on a Palitoy Bradgate UK exclusive blister card package that was only available overseas. The blister card artwork is different, much more colorful, and extremely rare. Because I have not seen these for sale or listed in any recent book, I will not attempt to estimate their value.

Neptunian, series one Alien, Mego, 1975.

Neptunian, No. 51203/1, green and yellow outfit. Accessories: Fitted green plastic webbed feet and gloved webbed hands.

This is the only figure in the Mego Star Trek line that does not represent in look or name any actual character from the television show. Neptunians have been found with either green or yellow wings. Some collectors believe that the green material used for the wings simply "yellows" with age, while others believe that these are actually two different figure variations. The yellow wings seem to be found mostly on the "10-back" cards and the green wings mostly found on the "14-back" cards. Whichever is the case, the value on those with green wings is usually double of those with yellow wings especially since the "14-back" cards are the rarer of the two.

Neptunian with green wings on 10-back card.
$200   **$300**

Neptunian with yellow wings on 14-back card.
$100   **$200**

The Keeper, series one Alien, Mego, 1975.

The Keeper, No. 51203/2, white robe with light orange or dark orange trim. No accessories.

The Keeper looks more like the Balok puppet in *The Original Series* episode, "The Corbomite Maneuver," than the Talosian Keeper from the pilot episode, "The Cage," or two-part episode, "The Menagerie," it is apparently based on. Like the Neptunian, some collectors believe the light or dark orange trim exists because these were two variants, and not because of fading. The earlier 10-back cards seem to verify this since it has been well documented that the lighter orange trim is mostly found on the first series 10-back cards and the darker orange trim found mostly on the later 14-back cards.

Keeper with light orange trim on 10-back card.
$150   **$250**

Keeper with dark orange trim on 14-back card.
$200   **$300**

The Gorn, series one Alien, Mego, 1975.

The Gorn, No. 51203/3, same outfit as Klingon. Maroon and brown shirt and brown tights. Accessories: Black knee-high boots, black belt with red Communicator and Phaser.

The Gorn seems to have suffered the most from Mego's cost cutting measures. It was created using outfits and body parts from Mego's line, the World's Greatest Super Heroes, and its Planet of the Apes line. The head is a WGSH Lizard head cast in brown, and the body is a Soldier Ape piece from its POTA line. The outfit is the same as the Klingon including the brown tights, while the belt and weapons are the same Starfleet issue as the Enterprise crew, with the Phaser and Communicator molded in red plastic instead of blue.

$200 $300

Cheron, series one Alien, Mego, 1975.

Cheron, No. 51203/4, half black dyed plastic, half white painted body with half black, half white fabric outfit. The head is white plastic with half painted black. Accessories: One black boot and one white boot.

Cheron figures are known for the black dyed plastic body to stain into the white fabric outfit over time. This figure seems to be based on the Bele character as seen in *The Original Series* episode, "Let That Be Your Last Battlefield." As with the Bele character, the Cheron figure is white on his left side, while Lokai was white on his right side. Mego seems to have gone overboard, however, with the half-black, half-white effect as even the character's outfit was treated to the black and white two-tone color scheme. Though Cheron is one of the easier Aliens series characters to find, it is somewhat rare to see it mint to near mint on the card with the white section of fabric still all white and unstained.

$100 $200

THIRD SERIES: ALIENS SERIES TWO, 1976

Talos, series two Alien, Mego, 1976.

The Romulan, series two Alien, Mego, 1976.

Talos, No. 51204/2, yellow jump suit with large brown collar and black belt. Accessories: Orange boots.

Another Alien figure that has many collectors scratching their heads. With only a few similarities to the actual character it was apparently based on, one can only try to imagine how the design for Talos made it from the drawing board to actual production. If The Keeper figure could swap its head with Talos, then at least one of the two figures might be a bit more accurate looking.

Note: Talos is the only one of all of the Star Trek Mego figures that uses a smaller blister card bubble to help keep the diminutive Talos from rattling around while still sealed on the card.

$250 $500

The Romulan, No. 51204/1, black and silver material bodysuit with a sewn-on over-the-shoulder black sash and black cuffs on the ends of the sleeves. Accessories: Black belt with red Communicator and Phaser, gold helmet, and brown boots.

The Romulan Alien seems to be a cross between the Romulan Commander seen in *The Original Series* episode, "Balance of Terror," and the lower-ranked Centurions of the same episode. The face sculpt has a likeness to the face of Mark Lenard who played the Romulan Commander in that episode. The gold helmet, however, looks like it belongs on the Centurion. The Romulan is also the only one of the Alien figures that uses a standard Type 2 body.

$850 $1,700

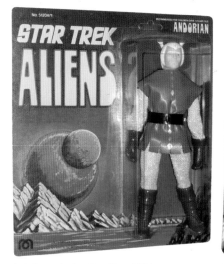

Andorian, No. 51204/2, silvery sparkled white bodysuit covered by a brown doublet detailed with painted silver diamonds and a wide black plastic belt with a diamond effect molded in the center. Accessories: A pair of brown boots and brown gloves.

As you can see, the Andorian is one of the most accurate of the Aliens Mego produced.

$500   **$1,000**

Andorian, series two Alien, Mego, 1976.

The back of the Andorian package, showing other action figures and toys to collect.

Mugato, No. 51204/4, green shirt with red dots inserted on a wide black low V-neck overlay with white string frills on end of sleeves. Also includes red pants with the white string frills on bottom of legs, and a black belt with silver buckle. No accessories.

Though this figure is obviously based on the alien Mugato character from *The Original Series* episode, "A Private Little War," it is still hard to imagine where the creative team at Mego came up with some of the ideas for its design. Overall, it is a spectacular-looking figure, especially on its 14-back blister card, and displays well loose or carded.

$600   **$1,200**

Mugato, series two Alien, Mego, 1976.

STAR TREK: THE MOTION PICTURE, MEGO, 1979

12" fully poseable authentically costumed action figures. Each box was the same except for the small text below the display window stating the character's name.

Full set of six.

$250   **$350**

Full set of six 12" *Star Trek: The Motion Picture* figures, Mego, 1979.

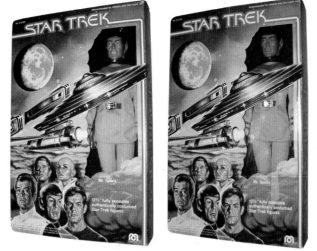

Captain Kirk, 12" *Star Trek: The Motion Picture* figure, Mego, 1979.

Captain Kirk, blue and white uniform. Accessories: Phaser and Belt Buckle.

$35   **$45**

Mr. Spock, 12" *Star Trek: The Motion Picture* figure, two variants: One with greenish-colored face, one with flesh-colored face, Mego, 1979.

Mr. Spock, gray uniform. Accessories: Phaser and Belt Buckle. Two variants: One with greenish-colored face, one with flesh-colored face.

$35   **$45**

Decker, 12" *Star Trek: The Motion Picture* figure, Mego, 1979.

Decker, gray uniform. Accessories: Phaser and Belt Buckle.

$65   **$85**

Ilia, 12" *Star Trek: The Motion Picture* figure, Mego, 1979.

Ilia, white mini-dress. Accessories: Phaser and orange necklace.

$35   **$45**

Klingon, 12" *Star Trek: The Motion Picture* figure, Mego, 1979.

Klingon, black and silver uniform. Accessories: Belt, breastplate and weapon.

$55   **$75**

Arcturian, 12" *Star Trek: The Motion Picture* figure, Mego, 1979.

Arcturian, wrinkle-faced alien with long white uniform shirt and beige pants.

$65   **$85**

Decker, 12" *Star Trek: The Motion Picture* figure in rare Spock packaging error, Mego, 1979.

Decker in Spock packaging error.

$45   **$65**

STAR TREK: THE MOTION PICTURE, MEGO, 1979

3-3/4" action figures.

FIRST SERIES

Kirk, 3-3/4" *Star Trek: The Motion Picture* figure on card, front and back, Mego, 1979.

Kirk, No. 91200/1, gray and white uniform.

$25   **$35**

Mr. Spock, 3-3/4" Motion Picture figure on card, Mego, 1979.

Mr. Spock, No. 91200/2, gray uniform.

$25   **$35**

Dr. McCoy, 3-3/4" Motion Picture figure on card, Mego, 1979.

Dr. McCoy, No. 91200/6, white shirt with gray pants.

$25   **$35**

Scotty, 3-3/4" Motion Picture figure on card, Mego, 1979.

Scotty, No. 91200/5, gray uniform.

$25   **$35**

Decker, 3-3/4" Motion Picture figure on card, Mego, 1979.

Decker, No. 91200/3, yellow uniform.

$25   **$35**

Ilia, 3-3/4" Motion Picture figure on card, Mego, 1979.

Ilia, No. 91200/4, gray and white uniform.

$25   **$35**

SECOND SERIES

The aliens were never available carded in the U.S. The Aliens were only sold carded in Canada and overseas in Italy. You could only get the Aliens by catalog sold in groups of three shipped bagged loose in a brown catalog mailer box. The Canadian versions do not have the character names on the card. Carded Alien 3-3/4" figures are extremely rare.

Klingon, 3-3/4" Motion Picture figure loose, Mego, 1979.

Arcturian, 3-3/4" Motion Picture figure loose, Mego, 1979.

Rigellian, 3-3/4" Motion Picture figure loose, Mego, 1979.

Klingon, No. 91200/7, black and silver uniform.

$65   **$85**

Arcturian, No. 912001/1, wrinkled-face alien with yellow uniform.

$150   **$250**

Betelgeusian, No. 91200/9, spiked tall black hair with silver outfit and red robe.

$250   **$350**

Megarite, No. 91201/1, dual lipped alien with black outfit and robe.

$250   **$300**

Rigellian, No. 91201/3, purple alien with white uniform.

$150   **$200**

Zaranite, No. 91200/8, silver masked alien with gray outfit.

$250   **$350**

KNICKERBOCKER, 1979

Star Trek: The Motion Picture soft poseable 12" doll figures in window boxed packaging.

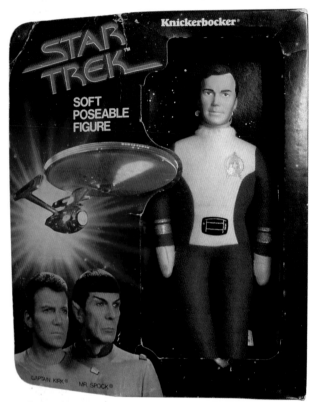

Captain Kirk, Knickerbocker, 1979.

Captain Kirk, grayish blue and white uniform.
$25   **$35**

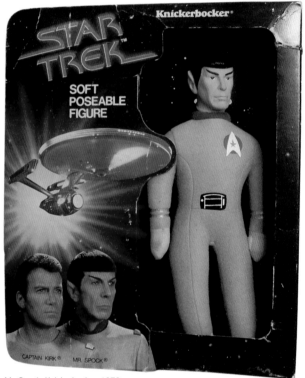

Mr. Spock, Knickerbocker, 1979.

Mr. Spock, gray uniform.
$25   **$35**

CUSTOMS

Talented fans have produced quite a lot of custom-made toys, props, action figures, packaging, and playsets. Other than props, the second most popular customs are figures and packaging that look similar to the Mego line. Web sites like www.megomuseum. com have members that display customs of unreleased characters including Sulu, Chekov, Nurse Chapel, Lt. Kyle, and Khan. These types of custom-made figures can be seen on Internet fan sites and forums as well as on eBay. The backer cards have also been custom made to represent the correct custom characters represented in the bubble.

Custom window box figures are another popular Mego-style custom. In the 1970s, Mego created window box packaging for its Planet of the Apes action figure line. Many collectors wished that Mego had also offered the Star Trek figures in the window box packaging, so a few creative people created custom versions for the 8" Mego Star Trek figures. Though these are custom made, they look like they belonged on a toy store shelf back in the mid-'70s.

Capt. Kirk Mego figure in custom box.

Complete 1975 Mego Capt. Kirk in custom box.
$45   **$65**

Mr. Spock Mego figure in custom box.

Complete 1975 Mego Mr. Spock in custom box.
$45   **$65**

Dr. McCoy Mego figure in custom box.

Complete 1975 Mego Dr. McCoy in custom box.
$45   **$65**

Mr. Scott Mego figure in custom box.

Complete 1975 Mego Mr. Scott in custom box.

$65   **$85**

Lt. Uhura Mego figure in custom box.

Complete 1975 Mego Lt. Uhura in custom box.

$45   **$65**

Klingon Mego figure in custom box.

Complete 1975 Mego Klingon in custom box.

$45   **$65**

Cheron Mego figure in custom box.

Complete 1975 Mego Cheron in custom box.

$75   **$95**

Capt. Kirk Mego figure in Playmates casual attire in custom box.

Complete 1975 Mego Capt. Kirk in custom box, casually attired in a shirt from a 9" Playmates' figure.
$65   **$85**

Custom made Mego style Horta creature.

Custom-made Mego-style Horta creature scaled for use with any 8" action figures. (Also see Props.)
$25   **$35**

RETRO CLOTH SERIES, DIAMOND SELECT, 2007

Customs have become so popular with fans that one of the more famous customizers, Paul "Dr. Mego" Clarke, www.megodoctor.com, was offered a contract with Diamond Select toys to create Mego-style reissues of the Mego 8" figure line. Called 8 Inch Retro Cloth Figures, they are being released in sets of two and are packaged in a unique clear blister design that allows the blister bubble card to be opened and resealed. As of this writing, the first six of the "Retro Cloth" action figures have been released.

FIRST SET

Capt. Kirk.
    Suggested retail: **$17.99**
Klingon.
    Suggested retail: **$17.99**

Capt. Kirk, first set 8" "Retro Cloth" Figure, Diamond Select, 2007.

Klingon, first set 8" "Retro Cloth" Figure, Diamond Select, 2007.

SECOND SET

Mr. Spock.
  Suggested retail: **$17.99**

Andorian.
  Suggested retail: **$17.99**

Mr. Spock, second set 8" "Retro Cloth" Figure, Diamond Select, 2007.

Andorian, second set 8" "Retro Cloth" Figure, Diamond Select, 2007.

THIRD SET

Dr. McCoy.
  Suggested retail: **$17.99**

Romulan.
  Suggested retail: **$17.99**

Dr. McCoy, third set 8" "Retro Cloth" Figure, Diamond Select, 2007.

Romulan, third set 8" "Retro Cloth" Figure, Diamond Select, 2007.

FOURTH SET

Scheduled release date: June 2008.

Mr. Scott (Scotty).
  Suggested retail: **$18.99**
The Keeper.
  Suggested retail: **$18.99**

HASTINGS AND PLANET X STORE EXCLUSIVE

Scheduled release date: July 2008.

Khan, the first Mego-style character never before officially released. Said to be a stand-alone figure and not part of a set.
  Suggested retail: **$18.99**

FIFTH SET

Scheduled release date: August 2008.

Lt. Uhura.
  Suggested retail: **$18.99**
Mugato. Said to be more accurate than the Mego version.
  Suggested retail: **$18.99**

SIXTH SET

Scheduled release date:
October 2008.

Chekov, the second Mego-style character never before officially released.
Suggested retail: **$18.99**
Cheron.
Suggested retail: **$18.99**

SEVENTH SET

Scheduled release date:
December 2008.

Sulu, the third Mego-style character never before officially released.
Suggested retail: **$18.99**
The Gorn, said to be more accurate than the Mego version.
Suggested retail: **$18.99**

Note: Due to a manufacturing error, the first run of Mr. Spock and Dr. McCoy figures have silver stripes on their sleeves instead of the correct gold color.

The first run Romulan figures were shipped with a red Tricorder, something that was never before produced. It is reported that these unique errors will be quickly remedied which could make these first-run Spock, McCoy, and Romulan figures more valuable.

PLAYMATES, 1992-99

Ad for Playmates action figures, 1993.

Ad for Playmates action figures.
$10   **$15**

Captain James T. Kirk, 9" Casual Attire, Playmates.

ACTION FIGURES, 9", 1995

Figure accessories included Phaser, Communicator, Tricorder, and display base unless otherwise noted.

Captain James T. Kirk-Casual Attire, No. 65292, Warp Factor Series 3, in green casual attire as seen in *The Original Series*. Accessories: Starfleet Phaser, two Tribbles, Communicator, and action base.
$25   **$45**

Captain James T. Kirk-Dress Uniform, No. 6288, in Starfleet dress uniform as first seen in *The Original Series* episode, "Court Martial," and in later episodes, "Journey to Babel," and "The Savage Curtain." Accessories: Phaser, Communicator, Tricorder, Spacecap, and command display base.
$25   **$45**

Mr. Spock, No. 6291, in blue science division uniform as seen in *The Original Series*. Accessories: Vulcan Harp, Phaser, Tricorder, Spacecap, and display base. Playmates made an error and shipped Mr. Spock with a TNG base instead of the science division display base.

$55   **$95**

Dr. McCoy, No. 6292, in blue science division uniform as seen in *The Original Series*. Accessories: Communicator, Medical Tricorder, test tubes, and science division display base.

$55   **$75**

Montgomery Scott, No. 6293, in red engineering uniform as seen in *The Original Series*. Accessories: Phaser, multi-range light source, engineering tool, and engineering display base.

$65   **$85**

Lieutenant Nyota Uhura, No. 6294, in red Star Fleet uniform as seen in *The Original Series*. Accessories: Phaser, Communicator, Tricorder, and engineering base.

$75   **$95**

Ensign Pavel Chekov, No. 16185, Federation Edition, in beige uniform as seen in *The Original Series*. Accessories: Phaser, Communicator, Tricorder, and command display base.

$25   **$35**

Nurse Christine Chapel, No. 65603, in nurse's uniform as seen in *The Original Series*. Accessories: Medical Tricorder, Communicator, test tubes, and Starfleet action base. Target Stores exclusive.

$55   **$75**

Lieutenant Hikaru Sulu, 9" Federation Edition, Playmates.

Trelane, 9" Limited Edition, Playmates.

Bele of Cheron, 9" Warp Factor Series 5, Playmates.

Lieutenant Hikaru Sulu, No. 16184, Federation Edition, in beige uniform as seen in *The Original Series*. Accessories: Phaser, Communicator, Tricorder, and command base.

$35   **$55**

Trelane, No. 65703, as seen in *The Original Series* episode, "The Squire of Gothos." Accessories: Sword, dueling pistol, Phaser, and action base. Limited edition of 5,000.

$45   **$65**

Bele of Cheron, No. 65298, Warp Factor Series 5, as seen in *The Original Series* episode, "Let That Be Your Last Battlefield." Accessories: Lantern bottle, fluted glass, fluted bottle, stemmed glass, Acorn top bottle, and action base.

$25   **$35**

Talosian Keeper, 9" Warp Factor Series 5, Playmates.

Talosian Keeper, No. 65295, Warp Factor Series 5, as seen in *The Original Series* pilot episode, "The Cage." Accessories: Talosian viewer and action base.

$35 $45

Captain Christopher Pike, No. 16183, Collector Edition, as seen in *The Original Series* pilot episode, "The Cage." Accessories: Laser pistol, Tricorder, and Starfleet action base.

$25 $35

Captain James T. Kirk, No. 16096, Collector Edition, in early 2nd pilot uniform from *The Original Series* episode, "Where No Man Has Gone Before." Accessories: Phaser, Communicator, Tricorder, and Starfleet action base. A Target Stores exclusive.

$35 $55

Mr. Spock, No. 16097, Collector Edition, in early 2nd pilot uniform from *The Original Series* episode, "Where No Man Has Gone Before." Accessories: Phaser, Communicator, Vulcan harp, and Starfleet action base. A Target Stores exclusive.

$45 $65

Montgomery Scott, No. 16098, Collector Edition, in early 2nd pilot uniform from *The Original Series* episode, "Where No Man Has Gone Before." Accessories: Phaser, Multi-range lightsource, Engineering diagnostic tool, and Starfleet action base. A Target Stores exclusive.

$45 $65

Captain James T. Kirk, 9" Collector Edition, Playmates.   Mr. Spock, 9" Collector Edition, Playmates.   Montgomery Scott, 9" Collector Edition, Playmates.

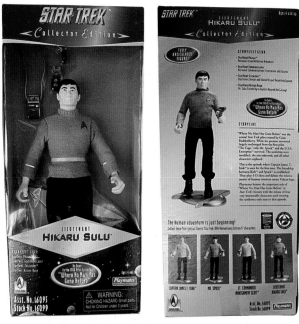

Lieutenant Hikaru Sulu, 9" Collector Edition, Playmates.

Lieutenant Hikaru Sulu, No. 16099, Collector Edition, in early 2nd pilot uniform from *The Original Series* episode, "Where No Man Has Gone Before." Accessories: Phaser, Communicator, Tricorder, and Starfleet action base. A Target Stores exclusive.

$25 **$45**

Captain James T. Kirk, No. 16091, as seen in *The Original Series*, "A Piece of the Action." Accessories: Machine Gun, Communicator, Phaser, and Starfleet action base. KB Toys exclusive of 5,000.

$65 **$85**

Mr. Spock, No. 16092, as seen in *The Original Series* episode, "A Piece of the Action." Accessories: Machine Gun, Communicator, Phaser and Starfleet action base. KB Toys exclusive of 5,000.

$75 **$95**

Captain James T. Kirk, No. 65260, as seen in *The Original Series* episode, "The City on the Edge of Forever." Accessories: Phaser, Communicator, Tricorder, and Starfleet action base. KB Toys exclusive of 6,000.

$65 **$85**

Mr. Spock, No. 65261, as seen in *The Original Series* episode, "The City on the Edge of Forever." Accessories: Phaser, Communicator, Tricorder, and Starfleet action base. KB Toys exclusive of 6,000.

$65 **$85**

Edith Keeler, 9" figure from "City on the Edge of Forever," Playmates.

Captain James T. Kirk, 9" figure from "Mirror, Mirror," Playmates.

Edith Keeler, No. 65704, as seen in *The Original Series* episode, "The City on the Edge of Forever." Accessories: Coffee mug, coffee pot and action base. KB Toys exclusive of 5,000.

$65 **$85**

Captain James T. Kirk, No. 65211, as seen in *The Original Series* episode, "Mirror, Mirror." Accessories: Mirror Universe Agonizer, Mirror Universe knife, Phaser, and Mirror Universe action base. KB Toys exclusive of 7,200.

$75 **$95**

Mr. Spock, No. 65212, as seen in *The Original Series* episode, "Mirror, Mirror." Accessories: Mirror Universe Agonizer, Mirror Universe knife, Phaser, and Mirror Universe action base. KB Toys exclusive of 7,200.

$75 **$95**

Mr. Spock, 9" from "Mirror, Mirror," Playmates.

Dr. McCoy, No. 65201, as seen in *The Original Series* episode, "Mirror, Mirror." Accessories: Mirror Universe Agonizer, Mirror Universe knife, Phaser, and Mirror Universe action base. KB Toys exclusive of 7,200.

   $65   **$85**

Lieutenant Uhura, No. 65202, as seen in *The Original Series* episode, "Mirror, Mirror." Accessories: Mirror Universe Agonizer, Mirror Universe knife, Phaser, and Mirror Universe action base, KB Toys exclusive of 7,200.

   $75   **$95**

Security Chief Sulu, No. 65701, as seen in *The Original Series* episode, "Mirror, Mirror." Accessories: Mirror Universe knife, Mirror Universe Agonizer, Phaser, and Mirror Universe action base. KB Toys exclusive of 7,200.

   $45   **$55**

Lt. Marlena Moreau, 9" figure from "Mirror, Mirror," Playmates.

Lt. Marlena Moreau, No. 65702, as seen in *The Original Series* episode, "Mirror, Mirror." Accessories: Mirror Universe knife, Mirror Universe Agonizer, Phaser, and Mirror Universe action base. KB Toys exclusive of 7,200.

   $45   **$65**

Captain James T. Kirk in Environmental Suit, No. 65601, as seen in *The Original Series* episode, "The Tholian Web." Accessories: Phaser, Communicator, and Starfleet action base. Target Stores exclusive.

$65   **$75**

Mr. Spock in Environmental Suit, No. 65251, as seen in *The Original Series* episode, "The Tholian Web." Accessories: Phaser, Communicator, and Starfleet action base. Target Stores exclusive.

$55   **$65**

Dr. Leonard McCoy, 9" loose figure from "The Tholian Web," Playmates.

Ensign Pavel Chekov, 9" figure from "The Tholian Web," Playmates.

Ensign Pavel Chekov, No. 65252, as seen in *The Original Series* episode, "The Tholian Web." Accessories: Phaser, Communicator, and Starfleet action base. Target Stores exclusive.

$25   **$45**

Dr. Leonard McCoy in Environmental Suit, No. 65002, as seen in *The Original Series* episode, "The Tholian Web." Accessories: Phaser, Communicator, and Starfleet action base. Target Stores exclusive.

$45   **$55**

Captain James T. Kirk, 9" figure from "Amok Time," Playmates.

Captain James T. Kirk, No. 65705, as seen in *The Original Series* episode, "Amok Time." Accessories: Vulcan Lirpa, Hypospray, and action base. KB Toys exclusive limited edition of 5,000.

$55   **$75**

Mr. Spock, No. 65706, as seen in *The Original Series* episode, "Amok Time." Accessories: Vulcan Harp, Vulcan Lirpa, Plomeek Soup, and action base. KB Toys exclusive limited edition of 5,000.

$65   **$85**

The Command Edition: Captain James T. Kirk, No. 6068, in yellow uniform as seen in *The Original Series*. Accessories: Phaser, Communicator, Tricorder, Collector Card, and display base.

$45   **$65**

ACTION FIGURES, 12", 1997

Captain James T. Kirk, No. 6500, Masterpiece Edition, includes a full color book with photos on the history of *Star Trek* and a certificate of authenticity. Limited edition of 10,000.

$150   **$200**

Mr. Spock, No. 65501, Classic Edition. Accessories: Vulcan harp, Communicator, Phaser, and Tricorder. Limited edition of 7,500.

$75   **$100**

Dr. McCoy, No. 65521, Classic Edition. Accessories: Communicator, Phaser and Tricorder. Limited edition of 7,500.

$55   **$75**

Montgomery Scott, No. 65522, Classic Edition. Accessories: Communicator, Phaser, and Tricorder. Limited edition of 7,500.

$45   **$65**

Lieutenant Nyota Uhura, No. 65532, Classic Edition. Accessories: Communicator, Phaser, and Tricorder. Limited edition of 7,500.

$85   **$125**

Ensign Pavel Chekov, No. 65531, Classic Edition. Accessories: Communicator, Phaser, and Tricorder. Limited edition of 7,500.

$35   **$45**

Lieutenant Hikaru Sulu, No. 65523, Classic Edition. Accessories: Communicator, Phaser, and Tricorder. Limited edition of 7,500.

$35   **$45**

Andorian Ambassador Shras, No. 65051, Classic Edition, as seen in *The Original Series* episode, "Journey To Babel." Accessories: Four drinking glasses. Limited edition of 7,500.

$65   **$85**

Captain James T. Kirk, 12" "Masterpiece Edition," Playmates.

Mr. Spock, 12" Classic Edition, Playmates.

Montgomery Scott, Classic Edition, Playmates.

Lieutenant Hikaru Sulu, Classic Edition, Playmates.

Andorian Ambassador Shras, Classic Edition, shown loose, Playmates.

Mugato, Classic Edition, shown loose, Playmates.   Gorn Captain, Classic Edition, figure shown in window box closed, opened and loose, Playmates.

Mugato, No. 65061, Classic Edition, as seen in *The Original Series* episode, "A Private Little War." Accessories: None. Limited edition of 7,500.

$35   **$45**

Gorn Captain, No. 65052, Classic Edition, as seen in *The Original Series* episode, "Arena." Accessories: Stick, Chiseled rock, and Universal Translator. Limited edition of 7,500.

$45   **$65**

Captain Christopher Pike, No. 65536, Classic Edition, as seen in *The Original Series* episode, "The Cage." Accessories: Laser Pistol, Communicator, and Tricorder. Limited edition of 7,500.

$75   **$100**

Captain Kirk As Romulan, No. 65514, Classic Edition, as seen in *The Original Series* episode, "The Enterprise Incident." Limited edition of 3,500.

$85   **$125**

Captain James T. Kirk, No. 65608, Classic Edition, as seen in *The Original Series* episode, "A Piece of the Action." Accessories: Blue hat with blue stripe, Phaser, Communicator, and Tommy Gun. Limited edition of 1,000.

$65   **$85**

Mr. Spock, No. 65609, Classic Edition, as seen in *The Original Series* episode, "A Piece of the Action." Accessories: Brown hat, Phaser, Communicator, and Tommy Gun. Limited edition of 1,000.

$75   **$85**

Captain James T. Kirk, No. 65707, as seen in the movie, *Star Trek II: The Wrath of Khan*. KB Toys exclusive. Limited Edition of 5,000.

$65   **$85**

Mr. Spock, No. 65708, as seen in the movie, *Star Trek II: The Wrath of Khan*. Accessories: Radiation gloves. KB Toys exclusive. Limited edition of 5,000.

$65   **$85**

5" ACTION FIGURES, 30TH ANNIVERSARY CLASSIC SERIES

All figures included a 30th Anniversary Action Base.

Captain Christopher Pike, No. 6448, as seen in *The Original Series* episode, "The Cage." Purple accessories: Laser pistol, Communicator, Warrior's Shield, Rigelian Spear, and action base.

$15   **$25**

Captain Christopher Pike, 5" 30th Anniversary Classic Series, Playmates.

Talosian Keeper, from "The Cage," Playmates.

Mr. Spock, from "The Cage," Playmates.

Captain James T. Kirk, casual attire, Playmates.

Nurse Christine Chapel, in nurse's uniform, Playmates.

Vina, Orion Animal Woman, No. 16040, as seen in *The Original Series* episode, "The Cage." Orange or blue accessories: Torch and fountain. Character description error: In the episode the character of Vina was referred to as an Orion Slave Girl, not Animal Woman.

$35   **$45**

Talosian Keeper, No. 16039, as seen in *The Original Series* episode, "The Cage." Black accessories: Nourishment vial, gas sprayer, Talosian viewscreen, and action base.

$20   **$30**

Mr. Spock, No. 16038, as seen in *The Original Series* episode, "The Cage." Black accessories: Laser Pistol, Communicator, landing party case, desktop monitor, and action base.

$25   **$35**

Captain James T. Kirk, Casual Attire, No. 16031, in casual attire as first seen in *The Original Series* episode, "Charlie X." Accessories: Phaser, Communicator, Tricorder, Captain's Log, and action base.

$35   **$55**

Dr. McCoy, No. 16155, in dress uniform as seen in *The Original Series* episode, "Court Martial." Includes accessories. Limited edition of 10,000.

$55   **$75**

Montgomery Scott, No. 16045, in early uniform as seen in *The Original Series* 2nd pilot episode, "Where No Man Has Gone Before." Spencer Gifts Limited edition of 10,000.

$55   **$75**

Lieutenant Hikaru Sulu, No. 16046, in early uniform as seen in *The Original Series* 2nd pilot episode, "Where No Man Has Gone Before." Spencer Gifts Limited edition of 10,000.

$45   **$65**

Nurse Christine Chapel, No. 6447, in nurses uniform as seen in *The Original Series*. Accessories: Medical Tricorder, Anabolic Protoplaser, Hypospray, Medical Scanner, and action base.

$25   **$35**

Yeoman Janice Rand, No. 6449, in red uniform as seen in *The Original Series*. Accessories: Tricorder, Communicator, Phaser, PADD, and action base.

$35   **$45**

Harry Mudd, No. 16154, as seen in the episode, "Mudd's Women." Red accessories: Goblet, Lithium Crystals, Venus Drug, Communicator, and action base.

$20   **$30**

Gorn, No. 16041, as seen in the episode, "Arena." Brown accessories: Primitive cannon, diamond projectiles, Metron recorder/universal translator, chiseled stone spike, and Gorn action base.

$35   **$55**

Yeoman Janice Rand, in original series red uniform, Playmates.

Harry Mudd, from "Mudd's Women," Playmates.

Mugato, No. 16042, as seen in the episode, "A Private Little War." Brown accessories: Flintlock, Mako Root, Hill People's drum, Phaser, and Alien action base.

$25 $35

Kirk in Environmental Suit, No. 16048, as seen in the episode, "The Tholian Web." Black accessories: Tricorder, Phaser, desktop monitor, Tri-Ox compound, and action base.

$35 $45

Captain Koloth, No. 65111, Warp Factor Series 1, 1997, as seen in the episode, "The Trouble With Tribbles." Accessories: Three plastic Tribbles, Klingon disruptor pistol, D'K Tahg knife, and Klingon action base.

$25 $35

Ilia Probe, No. 65102, Warp Factor Series 2, 1997, as seen in *Star Trek: The Motion Picture*. Blue or Silver accessories: V'Ger and action base. Triple Tribbles game pieces included with WF Series 2 figures.

$20 $30

Edith Keeler, No. 65114, Warp Factor Series 3, 1997, as seen in the episode, "The City on the Edge of Forever." Accessories: Coffee pot, handbag, typewriter, coffee mug, and action base.

$25 $35

Mr. Spock, No. 65105, Warp Factor Series 3, 1997, as seen in the episode, "Mirror, Mirror." Accessories: Phaser, Agonizer, desktop computer, knife, and action base.

$35 $45

Trelane, No. 65122, Warp Factor Series 4, 1998, as seen in the episode, "The Squire of Gothos." Accessories: Mirror machine, sword, pistol, and action base.

$20 $30

Andorian Alien, No. 65120, Warp Factor Series 4, 1998, as seen in the episode, "Whom Gods Destroy." Accessories: Chair Ultrasound Neutralizer, Andorian Serape, and action base.

$25 $35

Captain Kirk, No. 65128, Warp Factor Series 5, 1998, as seen in the episode, "The City on the Edge of Forever." Accessories: Phaser, coffee pot, coffee mug, and action base.

$45 $55

Mr. Spock, No. 65129, Warp Factor Series 5, 1998, as seen in the episode, "The City on the Edge of Forever." Accessories: Vacuum tubes, primitive computer, coffee mug, and action base.

$55 $65

5" ACTION FIGURES, MOVIE SERIES, 1995

Classic Assortment, Wave 1.

Admiral Kirk from *Star Trek: The Motion Picture*, Playmates.

Mr. Spock from *Star Trek: The Motion Picture*, Playmates.

Dr. McCoy from *Star Trek: The Motion Picture*, Playmates.

Admiral Kirk, No. 6451, in Star Fleet uniform as seen in *Star Trek: The Motion Picture*. Red accessories: Phaser, wrist Communicator, PADD, V'GER spacecraft section, and action base.

$20 $25

Mr. Spock, No. 6452, in Star Fleet uniform as seen in *Star Trek: The Motion Picture*. Green accessories: Tricorder, engineering tool, Kolinahr necklace, V'GER spacecraft section, and action base.

$25 $35

Dr. McCoy, No. 6453, in Star Fleet uniform as seen in *Star Trek: The Motion Picture*. Purple accessories: Medical Tricorder, medical kit, neurological scanner, V'GER Spacecraft section, and action base.

$35 $45

Martia the Shape-Shifter from *Star Trek VI: The Undiscovered Country*, Playmates.

General Chang from *Star Trek VI: The Undiscovered Country*, Playmates.

Commander Kruge from *Star Trek III: The Search For Spock,* Playmates.

Lt. Sulu, No. 6454, in Star Fleet uniform as seen in *Star Trek: The Motion Picture*. Blue accessories: Phaser, wrist Communicator, Tricorder, V'GER Spacecraft section, and action base.
 $20   **$30**

Lt. Nyota Uhura, No. 6455, in Star Fleet uniform as seen in *Star Trek: The Motion Picture*. Green accessories: Tricorder, wrist Communicator, PADD, V'GER Spacecraft section, and action base.
 $20   **$30**

Khan, No. 6456, as seen in *Star Trek II: The Wrath of Khan*. Gray accessories: Phaser, Ceti Eels, Genesis Torpedo, Genesis control box, and action base.
 $45   **$55**

Martia the Shape-Shifter, No. 6457, as seen in *Star Trek VI: The Undiscovered Country*. Orange accessories: Laser drill, flare, drilling mask, leg irons, and action base.
 $20   **$30**

General Chang, No. 6458, as seen in *Star Trek VI: The Undiscovered Country*. Gold accessories: Klingon Communicator, glass of Romulan Ale, Klingon Disruptor, Klingon staff, and action base.
 $20   **$30**

Commander Kruge, No. 6459, as seen in *Star Trek III: The Search For Spock*. Brown accessories: Klingon Communicator, Klingon Tricorder, Klingon Disruptor, Klingon Rifle, and action base.
 $20   **$30**

Lt. Saavik, No. 6460, in red Star Fleet uniform as seen in *Star Trek II: The Wrath of Khan*. Turquoise accessories: Phaser, Tricorder, Communicator, Starfleet duffel bag, and action base.
 $30   **$40**

Ilia Probe, No. 65102, as seen in *Star Trek: The Motion Picture*. Accessories: Blue or silver V'Ger and action base. Also part of the Warp Factor Series 2 figures, 1997.
 $20   **$30**

TRANSPORTER SERIES

Transporter display features flickering lights and beaming transporter sound.

Captain Kirk, Transporter series, Playmates.

Mr. Spock, Transporter series, Playmates.

Montgomery Scott, Transporter series, Playmates.

Nurse Christine Chapel, Transporter series, Playmates.

Yeoman Janice Rand, Transporter series, Playmates.

Captain Kirk, No. 65401.

$55   **$65**

Dr. McCoy, No. 65403.

$55   **$65**

Montgomery Scott, No. 65405.

$65   **$75**

Lt. Sulu, No. 65232.

$45   **$55**

Yeoman Janice Rand, No. 65442.

$55   **$65**

Mr. Spock, No. 65402.

$65   **$75**

Lt. Nyota Uhura, No. 65404.

$55   **$65**

Pavel Chekov, No. 65231.

$45   **$55**

Nurse Christine Chapel, No. 65441.

$55   **$65**

PLAYMATES, FIGURES, AND SETS:

Classic Bridge Figures, No. 6090, Captain Kirk, Mr. Spock, Dr. McCoy, Scotty, Uhura, Sulu, Chekov.

$75   **$125**

Captain Kirk, Balok, and Puppet Set, No. 65182, as seen in *The Original Series* episode, "The Corbomite Maneuver."

$35   **$55**

Captain Kirk - Mr. Spock Tholian Web Set, No. 65174, as seen in *The Original Series* episode, "The Tholian Web." Target Stores exclusive.

$55   **$75**

Captain Kirk - Mr. Spock Amok Set, No. 65172, as seen in *The Original Series* episode, "Amok Time." Store Exclusive of only 3,000.

$65   **$85**

5" EXCLUSIVE OR LIMITED FIGURES

Captain Kirk, No. 65525, as seen in *The Original Series* episode, "A Piece of the Action." Toy Fare Exclusive of 10,000.

$25   **$35**

Mr. Spock, No. 65523, as seen in *The Original Series* episode, "The Tholian Web." Exclusive of 12,000.

$35   **$45**

Captain Mackenzie Calhoun, From the Pocket Book series, *Star Trek New Frontier*. Accessories includes the Xenex sword. Exclusive of 10,000.

$20   **$30**

Captain Kirk, "A Piece of the Action," Playmates.

Captain Mackenzie Calhoun, "Star Trek New Frontier," Playmates.

5" STAR TREK TEENAGE MUTANT NINJA TURTLES

Set of four 5" Star Trek Teenage Mutant Ninja Turtles.

An interesting and unique toy crossover between Star Trek and The Ninja Turtles.

Captain Leonardo, Star Trek Teenage Mutant Ninja Turtle, Playmates.

First Officer Donatello, Star Trek Teenage Mutant Ninja Turtle, Playmates, 1997.

Chief Medical Officer Raphael, Star Trek Teenage Mutant Ninja Turtle, Playmates, 1997.

Chief Engineer Michaelangelo, Star Trek Teenage Mutant Ninja Turtle, Playmates, 1997.

Captain Leonardo, No. 3451, includes bonus collector card Kowabunga Classic Phaser, Classic Turtle-tech Tricorder, Cool Classic Communicator, Hi-Trek Katana, and shell action base.

$25   **$35**

First Officer Donatello, No. 3454, the Subspace shelled Science Officer. Includes bonus collector card, Classic Subsauce Phaser, Classic Sewer Science Tricorder, Pure Logic Classic Communicator, Pon Farr Battle Bo, and shell action base.

$25   **$35**

Chief Medical Officer Raphael, No. 3453, includes bonus collector card, Classic Foot Chasin' Phaser, Mutant Medical Classic Tricorder, Classic Medical Officers Kowabunga Communicator, Subspace Sais, and shell action base.

$25   **$35**

Chief Engineer Michaelangelo, No. 3452, includes bonus collector card Kowabunga Classic Foot Findin' Phaser, Mutant Engineerin' Taste-testin' Tricorder, Pizzarium-powered Thin Crust Classic Communicator, Warp Engine Defendin' Nebula Nunchukas, and shell action base.

$25   **$35**

Playmates dropped the *Star Trek* license in 2000 and it was quickly picked up by a small company called Palisades. With the 35th Anniversary of *Star Trek* just around the corner in 2001, Palisades created a prototype 6" scale action figure set featuring Captain Kirk in his Captain's chair with Gene Roddenberry beside him. Though a unique idea, the set never made it into production.

As quickly as Palisades was in, it was out, and Art Asylum picked up the license. I look forward to showcasing the Diamond Select/Art Asylum line-up in the future.

As of this writing, Playmates was announced as the official license holder for the new *Star Trek* movie currently scheduled for release in May 2009.

DANBURY MINT, 1991

Star Trek Danbury Mint Porcelain Figures.
Set of 12 sold individually with certificate.

ENTERPRISE CREW:			ALIENS:		
Captain Kirk.			Talosian.		
	$20	$30		$20	$30
Mr. Spock.			Khan.		
	$20	$30		$25	$35
Dr. McCoy.			Andorian.		
	$20	$30		$20	$30
Mr. Scott.			Romulan.		
	$25	$30		$20	$30
Lt. Uhura in chair.			Klingon.		
	$35	$45		$25	$35
Lt. Sulu with sword.			Display stand.		
	$40	$55		$25	$50
Ensign Chekov with Tribbles.					
	$20	$30			

Set of 12 Star Trek Porcelain Figures in display stand, Danbury Mint.

The empty display stand shows the graphic of the Enterprise.

ERTL, 1984

Die-cast figures from *Star Trek III: The Search for Spock.*

Captain Kirk, accessories:			Scotty, accessories: Phaser.		
Communicator.				$10	$20
	$10	$20	Klingon Leader, accessories:		
Mr. Spock, accessories: Phaser.			Pet.		
	$10	$20		$10	$25

Captain Kirk die-cast figure on card, front and back, ERTL, 1984.

GALOOB, 1989

Limited edition set of five *Star Trek V: The Final Frontier* action figures: Captain James T. Kirk, Mr. Spock, Dr. Leonard McCoy, Sybok, Klaa.

$25   **$45 each**

Captain James T. Kirk, Galoob, 1989.

HAMILTON GIFTS, 1991

10-1/2" molded vinyl *The Original Series* figures were sold loose with a hang tag. Arms and legs were jointed at the body only. Each figure includes a separate plastic base.

Kirk, Spock, McCoy, Scotty.

$1   **$5**

Andorian.

$2   **$6**

Gorn, Mugato, Talosian, Tellarite.

$5   **$10**

10-1/2" vinyl *The Original Series* figures, Hamilton Gifts, 1991.

MATTEL, 1996

30th Anniversary Barbie and Ken Set. Due to the cross-collectable nature of Barbie figures, the values can become quite volatile at times if both Star Trek collectors and Barbie/doll collectors compete for the same items.

$45   **$65**

Individually boxed Star Trek Barbies obtained in Riviera packaging.

$25   **$35**

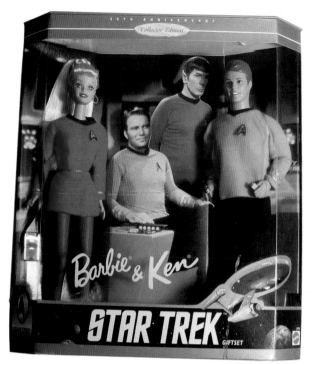

30th Anniversary Barbie and Ken Set, Mattel, 1996.

Star Trek Barbie in Riviera packaging, Mattel.

SIDESHOW, 2002

Detailed Polystone busts of some of the classic *Star Trek* characters. Though these Series 1 busts are not exactly action figures, they are not exactly toys either.

Captain Kirk, Mr. Spock, Dr. McCoy, Engineer Scott.

$35   **$45**

Web exclusives: Gorn Captain and Captain Koloth.

$55   **$75**

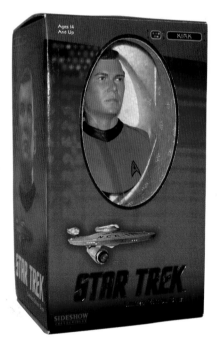

Captain Kirk bust, Sideshow, 2002.

Mr. Spock bust, Sideshow, 2002.

Kirk bank, Play Pal, 1976.

Spock bank, Play Pal, 1976.

Banks

Thanks to the Internet and auction sites such as eBay, I was finally able to obtain some of the more obscure and harder-to-find pieces for my collection like the Play Pal banks.

PLAY PAL, 1976

Colorful plastic banks with either a clear or white stopper in the base:

Kirk bank, Kirk standing in front of a copper-colored computer console holding a closed Communicator in his right hand while gripping a handle from the console in his left.

$55 **$75**

Spock bank, Spock standing in front of a copper-colored computer console holding a closed Communicator in his right hand.

$65 **$85**

Bedding and Curtains

A variety of companies known for quality fabric products delved into *Star Trek IV: The Final Frontier* and released everything from afghans to bed sheets with Star Trek imagery.

AFGHAN

PARAMOUNT PROMOTIONAL, 1992

Star Trek IV: The Final Frontier 4' x 6' fringed with image of movie poster, very rare.

$250 **$350**

BEACH TOWELS

CANON, 1975

Kirk and Spock portraits, Enterprise.

$65 **$75 each**

Beach towel, Spock Portrait, Canon, 1975.

Beach towel, Kirk and Spock Portraits, Canon, 1975.

Beach towel, Spock on a planet, Franco, 1975.

Beach towel, Enterprise over a planet, Franco, 1975.

Beach towel, Kirk, Spock, and McCoy with Aliens, Franco, 1975.

Beach towel, Spock shooting three-headed snake, Franco, 1975.

CECIL SAYDAH CO., 1993

Features color artwork of Kirk, Spock and McCoy from *The Original Series* on a black background.

$45	**$55**

FRANCO, 1975

Kirk, Spock and McCoy with Aliens in front of Rigel Castle.

Enterprise over a planet.

Spock Shooting three-headed snake.

Spock on a planet.

$75	**$95 each**

FRANCO, 1976

Enterprise battling Klingon Cruiser.

Kirk and Spock.

Spock (holding communicator and phaser).

$75	**$95 each**

BED LINENS

CANON, 1979

Features artwork of scenes from *Star Trek: The Motion Picture*.

Pillow cases.

$25	**$35**

Sheets (twin).

$75	**$100**

FASHION MANOR, 1976

Features original crew and ship scenes.

Fitted sheet and pillowcase set.

$45	**$65**

Sheet only.

$35	**$45**

Pillow case only.

$15	**$20**

PACIFIC MILLS, 1975

Features *The Original Series* Enterprise and crew on a dark or light blue space background.

Bed spread (twin).

$150	**$200**

Fitted sheets (twin) and pillowcase set.

$55	**$75**

Sheet only (twin).

$35	**$45**

Pillow case only.

$25	**$30**

PARAMOUNT, 1976

Pillowcase, features starships.

$25	**$45**

STAR DREAM, 1995

Star Trek: Generations movie poster artwork on bedding. Limited-edition set made in Germany included coverlet and pillow case.

$100	**$150**

BLANKETS

KOKOMO, 1993

Limited-edition wool blanket with artwork of the U.S.S. Enterprise NCC-1701-A and command insignia in blue.

$150	**$200**

COMFORTER

Twin comforter, Aberdeen, 1986.

ABERDEEN, 1986

Features original crew and ship scenes.

Twin bed.

$100	**$150**

Full bed.

$125	**$175**

CURTAINS, SHEETS, AND PILLOW CASES

Star Trek: The Motion Picture themed curtains, Canon, 1979.

CANON, 1979

Curtains, feature artwork of ships and crew from *Star Trek: The Motion Picture*.

$25 $45

PACIFIC MILLS, 1975

Features original crew and ship scenes:

Curtains.

$50 $100

Enterprise and Crew curtains, Pacific Mills, 1975.

Enterprise and Crew sheets, Pacific Mills, 1975.

Sheets.

$25 $50

Pillow cases.

$25 $35

Enterprise and crew pillow cases, Pacific Mills, 1975.

Ships and crew pillow cases, Stephens, 1975.

STEPHENS, 1975

Features original crew and ship scenes:

Pillow cases.

$20 $25

Twin sheets.

$35 $45

Full sheets.

$45 $55

DUST RUFFLE

ABERDEEN, 1986

Features star pattern on dark blue fabric matching other Aberdeen Star Trek bedding items. No ships or crew images on the ruffle, just the star pattern.

$25 $45

FABRIC

FABRIC, 1976

Features Enterprise and K-7 Space Station repeating pattern; per yard:

$15 $25

Pillow made from fabric.

$15 $20

Enterprise and K-7 Space Station fabric, 1976.

Enterprise and K-7 Space Station fabric pillow.

PILLOW SHAM

ABERDEEN, 1986

Features ships and scenes from the Star Trek movies on a dark blue fabric background.

$25 $35

THROW RUGS

THROW RUGS, 1976

Standard-size plush fur rugs feature color artwork from scenes from the original series and from poster artwork: Bridge scene, crew, Enterprise, episode photo collage (same collage used in the 1976 Langley Associates collage poster).

$150 $200 each

Belts and Belt Buckles

Many collectible belt buckles serve display duty only and never see duty on a belt. Thus, it is not unusual to find these in excellent condition.

BELT BUCKLES

Enterprise-shaped buckle, Baron Buckle, 1978.

BARON BUCKLE, 1978

Enterprise-shaped buckle.

$25 $35

HEROES WORLD, 1980

Star Trek: The Motion Picture Starfleet belt buckle.

$10 $20

Enterprise with Saturn: "Space the Final Frontier," Indiana Metal Co., 1982.

INDIANA METAL CO., 1982

Enterprise with Saturn: "Space the Final Frontier," 2-1/2".

$15 $20

LEE BELTS, 1976

Kirk and Spock profile buckle:

First version.

$25 $30

Second version.

$15 $20

Third version.

$20 $25

Spock profile oval buckle.

$15 $20

Spock profile round with red enamel trim.

$20 $25

Original television series Enterprise Orbiting Planet oval brass-tone buckle.

$25 $30

Enterprise NCC-1701.

$20 $30

Enterprise NCC-1701.

$15 $20

Enterprise NCC-1701 with blue enamel trim.

$25 $30

Kirk and Spock profile buckle, third version, Lee Belts, 1976.

Spock profile round with red enamel trim, Lee Belts, 1976.

Kirk and Spock profile version, first version, Lee Belts, 1976.

Kirk and Spock profile buckle, second version, Lee Belts, 1976.

Enterprise NCC-1701, Lee Belts, 1976.

Enterprise NCC-1701, Lee Belts, 1976.

Enterprise NCC-1701, Lee Belts, 1976.

LEE BELTS, 1979

Star Trek logo metal buckle.

$15 $20

LINCOLN ENTERPRISES, 1980

Star Trek: The Motion Picture U.S.S. Enterprise Commemorative belt buckle:

Minted in bronze.

$20 $30

Minted in sterling silver with 24k gold highlights.

$45 $55

BELTS

BELT DESIGNS

Web belt with logo buckle.

$20 $25

LEE, 1976

Original Enterprise and Star Trek elastic cloth belt in assorted colors.

$45 $55

Brown or black vinyl with television Enterprise on buckle.

$45 $55

LEE, 1979

Star Trek: The Motion Picture stretch cloth belt in blue.

$35 $45

Vinyl belt with Kirk and Spock on brass buckle.

$25 $35

LEE, 1982

Star Trek characters and ships on brown leather belt.

$35 $45

Movie belt and buckle, Star Trek II through VI.

$10 $25

Web belt with logo buckle, Belt Designs.

Star Trek characters and ships on brown leather belt, Lee, 1982.

Movie belt and buckle (Star Trek II through VI).

Star Trek characters and ships on brown leather belt, Lee, 1982.

Blueprints

Franz Joseph may have done as much to ignite the imagination of Star Trek fans as anyone in the show's storied history. His technical manual and Enterprise blueprints were released in 1975 as Star Trek finally found its audience in syndication and its popularity soared.

These were the most amazing pieces of Star Trek memorabilia fans had seen to date, and for the thousands of Star Trek fans starving at the time for anything and everything Star Trek, he launched a collecting phenomenon.

Star Trek Blueprints by Franz Joseph, Balantine Books, 1975. Features the complete set of 12 blueprints of the Enterprise.

14 Official Blueprints, Star Trek: The Motion Picture, Balantine Books, 1975.

BALANTINE BOOKS, 1975

Star Trek Blueprints, features the set of 12 Enterprise blueprints, by Franz Joseph, who is also famous for the original 1975 technical manual.

$45 $55

14 Official Blueprints, Star Trek: The Motion Picture, New Enterprise & Bridge, Klingon Cruiser and bridge and more.

$25 $35

Bridge Blueprints: U.S.S. Enterprise Bridge by Michael McMaster:

First edition: Vertical cover format w/blue ink.

$25 $35

Second edition: Horizontal format cover, red w/blue ink.

$20 $30

Third edition: Horizontal format cover w/black ink.

$20 $30

Bridge Blueprints: Revised by Michael McMaster.

$15 $20

Bridge Blueprints: U.S.S. Enterprise Bridge by Lawrence Miller.

$20 $30

Bookmarks, Bookplates, and Journals

While most people put bookmarks to their intended use, collectors put them on display or carefully store them. Condition is important toward value, so make sure they are unbent and any tassels are intact.

BOOKMARKS

ANTIOCH PUB. CO., 1985

Standard-size bookmark, "Beam Me Up Scotty, There's No Intelligent Life Down Here."

$1 $5

Original series bookmarks, Antioch Pub. Co., 1991-1993.

ANTIOCH PUB. CO., 1991-93

Standard-size bookmarks with *The Original Series* characters and ships:

Enterprise "To Boldly Go Where No Man Has Gone Before."

Captain Kirk in Transporter.

Mr. Spock in Transporter.

Dr. McCoy "I'm a doctor, not a..."

Mr. Scott "I can't change the laws of physics."

Lt. Uhura "Hailing Frequencies Open."

$1 $5 each

POCKET BOOKS, 1979

Bookmark reads, "The Human Adventure is Just Beginning." This was a special give-away promotion by Pocket Books to help advertise the release of *Star Trek: The Motion Picture* novel.

$5 $10

POCKET BOOKS, 1987

Bookmark features *The Original Series* Enterprise on one side and reads "Strangers in the Sky Star Trek Novel by Margaret Wander Bonanno" on the other. This was a special give-away Pocket Books promotion given out at bookstores to those purchasing the book.

$5 $10

T-K GRAPHICS, 1987

Standard-size bookmarks:

"Beam Me Up."

"Star Fleet Command Intelligence Division."

"Tribble Breeding is a Hairy Experience."

"Star Trek Forever" (with Janus Head logo).

"Star Fleet tactical Operations Center" (with UFP logo).

"U.S.S. Enterprise" (with schematic drawing).

$1 $5 each

BOOKPLATES

T-K GRAPHICS, 1984

Self-sticking bookplates feature a space to personalize under the Star Trek artwork where it reads "From the library of":

Khan.

$10 $15

Starfleet Academy Library.

$20 $25

ANTIOCH, 1991

Self-sticking bookplates feature a space to personalize under the Star Trek artwork where it reads, "From the collection of":

Command Insignia (circled by U.S.S. Enterprise NCC-1701 text).

U.S.S. Enterprise (with classic Star Trek text).

$10 $15 each

Self-sticking Star Trek bookplates, Antioch, 1991.

Mr. Spock Journal with bookmark, Antioch Pub. Co., 1991.

Limited-edition Command Insignia Journal, Antioch Pub. Co., 1997.

JOURNALS

ANTIOCH PUB. CO., 1991

Mr. Spock Journal with bookmark.

$15 $20

ANTIOCH PUB. CO., 1997

Limited-edition Command Insignia Journal with Enterprise bookmark, Enterprise identification card, and command insignia bridge pass.

$20 $25

Books

For centuries, bibliophiles have accumulated collections of their favorite titles. Great and small, these collections reflect the diverse interests of their owners. Before *Star Trek*, the science fiction genre enjoyed a small, but devoted, following. *Star Trek* brought science fiction to the masses on an unprecedented scale, and the once-small cadre of fans turned legion.

After you've seen every television episode and watched all of the films, the wide variety of books are the ideal way to carry on the adventure.

Self-sticking book plates, Antioch, 1991.

The Making of Star Trek by Stephen Whitfield and Gene Roddenberry, first edition, Ballantine, 1968.

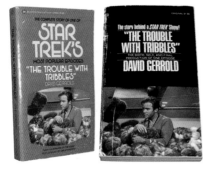

The Trouble With Tribbles by David Gerrold, Ballantine, 1973.

World of Star Trek by David Gerrold, Ballantine, 1973.

David Gerrold's written letter.

ACE, 1979

William Shatner: Where No Man Has Gone Before by Shatner, Marshak, Culbreath. The authorized biography of William Shatner.

$50   **$70**

ANIMA, 1977

Meaning in Star Trek by Karen Blair. The first published attempt to analyze the psychology of the original *Star Trek* series and characters. It is also a fascinating look into the early days, describing in detail of how it transformed from a cancelled television show into a pop culture phenomenon.

$30   **$35**

BALLANTINE, 1968

The Making of Star Trek, Stephen Whitfield and Gene Roddenberry. Written in 1968 between the second and third series, it is a well written and detailed account documenting much of what is involved in producing a weekly sci-fi television series.

First edition.
$35   **$45**
Later editions.
$15   **$20**

BALLANTINE, 1973

Trouble with Tribbles by David Gerrold. Gerrold's novel adaptation of his popular episode of the same name. Only days after watching *Star Trek* premier on television in 1966, David Gerrold submitted quite a few different story ideas to producer Gene L. Coon at Paramount. One in particular called "The Fuzzies," though initially rejected, was later reconsidered when Mr. Coon contacted Mr. Gerrold's agent asking to have it reworked into a full story. Mr. Gerrold reworked it into "A Fuzzy Thing Happened To Me," which eventually became "The Trouble With Tribbles" and, of course, the rest is now history. It is interesting to note that in his novelization, Mr. Gerrold changed or completely removed some key parts that took place in the television episode. Most notably he removed the briefing room scene, changed the Spican flame gems and Antarean glow water to Argilian flame gems and Sirian glow water, removed the brawl between the Klingons and the Enterprise crew and so also removed the lineup questioning on the Enterprise afterwards as well. He also changed Mr. Scott's last line, "They'll be no Tribble at all," to "All their Tribbles will be big ones." He also added an interesting introduction on Tribbles.

$25   **$45**

Letter from David Gerrold addressing the large fan response to his book.
Price unknown

World of Star Trek by David Gerrold. A behind-the-scenes look into *The Original Series* with rare photos of the cast, props and sets.

$25   **$30**

Sample page of *Starfleet Technical Manual* by Franz Joseph, Ballantine, 1975.

Manual with 20th Anniversary reissue, *Starfleet Technical Manual* by Franz Joseph, Ballantine, 1975.

Star Trek Log Books, Ballantine, 1974-1978.

Advertisement/flyer for technical manual, Ballantine Books flyer, 1975.

Starfleet Technical Manual by Franz Joseph, Ballantine, 1975.

Star Trek Enterprise Blueprints by Franz Joseph, Ballantine, 1975.

Inside front cover of *Starfleet Technical Manual* by Franz Joseph, Ballantine, 1975.

Star Trek Lives! by Jacqueline Lichtenberg, both cover versions, Ballantine/Corgi, 1975.

BALLANTINE, 1974-1978

Star Trek Log Books Logs One through Ten, Alan Dean Foster. Novelizations of *Star Trek: The Animated Series.*

$5   **$15 each book**

Ballantine Books flyer, 1975, advertisement/ flyer for Technical Manual.

$1   **$5**

BALLANTINE, 1975

Starfleet Technical Manual, Franz Joseph. Book features detailed technical information about Starfleet, ships and personnel. It was also used as the basis for the strategy game Starfleet Battles and though not recognized officially as canon, was also used as reference in three films. The history on this book goes that in 1973, Franz Joseph and his daughter were members of a Trek society called STAR where members made their own props and costumes of the show. With his aerospace design abilities, Mr. Joseph created technical drawings of many of the ships and equipment. Gene Roddenberry, who saw many of these technical drawings, was impressed and got his wife Majel Barrett's company, Lincoln Enterprises, involved to help Mr. Joseph create a technical manual. This gave Mr. Joseph privileged access to many of the original props and carpenters' blueprints. Published by Ballantine books in 1975, the manual quickly became the number one seller on the *New York Times* trade paperback list, breaking all other existing sales records. The huge success of the manual was the first hint of what was to come of *Star Trek's* growing popularity.

$50   **$90**

Star Trek Enterprise Blueprints, set of 12 by Franz Joseph.

$45   **$55**

BALLANTINE/ CORGI, 1975

Star Trek Lives! by Jacqueline Lichtenberg.

Both cover versions.

$5   **$15**

Star Trek Concordance, Ballantine, 1976.

Original first printing, *First Season Star Trek Concordance*, Independent Printing, 1968.

Third Season supplement, *Star Trek Concordance*, Independent Printing, 1968.

Reprint *Star Trek Concordance*, Titan Books, 1995.

Star Trek Concordance Color Book, Mathom House Enterprises, 1973.

Star Trek book order form, Ballantine.

Letters to Star Trek by Susan Sackett, Ballantine, 1977.

Starfleet Medical Reference by Eileen Palestine, Ballantine, 1977.

Trek or Treat by Flanagan and Ehrhardt, Ballantine, 1977.

Price of the Phoenix by Marshall and Culbreath, Ballantine, 1977.

Planet of Judgment by Joe Haldeman, Ballantine, 1977.

BALLANTINE, 1976

Star Trek Concordance. This is based on a privately printed fandom publication created by Dorothy Jones and Bjo Trimble in 1968. It was then written into a reference book about *The Original Series* and the animated series, which was then published by Ballantine Books in 1976.

$25   **$35**

INDEPENDENT PRINTING, 1968

Star Trek Concordance. Original rare first printing, first season.

$55   **$75**

Second season supplement.

$55   **$75**

Third season supplement.

$55   **$75**

CAROL PUBLISHING CORPORATION, 1995

Star Trek Concordance reprint.

$10   **$15**

TITAN BOOKS, 1995 (FOREIGN PUBLICATION)

Star Trek Concordance reprint.

$5   **$20**

MATHOM HOUSE ENTERPRISES, 1973

Star Trek Concordance Color Book, collection of artwork by Alicia Austin, George Barr, Greg Bear, Greg Jein, and Bjo Trimble from the original *Star Trek Concordance* published in 1969.

$100   **$200**

Ballantine Star Trek books order form.

$5   **$10**

BALLANTINE, 1977

Letters to Star Trek by Susan Sackett. Gene Roddenberry shares with us the best of the many thousands of fan letters that he and the cast of Star Trek received since the television show first aired.

$15   **$25**

Starfleet Medical Reference by Eileen Palestine. Detailed reference book on all things Medical in Star Fleet. The book's first printing was packaged as a large paperback with a silver colored cardstock over the front cover with the Star Trek logo.

$30   **$35**

Trek or Treat by Flanagan and Ehrhardt. Photos from *The Original Series* with humorous sayings added as can be seen on the front cover.

$10   **$15**

Planet of Judgment by Joe Haldeman. The crew of the Enterprise beams down and gets trapped on an unknown planet that obeys no known laws of science and shouldn't even exist.

$7   **$8**

Price of the Phoenix by Marshall and Culbreath. Mr. Spock investigates the death of Captain Kirk in a house fire on an unnamed planet and confronts the ruler who holds many secrets.

$7   **$9**

BALLANTINE, 1979

Star Trek The Motion Picture Blueprints.
Detailed blueprints of the movie Enterprise,
Klingon, Vulcan ships and more from the
motion picture.

$25 $35

BANTAM, 1967

Star Trek Volumes 1-12, James Blish.
Adaptations of the original television
episodes. James Blish passed away midway
through writing *Star Trek 12*. His wife, J. A.
Lawrence, completed the book and then
later also completed the adaptations in the
book *Mudd's Angels*.

$5 $10 each

British versions published by Corgi:

Hard cover.

$10 $15

Paperback.

$5 $10

Books were also sold in boxed sets of 4 to 5
books per "box."

$25 $45

BANTAM, 1970

Spock Must Die by James Blish. This was
the first original *Star Trek* novel published
by Bantam Books and has had a few cover
artwork variations. It is a sequel to *Errand of
Mercy* by James Blish. A transporter accident
creates two Mr. Spocks and one of them
must be destroyed.

$5 $15

BANTAM, 1975

Star Trek Lives!, Jacqueline Lichtenberg
Sondra Marshak and Joan Winston. The book
discusses the popularity and ideas of *The
Original Series* while also focusing on the
growing fandom.

$10 $20

BANTAM, 1976

Spock Messiah, Theodore Cogswell and
Charles Spano, Jr. A defective mind-link
experiment with telepathic implants goes
terribly wrong, causing the usually logical Mr.
Spock to go mad and leave the Enterprise
only to become the Messiah of the hostile
planet Kyros, which launches a holy war on
the rest of the world.

$7 $8

Hardcover *Star Trek* volumes by James Blish,
Bantam, 1967.

Star Trek The Motion Picture Blueprints, Ballantine,
1979.

Star Trek, Volumes 1-12, by James Blish, Bantam
1967.

Boxed sets of *Star Trek* volumes by James Blish,
Bantam, 1967.

Three different book/cover versions of *Star Trek* by
James Blish, #1, Bantam, 1967.

Spock Must Die! by James Blish, Bantam, 1970.

Three different book/cover versions of *Star Trek* by
James Blish, #9, Bantam, 1967.

Star Trek Lives! by
Jacqueline Lichtenberg,
Sondra Marshak and
Joan Winston, Bantam,

Spock Messiah by
Theodore Cogswell
and Charles Spano, Jr.,
Bantam, 1976.

Paperback *Star Trek* by James Blish, Bantam, 1967.

Paperback *Star Trek Puzzle Manual* by James Razzi, Bantam, 1976.

Large format *Star Trek Puzzle Manual* by James Razzi, Bantam, 1976.

Star Trek: The New Voyages by Marshak and Culbreath, Bantam, 1976.

Fotonovel, series of 12 books, Bantam, 1977-1978.

Fotonovel #1, City on the Edge of Forever, Bantam, 1977.

Fotonovel #2, Where No Man Has Gone Before, Bantam, 1977.

Fotonovel #3, The Trouble With Tribbles, Bantam, 1977.

Fotonovel #4, A Taste of Armageddon, Bantam, 1978.

Fotonovel #5, Metamorphosis, Bantam, 1978.

Fotonovel #6, All Our Yesterdays, Bantam, 1978.

Star Trek Puzzle Manual, James Razzi:

Paperback.

| $5 | $10 |

Large format.

| $20 | $30 |

Star Trek: The New Voyages, Marshak and Culbreath. Collection of original short stories based on *The Original Series* includes: "Ni Var" by Claire Gabriel, "Intersection Point" by Juanita Coulson, "The Enchanted Pool" by Marcia Ericson, "Visit to a Weird Planet Revisited" by Ruth Berman, "The Face on the Barroom Floor" by Eleanor Arnason and Ruth Berman, "The Hunting" by Doris Beetem, "The Winged Dreamers" by Jennifer Guttridge and "Mind-Sifter" by Shirley Maiewski.

| $10 | $15 |

BANTAM, 1977-1978

Fotonovel series of 12 books (and later two movie novels). Each "fotonovel" episode book is made up of hundreds of color photos from each episode laid out in the style of a graphic novel.

#1 *City on the Edge of Forever*, 1977.

#2 *Where No Man Has Gone Before*, 1977.

#3 *The Trouble With Tribbles*, 1977.

#4 *A Taste of Armageddon*, 1978.

#5 *Metamorphosis*, 1978.

#6 *All Our Yesterdays*, 1978.

#7 *The Galileo*, 1978.

#8 *A Piece of the Action*, 1978.

| $10 | $15 each |

Fotonovel #7, The Galileo, Bantam, 1978.

Fotonovel #8, A Piece of the Action, Bantam 1978.

Fotonovel #9, Devil in the Dark, Bantam, 1978.

Fotonovel #11, The Deadly Years, Bantam, 1978.

Fotonovel #10, Day of the Dove, Bantam, 1978.

Fotonovel #12, Amok Time, Bantam, 1978.

Boxed sets of Fotonovels, Bantam, 1977-1978.

Star Trek: The Motion Picture "Fotonovel" Photostory, Bantam, 1979.

Mudd's Angels by J.A. Lawrence, Bantam, 1978.

#9 *Devil in the Dark*, 1978.

#10 *Day of the Dove*, 1978.

#11 *The Deadly Years*, 1978.

#12 *Amok Time*, 1978.

Box sets.

$25 $40

BANTAM, 1977

Star Trek Intergalactic Puzzles by James Razzi. Assorted *Star Trek*-themed puzzles and brain teasers.

$20 $25

Star Trek: The New Voyages 2, Marshak and Culbreath. More original short stories including: "Surprise!" by Nichelle Nichols, Sondra Marshak and Myrna Culbreath, "Snake Pit" by Connie Faddis, "The Patient Parasites" by Russell Bates, "In the Maze" by Jennifer Guttridge, "Cave-In" by Jane Peyton, "Marginal Existence" by Connie Faddis, "The Procrustean Petard" by Sondra Marshak and Myrna Culbreath and "The Sleeping God" by Jesco von Puttkamer.

$10 $15

BANTAM, 1978

Mudd's Angels, J.A. Lawrence. Book is comprised of three stories featuring Harry Mudd: "Mudd's Woman," adapted from the script by Stephen Kandel; "I, Mudd," adapted from the script also by Stephen Kandel; and "The Business, As Usual, During Altercations," a new story by J.A. Lawrence. J.A. Lawrence was James Blish's wife and after his death she completed his last two episode novelizations while adding a third original story of her own. The book was originally intended to contain all of the Harry Mudd episode stories including the animated episode "Mudd's Passion," but at that time, the rights to all of the animated stories were owned by Ballantine Books.

$20 $25

Official Star Trek Cooking Manual, Ann Picard. A galaxy of Star Trek recipes, with over 100 favorites of the starship Enterprise.

$50 $75

Starless World, Gordon Eklund. Inside a hollow shell of a remote planet, the Enterprise crew discover a planet within a planet energized by a white dwarf star. The planet seems like a lost Eden populated by a race of small, gentle, furry humanoids, but the planetoid is in peril and falling toward a black hole and inescapable doom, taking the Enterprise crew with it.

$12 $20

Vulcan, Kathleen Sky. After a series of freak ion storms, the Neutral Zone between Federation space and the Romulan Empire will soon shift, placing the planet Arachnae entirely within Romulan space. The Enterprise crew is sent to seek out intelligent life on Arachnae and offer Federation protection.

$18 $22

BANTAM, 1979

Devil World, Gordon Eklund. The crew of the Enterprise travels to the quarantined planet of Heartland, seeking the infamous traitor Jacob Kell who had once sold out the Federations to the Klingons. The Enterprise landing party beams down to discover a strange world where evil and immortality rule.

$15 $20

The Fate of the Phoenix, Marshak and Culbreath. Sequel to the earlier novel *The Price of the Phoenix*, where the evil black Omne had been defeated. This time, however, through the miracle of rebirth, this evil entity lives again. Captain Kirk, Mr. Spock and the rest of the Enterprise crew must fight hand-to-hand combat with the giant evil and immortal Omne, who has now not only vowed revenge against the Enterprise and her crew, but against the entire human race.

$7 $8

Trek to Madworld, Stephen Goldin. During an urgent mission of mercy to the dying colony of Epsilon Delta 4, the Enterprise is diverted by the unpredictable exile Enowil, who is in charge of a world gone mad. The exile has a Klingon and a Romulan warship already under his control and decides to put Captain Kirk and his crew through a very dangerous test of wits during which the colonists on Epsilon Delta 4 face certain death while they continue to wait for rescue by the now missing Enterprise.

$8 $12

Star Trek Annuals, BBC Productions, 1968.

Star Trek Annuals, BBC Productions, 1970.

Star Trek Annuals, BBC Productions, 1971-1972.

Star Trek Annuals, BBC productions, 1973.

Star Trek Annuals, BBC Productions, from top: 1976, 1975, and 1974.

Star Trek Annuals, BBC Productions, 1977-1980.

World Without End, Joe Haldeman. While the Enterprise orbits an alien planetoid-shaped starship, Captain Kirk and landing party become stranded after beaming over and get detained in a prison cell. During this time the Enterprise becomes ensnared by wires that begin draining off its power reserves at such an alarming rate that it forces the crew to decide between crashing into the planetoid's surface once all power is gone or beaming over where the captain and the landing party are now being held captive.

$10   **$15**

Star Trek: The Motion Picture "Fotonovel" Photostory. Actual photos from the movie with word balloons make up the book.

$25   **$35**

BBC PRODUCTIONS, 1968 TO 1990S

Star Trek Annuals. The UK released oversize hardcover books reprinting various Gold Key comics, as well as a variety of puzzles and photos.

$25   **$55**

Television Picture Story Book (UK), 1971, rare British story book featuring some great artwork.

$25   **$35**

BIBLE VOICE, 1978

Winkie Pratney. *Star Wars, Star Trek and the 21st Century Christians.* A unique short-volume book aimed at converting kids to Christianity using their interest in *Star Wars* and *Star Trek.*

$10   **$20**

Star Trek Annuals, BBC Productions, 1981 and up.

British Television Picture Story Book, 1971.

Star Trek: Space Ark Giant Story Coloring Book, Cav-Mart Inc., 1978.

CAV-MART INC., 1978

Star Trek: Space Ark Giant Story Coloring Book, 17" x 22"; (Liza Hamill; Don Dyen).

$25   **$35**

Profiles in History Presents the Star Trek Auction.

CELESTIAL ARTS, 1975

I Am Not Spock; Leonard Nimoy autobiography. This book was Leonard Nimoy's attempt to try and distance himself from *Star Trek* in the mid-1970s. Quite a few years later he finally came to peace with the fact that he will always be known as Mr. Spock and wrote a new book called, *I Am Spock*.

I Am Not Spock, hardcover.
$40 $60
I Am Not Spock, paperback.
$5 $10

DUTTON, 1970-1974

Star Trek Readers Vol. I-VI. A compilation of James Blish's *Star Trek* adaptations. Many believe that the first *Star Trek* reader by James Blish was the best, as it included Blish's attempt to slightly rework one of the most beloved of all of the *Star Trek* stories, "The City on the Edge of Forever." It becomes Blish's version because he reworked the story in a way to combine what he believed was the best of both Harlan Ellison's original script and the TV-produced version that aired. Blish admitted later that he worried that he might owe many apologies to *Star Trek* fans around the world, but to his surprise and delight his "version" was met with critical acclaim from most of the Trek community.
$15 $35

Profiles in History/eBay. Profiles in History Presents the *Star Trek* auction, featuring the collection of art director Matt Jefferies, among others.
$25 $45

GROSSET & DUNLAP, 1979

Star Trek Catalog by Gerry Turnbull. Available in both paperback and large format, the book includes detailed summaries of each of the 78 episodes including biographies on the cast and a catalog of related memorabilia.
$10 $15

Star Trek Memories by William Shatner and Chris Kreski, Harper, 1993.

Star Trek Movie Memories by William Shatner and Chris Kreski, Harper, 1994.

HARPER, 1993

Star Trek Memories by William Shatner and Chris Kreski. William Shatner looks back at his 25 years of being in *Star Trek*. Later released on VHS and then DVD, it features cast members from the television series and movies reminiscing with Shatner about the making of the series and the films and their opinions on why they feel the franchise has been so successful.

Hardcover.
$15 $20
Paperback.
$5 $10

Star Trek Catalog by Gerry Turnbull, Grosset & Dunlap, 1979.

HARPER 1994

Star Trek Movie Memories by William Shatner and Chris Kreski. William Shatner's on and off the set memories of making the feature films. Also see audio novels in records and tapes.
Hardcover.
$15 $20
Paperback.
$5 $10
Star Trek Unauthorized Star Trek Quiz Book.
$5 $10

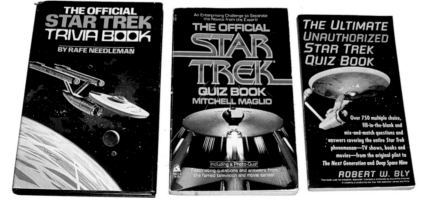

Star Trek Unauthorized Star Trek Quiz Book, Harper, 1994.

Star Trek, Japanese version, Hayakawa Tokyo Books.

Star Trek, Japanese version, Hayakawa Tokyo Books.

Star Trek, Japanese version, Hayakawa Tokyo Books.

Star Trek, Japanese version, Hayakawa Tokyo Books.

Artwork in Japanese versions of James Blish's novel adaptations, Hayakawa Tokyo Books.

Star Trek, Japanese version, Hayakawa Tokyo Books.

Star Trek, Japanese version, Hayakawa Tokyo Books.

Star Trek, Japanese version, Hayakawa Tokyo Books.

Star Trek, Japanese version, Hayakawa Tokyo Books.

HAYAKAWA TOKYO BOOKS

Japanese versions of James Blish novel adaptations of *The Original Series*. Asian books read from back to front which adds to the charm and collectibility of these unique books. They have spectacular cover artwork with a few of the books featuring unique artwork inside as well.

Individual books.

$10   **$25**

Set of 12.

$120   **$400**

Star Trek, Japanese version, Hayakawa Tokyo Books.

Star Trek, Japanese version, Hayakawa Tokyo Books.

Star Trek, Japanese version, Hayakawa Tokyo Books.

Star Trek, Japanese version, Hayakawa Tokyo Books.

HERITAGE, 1976

Who Was That Monolith I Saw You With? by Michael Goodwin. Black and white comic book-style artwork panels of funny happenings of the Starship Enterprise.

$5   **$15**

IMAGE PUBLISHING

The Making of Trek Films, James Van Hise. An illustrated history of *Star Trek* on the big screen exploring the success of the films and the cast while chronicling many of the onscreen and behind-the-scenes stories.

$10   **$15**

Who Was That Monolith I Saw You With? by Michael Goodwin, Heritage, 1976.

The Making of Trek Films by James Van Hise, Image Publishing.

Christmas Catalog, JCPenney, 1973-1975.

Christmas Catalog, JCPenney, 1976-1980.

JCPENNEY, 1973-75

Christmas catalog. Includes Star Trek toys, clothes, housewares, etc.

$35   **$65**

JCPENNEY, 1976-1980

Christmas catalog. Includes Star Trek toys, clothes, housewares, etc.

$25   **$45**

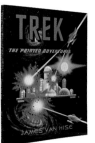

Star Trek Coloring Book,
Lincoln Enterprises.

*Star Trek Memorabilia
Catalog,* Memorabilia
Catalog Booklet.

*Star Trek and Star Wars Collectibles Price Guides,
Official Price Guides, 1983-1987.*

*Trek, The Printed
Adventures* by James
Van Hise, Pioneer
Press.

The History of Trek
by James Van Hise,
Pioneer Press.

Christmas catalogs, Montgomery Ward, 1973-1980.

*Official Star Trek: The
Motion Picture Movie
Premier Program,*
Paramount, 1979.

The Monsters of Star Trek by Daniel Cohen,
Pocket Books, 1980.

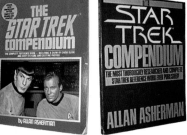

Star Trek Compendium, Guide to Star Trek by Allan
Asherman, Pocket Books, 1981.

LINCOLN ENTERPRISE

Star Trek coloring book; includes 24 artwork
scenes from *Star Trek: The Animated Series.*

$55   **$75**

*Memorabilia Catalog Booklet, Star Trek
Memorabilia Catalog.*

$5   **$15**

MONTGOMERY WARD, 1973-1980

Christmas catalogs; includes Star Trek toys,
clothes, housewares, etc.

$25   **$45**

OFFICIAL PRICE GUIDES, 1983-1987

*Star Trek and Star Wars Collectibles Price
Guides.* The first of the major sci-fi price
guides back when Star Trek and Star
Wars were just starting out as collectible
juggernauts and were combined together in
a single book.

$10   **$25**

PARAMOUNT, 1979

*Official Star Trek: The Motion Picture Movie
Premier* program. Features color photos
on thick glossy card stock pages from the
movie.

$25   **$45**

PARKERS RUN, 1978

Two different "Giant coloring books,"
Uncharted World and *War in Space.*

$30   **$40**

PIONEER PRESS

Trek, The Printed Adventures and *The History
of Trek,* both by James Van Hise.

$10   **$15 each**

POCKET BOOKS, 1980

The Monsters of Star Trek by Daniel Cohen.
The source book for the *Star Trek* fan on
the various life forms encountered in *The
Original Series.* Includes illustrations and
photos from various episodes.

$10   **$15**

POCKET BOOKS, 1981

Star Trek Compendium, Guide to Star Trek
by Allan Asherman. Two cover versions.
The book gives summaries and production
information on all three seasons of Trek and
the first motion picture. It also provides the
actual production schedule for each of the
episodes including script dates and when
each episode was filmed.

$10   **$15**

Star Trek: Phase II by Judith and Garfield Reeves-Stevens, Pocket Books.

Star Trek by Judith and Garfield Reeves-Stevens, Pocket Books, 1995.

Where No One Has Gone Before, Pocket Books, 1996.

These Are The Voyages 3-D Pop-Up Book, Pocket Books, 1996.

POCKET BOOKS

Star Trek: Phase II by Judith and Garfield Reeves-Stevens; "Story of the show that almost was." In 1977, Paramount Pictures had begun working on launching a new television network. Recognizing the large growing *Star Trek* fandom as well as a growing interest in science fiction programming, Paramount created plans to launch a new *Star Trek* series as the flagship program for its new network. The new series would follow the adventures of the Enterprise and crew on a second five-year mission, called Phase Two. Though Paramount's network deal would fall through thanks to the success of movies like *Star Wars* and *Close Encounters of the Third Kind* in the summer of 1977, the idea of a new *Star Trek* would not die and would soon become a major motion picture which would launch a whole new age of *Star Trek.*

$25   **$35**

POCKET BOOKS, 1995

The Art of Star Trek by Judith and Garfield Reeves-Stevens. No where else will you find this large a gallery of amazing and spectacular *Star Trek* artwork, which also becomes a tribute to the many designers, technicians and artists whose incredible imaginations created the unique and distinctive look that makes up the Star Trek universe.

$25   **$45**

POCKET BOOKS, 1996

Where No One Has Gone Before; "a history of *Star Trek* in pictures." A large volume "coffee table"-type book packed with photographs and tells the history of *Star Trek* from the beginning up to the latest incarnations. A must have for both casual and die-hard fans alike.

$25   **$35**

Voyages 3-D pop-up book, *Celebrating 30 years of Star Trek* in a 3-D pop-up display by Charles Kurts.

$10   **$25**

POCKET BOOKS, 1997

Star Trek: Federation Travel Guide by Michael Jan Friedman. This is considered the essential guide for any interstellar traveler and/or *Star Trek* fan. It features artwork created for a variety of the *Star Trek* series through the years and includes information on the many worlds in and around the Federation. One of the unique parts of this book is some of the essential phrases that are included by those who were involved in creating many of the interesting languages for *Star Trek* including the ever popular Klingon language.

$15   **$20**

Star Trek: Federation Travel Guide by Michael Jan Friedman, Pocket Books, 1997.

Giant in the Universe by Kay Wood, Random House, 1977.

RANDOM HOUSE, 1976

Star Trek Action Toy Book by James Razzi. This punch-out, fold and play book includes perforated graphics and printed instructions on how to make such things as a communicator that flips open, a Phaser with a working trigger or a Tricorder with a swivel open and close top among many other punch out toys.

$20   **$40**

RANDOM HOUSE, 1977

Giant in the Universe, Kay Wood. Captain Kirk, Mr. Spock, and Mr. Scott beam down to explore a gigantic unidentified planet and discover a giant who attempts to catch them.

$30   **$60**

Trillions of Trilligs by Cerf and Lerner, Random House, 1977.

The Truth Machine by Cerf and Lerner, Random House, 1977.

Star Trek Photograph Album, Robert Frederick LTD, 1998.

Star Trek: A Book to Color, Saalfield, 1967.

Star Trek Coloring Books – Spock, Saalfield, 1975.

Star Trek: An Analysis of a Phenomenon in Science Fiction, SC Enterprises, 1968.

Star Trek Quiz Book by Andrew and Dunning, Signet, 1977.

Mr. Scott's Guide to the Enterprise, written and illustrated by Shane Johnson, Simon and Schuster, 1987.

I Can Draw Star Trek by Tony Tallarico, Simon Spotlight, 1996.

Prisoner of Vega, Lerner and Cerf. The Enterprise crew discovers villains from the Klingon Empire are holding the beautiful ruler Queen Vanadala of Vega III prisoner.

$20 $25

Trillions of Trilligs, Cerf and Lerner. The Enterprise crew beams down to the planet Ynobe II to try and save the people of the planet who are being attacked by Trillions of Trillig robots that are everywhere.

$15 $30

The Truth Machine, Cerf and Lerner. The Enterprise crew encounters an alien race that has developed a fleet of powerful warships who are seeking the secret of warp drive so they can conquer the galaxy.

$15 $30

ROBERT FREDERICK LTD., 1998

Star Trek Photograph Album.

$15 $25

RUNNING PRESS, 1976

Star Trek Crossword Puzzle. Puzzle is shaped like the Enterprise and comes folded up in an envelope.

$10 $12

SAALFIELD, 1967

Star Trek: A Book to Color, based on the NBC television series by Robert Doremus.

$45 $55

SAALFIELD, 1975

Star Trek Coloring Books-Spock.

$10 $20

Star Trek Coloring Books-Spock and Kirk.

$10 $20

Star Trek Punch-Out and Play Album.

$20 $30

SC ENTERPRISES, 1968

Star Trek: An Analysis of a Phenomenon in Science Fiction, a rare and early publication, with 47 pages of photos and illustrations.

$25 $50

SEARS, 1974-1975

Wishbook Christmas catalogs; includes Star Trek toys, clothes, housewares, etc.

$45 $75

SEARS, 1976-1978

Wishbook Christmas catalogs; includes Star Trek toys, clothes, housewares, etc.

$25 $45

SEARS, 1979-1980

Wishbook Christmas catalogs; includes Star Trek toys, clothes, housewares, etc mostly from *Star Trek: The Motion Picture*.

$25 $45

SIGNET, 1977

Star Trek Quiz Book by Andrew and Dunning. Tests your knowledge of *Star Trek* from all three seasons of *The Original Series*.

$10 $15

SIGNET, 1978 TO 1991

The Best of Trek, Irwin and Love #1-#16. A compilation of the best of some of the original short stories.

$5 $20

SIMON AND SCHUSTER, 1987

Mr. Scott's Guide to the Enterprise, written and illustrated by Shane Johnson. "Based upon the engineering logs of Chief Engineer Montgomery Scott."

$5 $20

SIMON SPOTLIGHT, 1996

I Can Draw Star Trek by Tony Tallarico. Shows how to draw the spacecraft and other devices of *The Original Series*.

$10 $15

U.S.S. Enterprise
Officer's Manual,
Starfleet Publication
Office.

Line Officer
Requirements Vol. One,
Starfleet Academy
Training Command.

Line Officer Requirements Vol. Two, Starfleet
Academy Training Command.

Line Officer
Requirements
Supplement, Starfleet
Academy Training
Command.

Command &
Operations, Starfleet
Officers Requirements
Vol. One.

Detailed uniform specs,
Starfleet Uniform
Recognition Manual by
Shane Johnson.

Starfleet Academy
Training Command,
Starfleet Dynamics.

Weapons and Field Equipment Technical Reference
Manual by Shane Johnson.

Starship Designs and
Schematics, Starship
Design, 2280.

U.S.S. Enterprise
Officer's Manual.

STARFLEET
PUBLICATION OFFICE

U.S.S. Enterprise Officer's Manual.
 $20   **$25**
Starfleet Academy Training Command (red)

Line Officer Requirements Vol. One.
 $20   **$25**
Starfleet Academy Training Command (green)

Line Officer Requirements Vol. Two.
 $20   **$25**
Starfleet Academy Training Command (black)

Line Officer Requirements Supplement.
 $20   **$25**
Starfleet Officers Requirements Volume One
(purple)

Command & Operations.
 $20   **$25**
Starfleet Uniform Recognition Manual by
Shane Johnson. Has 80 pages of detailed
uniform specs.
 $15   **$20**
Starfleet Dynamics

Starfleet Academy Training Command.
Starfleet Officer requirements (25th
anniversary edition).
 $25   **$30**
Starship Design, 2280; book includes
Starship designs and schematics.
 $20   **$25**
U.S.S. Enterprise Officers Manual; spiral-
bound officers manual.
 $15   **$20**
*Weapons and Field Equipment Technical
Reference Manual* by Shane Johnson;
includes Star Trek weapons and field
equipment technical specs.
 $15   **$20**

Star Trek Lives!
International Star Trek
Convention Program,
1973.

Boston Star Trek
Convention Program,
1976.

The Star Trek
Convention Program,
1976.

STAR TREK CONVENTION PROGRAMS, 1972-PRESENT

Beginning in 1972, there has been at least one Star Trek convention each year. Here are a few examples of convention programs:

Star Trek Lives! International Star Trek Convention 1973.
$25 **$35**
Boston Star Trek Convention.
$15 **$25**
The Star Trek Convention 1976.
$15 **$25**
Convention Bag, Boston Star Trek Convention 1976.
$2 **$5**
Star Trek Bi-Centennial-10 Convention Bag.
$5 **$8**

TERRA ASTRA

German versions of the Blish's episode adaptations.
Each book.
$5 **$10**
Complete set of 15 books.
$75 **$150**

WALLABY, 1979

Make Your Own Costume Book, Lynn Edelman Schnurnberger.
$20 **$30**
Star Trek: The Motion Picture Peel-Off Graphics Book, Lee Cole.
$40 **$50**

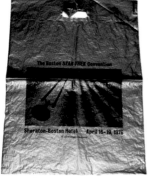

Convention Bag, Boston Star Trek
Convention, 1976.

Convention Bag, Star Trek
Bi-Centennial-10.

Complete set of 15 books, German version of Blish's episode adaptations, *Terra Astra*.

WANDERER, 1979

Star Trek Giant Coloring Book #1 and #2.
$10 **$20**
Star Trek Make-a-Game Book, Bruce and Greg Nash.
$20 **$30**
Star Trek: The Motion Picture Bridge Punch-Out Book.
$20 **$30**
Star Trek: The Motion Picture U.S.S. Enterprise Punch-Out Book.
$25 **$40**

Star Trek
Make-
a-Game
Book by
Bruce and
Greg Nash,
Wanderer,
1979.

WANDERER, 1980

Star Trek: The Motion Picture Pop-Up Book.

   $25   **$35**

WARNER, 1977

Meaning in Star Trek by Karen Blair. A fascinating look into the early days of *Star Trek* describing in detail on how it transformed from a canceled television show into a pop-culture phenomenon.

   $20   **$30**

WESTERN, 1968

Mission to Horatius, Mack Reynolds. This was the very first professional *Star Trek* novel published as well as the only novel to be published while *The Original Series* was still in production. An exhausted Enterprise crew answering a mysterious distress call in the far away Horatius system soon discover that they must find a way to help the Horatians without breaking the prime directive.

   $75   **$100**

Reprint.

   $20   **$25**

WHITMAN, 1978, COLORING BOOKS

A Blast of Activities.

A Launch Into Fun.

Far-Out Fun.

Futuristic Fun.

Jeopardy at Jutterdon.

Planet Ecnal's Dilemma.

Rescue at Raylo.

   $10   **$25 each**

WORLD DISTRIBUTORS, 1974

Unique *Star Trek* coloring book; includes artwork and a story.

   $45   **$65**

Book store advertisement poster advertising *Star Trek* books, shown at right. Note the reissues at the bottom showing a few older stories based on *The Original Series* and characters going through yet another reprinting.

Star Trek: The Motion Picture Pop-Up Book, Wanderer, 1980.

Mission to Horatius by Mack Reynolds, western, 1968.

Futuristic Fun Coloring Book, Whitman, 1978.

Star Trek Coloring Book, World Distributors, 1974.

Book store advertisement poster for *Star Trek* books by Pocket Books.

Bumper Stickers

APRIL PUBLICATIONS, 1984

Blue lettering on day-glo yellow background:

Caution...I Brake for Tribbles.

Honk If You Like Star Trek.

I've Visited Vulcan – Home of Spock.

Live Long and Prosper.

Star Trek Lives.

This Vehicle Equipped with Warp Drive.

Vulcan Power.

 $20   **$25 each**

AVIVA ENTERPRISES, 1979

Beam Me Up Mr. Spock.

Dr. McCoy Doesn't Make House Calls.

I Am a Trekkie.

Live Long and Prosper.

Star Trek (with Enterprise and Spock).

 $15   **$20 each**

BUMPER STICKERS, 1978

Beam Me Up Scotty.

Live Long And Prosper.

U.S.S. Enterprise NCC-1701.

"Hailing Frequencies Open."

 $10   **$15 each**

LINCOLN ENTERPRISES, 1984

Lincoln Enterprises is Majel Barrett Roddenberry's Star Trek fan merchandise store. She and her company were the first to offer unique Star Trek items for sale specially made for the fans. These items were first made available in the 1970s via catalogs and mail order and now can be found online at: www.roddenberry.com. All have black lettering on day-glo fluorescent background:

Star Trek Lives.

Live Long and Prosper.

I Grok Spock/Star Trek.

I Reserve the Right to Arm Klingons.

Government Vehicle/Vulcan Embassy.

Take a Human to Lunch Star Trek.

Smile...if you like Star Trek.

Vote YES on Star Trek.

Caution...Endangered Species.

Jaws is a Klingon Minnow.

Mr. Spock for President.

Don't Tailgate, This is a Klingon War Cruiser.

Trekker on Board.

Mr. Spock Phone Home.

I Am a Carbon Unit.

The Human Adventure is Just Beginning.

 $5   **$10 each**

MERE DRAGONS, 1988

At Warp Speed 9 – They All Look Green to Me.

Beam Me Up Scotty – It Ate My Phaser.

Brought to You By the Klingon Anti-Earth League.

Caution: This Vehicle Equipped with Photon Torpedos & a Trigger Happy Helmsman.

Engine by Scotty. 0 to warp 7 in fifteen seconds.

He's Dead Jim – You Grab His Tricorder, I'll Get His Wallet.

I'd Rather Be: Squishing Tribbles; Fleecing the Federation; Annoying Earthers; Guzzling Romulan Ale.

If You Can Read This, You Are in Phaser Range.

My Other Car is a Starship.

Nobody Knows the Tribbles I've Seen.

The Only Way to Fly (Picture of Enterprise).

There Are a Few Problems in the Galaxy That Can't Be Solved By a Suitable Application of Concentrated Phaser Fire.

Vulcan Power of Logical Enlightenment.

 $5   **$10 each**

Beam Me Up, Scotty, bumper stickers, 1978.

Live Long And Prosper, bumper stickers, 1978.

U.S.S. Enterprise NCC-1701, bumper stickers, 1978.

At Warp Speed 9 – They All Look Green To Me, Mere Dragons, 1988.

I'd rather be: squishing tribbles; fleecing the Federation; annoying Earthers, Guzzling Romulan Ale; Mere Dragons, 1988.

PEGASUS PUBLISHING

"Kirk to Enterprise, Beam Down Yeoman Rand and a Six-Pack."

 $5   **$10**

STAR TREK CONVENTION, NEW YORK CITY, 1972

"Star Trek Lives" in orange lettering on black background.

 $25   **$45**

STAR TREK ENTERPRISES, 1968

Rare stickers, especially the one from when fans were asked to write in to NBC to try and save *Star Trek* from cancellation.

"Save Star Trek - Write NBC" in fluorescent green on black background; "Spock It To Me" in black lettering on Day-Glo background.

 $45   **$55 each**

Buttons, Coins, Medallions, and Medals

Homemade and fan-made buttons, pins, and coins are so easy to create, that this chapter only documents the popular, company-manufactured offerings. Though not a complete list by any means, this will at least give you a sample of what is available to collectors.

BUTTONS

AVIVA, 1979

Star Trek: The Motion Picture buttons:

Crew on Bridge.

Kirk in uniform.

Kirk standing.

Kirk, Spock, McCoy.

Spock in uniform.

Spock in Vulcan clothing.

$1   **$5 each**

BUTTON-UP, 1984

Original series buttons:

Kirk head shot.

Kirk and McCoy.

Kirk and Spock.

Kirk, Spock, and McCoy.

McCoy, Uhura, and Chekov.

Sulu.

Enterprise.

Enterprise and Constellation.

$1   **$5 each**

Star Trek III: The Search for Spock buttons:

Kirk head shot.

Kirk wider head shot.

McCoy.

Spock Vulcan costume.

Chekov head shot.

Sulu head shot.

Uhura holding Phaser.

David Marcus wide head shot.

Saavik head shot.

Kruge head shot.

Star Trek III logo.

$1   **$5 each**

CALIFORNIA DREAMERS, 1987

Various buttons, California Dreamers, 1987.

Photos buttons; same images and sayings as the set of key chains also produced by California Dreamers:

Space the Final Frontier.

Live Long and Prosper.

Hang in There.

Beam Me up Scotty.

Superior Being.

Keep Your Shields Up.

I Hate Mondays.

Seek Out Strange New Worlds.

Fire All Phaser Weapons.

Spock for President.

The Captain.

$5   **$10 each**

LANGLEY & ASSOCIATES, 1976

Buttons, Langley & Associates, 1976.

Buttons featuring photos from the TV show:

Kirk head shot.	Chekov with crew.
Kirk in uniform.	Chekov frowning.
Kirk Trouble with Tribbles.	Chekov on bridge.
Kirk ready to beam down.	Chekov smiling.
Kirk with communicator.	Scott close-up.
Kirk behind bars.	Spock as Science Officer.
Pike, original commander.	Spock close-up.
McCoy close-up.	Spock laughing.
McCoy.	Spock logical-looking.
McCoy talking.	Spock smiling.
Enterprise with Star Trek.	Spock talking.
Enterprise above planet.	Spock head shot.
Enterprise rear view.	Spock with beard.
Enterprise with red planet.	Sulu.
Khan.	Sulu close-up.
Klingon ship.	Sulu looking up.
Uhura with headset.	Nurse Chapel.
Uhura by communication equipment.	Yeoman Rand.

$1 $5 each

LINCOLN ENTERPRISES, 1976

Buttons with photos from the original TV series:

Kirk.	Scotty.	Chekov.
Spock.	Uhura.	Chapel.
McCoy.	Sulu.	Enterprise.

$5 $10 each

PARAMOUNT PICTURES CORP, 1966

Black and white promotional buttons of Kirk and Spock.

$25 $45

PARAMOUNT PICTURES CORP., 1974

Promotional button, Star Trek original TV series crew.

$5 $10

PARAMOUNT PICTURES, TREKKIES

Trekkies promotional movie button, Paramount Pictures.

"They are the most powerful force in the universe"; promotional button for movie theater employees to wear to advertise the May 21 opening of the first *Trekkies* movie.

$5 $10

POCKET BOOKS, 1985-1989, PROMOTIONAL BOOK BUTTONS

"Read the Klingon Language," 1985.
"Star Trek: The Only Logical Books To Read," Spock, 1986.
"Star Trek: The Only Logical Books To Read," Spock, 1989.

$4 $8 each

STARPOST, 1987, SET OF COLOR BUTTONS FROM THE ORIGINAL SERIES

Spock.

Spock head shot.

Vian.

Talosian.

Mugato.

U.S.S. Enterprise (artwork).

Kirk, Spock, McCoy and Enterprise (artwork).
$10 $20 each

VIRGIL FINLEY, 1973

These were the first official Star Trek buttons as they were sold at the 1973 Star Trek Con, which was the first official Star Trek convention. Sold as a set of three buttons, these were artistic portraits of Mr. Spock created by Virgil Finley. After the convention, they were then advertised for sale in the *Monster Times* magazine from 1973 to 1974.

Green button with black and white drawing of Spock.
$25 $35 each

COINS

CHICAGOLAND PROCESSING, 1991, 25TH ANNIVERSARY COMMEMORATIVE COINS

Enterprise silver.

Kirk silver.

Spock silver.
$65 $75
Set of the three matching silver coins.
$150 $175
Set of the three matching coins in gold on silver; sold with matching number sets only.
$250 $300

25th Anniversary Commemorative Coin, Chicagoland Processing, 1991.

CONTINENTAL COIN COMPANY, 1992, MOVIE POSTER TRADING CARD INGOTS

Star Trek: The Motion Picture (Advance).
$55 $65
Star Trek: The Motion Picture (Style A).
$45 $55
Star Trek II: The Wrath of Khan.
$45 $55
Star Trek: IV: The Voyage Home (Advance).
$55 $65

Star Trek IV: The Voyage Home (Style A).
$45 $50
Star Trek V: The Final Frontier (Advance).
$55 $65
Star Trek VI: The Undiscovered Country (Advance).
$55 $65
Star Trek VI: The Undiscovered Country (Style A).
$45 $55

FRANKLIN MINT, 1990

Star Trek 25th Anniversary Coin.
$55   **$75**

HUCKLEBERRY, 1972

Large wooden nickel with drawing of Mr. Spock. Has "In Spock We Trust" and "Leonard Nimoy Wouldn't Lie" on back of coin.
$20   **$45**

LINCOLN ENTERPRISES, 1976

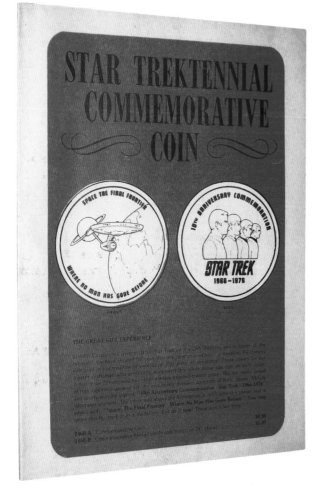

Star Trektennial Coin ad by Lincoln Enterprises, 1976.

Special Commemorative Coin celebrating the 10th Anniversary.

Star Trektennial Coin No. 2460-A.
$25   **$45**

Star Trektennial Commemorative Medallion No. 2460-B; coin mounted on 24" chain.
$45   **$55**

FRANKLIN MINT, 1993

Set of 12 solid silver coins. Each coin features one of the crew members on one side and their insignia symbols on the other. A blue and silver display case was provided for free after a customer had completed the entire set of coins.
$45   **$55 per coin**

Display case (originally free).
$75   **$100**

RARITIES MINT, 1989

Set of seven crew member coins. Each coin features an image of a crew member in a frosted-style relief on a mirrored background. Coins all have the Enterprise with the Star Trek text logo and each coin is numbered on the edge. An error occurs in the numbering sequence. Some numbering is much higher than the actual number of coins produced. These 1-ounce silver coins came in a velvet-like lined box with plastic holders.

Kirk.	McCoy.	Uhura.
Spock.	Scotty.	Sulu.
Chekov.		

$75   **$100 each**

Set of 7 coins.
$500   **$600**

The 1/4-ounce silver coins came in a key chain or necklace in a velvet-like lined box. Spock only.
$45   **$55**

The 1/4-ounce gold coins came in a velvet-like lined box with plastic holders:

Kirk.	McCoy.	Uhura.
Spock.	Scotty.	Sulu.
Chekov.		

$350   **$400 each**

Set of 7 coins.
$2,500   **$3,000**

The 1-ounce gold coins came in a special embossed leather display book. These were a special order set from Rarities Mint and only around 15 sets were actually produced.

Set of 7 coins.
$20,000   **$30,000**

Star Trek: The Final Frontier Coins, 1989. A variety of colored coins with images of the ships and characters. Note the name on the top of William Shatner's coin is Bacchus.

$1 $5 each

Various colored *Final Frontier* Coins, 1989.

MEDALLIONS AND MEDALS

FRANKLIN MINT, CALENDAR MEDALS

Coin features Kirk, Spock, McCoy, and Enterprise over the Command Insignia logo; 1991, 25th Anniversary:

Pewter.
$65 $75

Silver.
$200 $250

1994, *Star Trek: The Motion Picture* 15th Anniversary:

Pewter.
$55 $65

Silver.
$150 $200

HANOVER MINT, 1974 STAR TREK MEDALLIONS

The First Series Medallion features an image on the front of Kirk and Spock on a planet and the Enterprise on the back. Serial numbers are stamped on the edge of the coin and include a detachable rim piece for a necklace chain:

Bronze.
$75 $125

Gold plating over silver.
$200 $250

Silver.
$250 $300

Second Series produced in bronze only, with no stamped serial numbers.
$45 $55

Third Series produced in bronze only. Lesser-quality strikes now include a hole for a necklace chain with serial numbers on the rim of the coin.
$25 $35

LINCOLN ENTERPRISES, 1976

Tenth Anniversary Commemorative Medallion. Features Kirk, Spock, and McCoy on the front and the Enterprise orbiting a planet on the back; also includes the dates on back: 1966-1976.
$25 $35

LINCOLN ENTERPRISES, 1984

Star Trek III: The Search for Spock Commemorative Medallion. Features Kirk and Spock on the front and the Enterprise over a planet on the back; included coin rim with chain.
$20 $40

LINCOLN ENTERPRISES, 1986

Star Trek IV: The Voyage Home Commemorative Medallion. Features a bird of prey over the Golden Gate Bridge on the front with the Challenger and text on back. It included a molded bezel for a neck ribbon and was numbered on the bottom.

Bronze.
$25 $35

Gold plated.
$75 $85

Gold and silver plated.
$100 $150

Pewter.
$25 $35

LINCOLN ENTERPRISES, 1986

20th Anniversary Commemorative Medallion. Features Kirk and Spock on the front and the Enterprise on the back; includes the dates on back: 1966-1986.

$25   **$35**

Starland Metal medallion features a blue design printed on a polished center with a wreath design in the center. The back features an etched number with raised wreath design; limited edition to only 3,000.

UFP design.

$25   **$30**

UFP/Starfleet academy with command insignia symbol.

$25   **$35**

QVC 25TH ANNIVERSARY MEDALLION

Gold-plated medallion features an anniversary logo on one side and the original series Enterprise with "U.S.S. Enterprise" text on the other.

$25   **$35**

Calendars

Star Trek Stardate Calendar 1976, Ballantine Books, 1975.

Star Trek Stardate Calendar 1977, Ballantine Books, 1976.

Star Trek Stardate Calendar 1978, Ballantine Books, 1977.

BALLANTINE BOOKS, 1975

Star Trek Stardate Calendar 1976:

Boxed.
  $25   **$35**
Loose.
  $10   **$15**

BALLANTINE BOOKS, 1976

Star Trek Stardate Calendar 1977:

Boxed.
  $25   **$35**
Loose.
  $10   **$15**

BALLANTINE BOOKS, 1977

Star Trek Stardate Calendar 1978:

Boxed.
  $25   **$35**
Loose.
  $10   **$15**

FRANCO, 1977

Cloth hanging calendar.
  $45   **$55**

T-K GRAPHICS, 1979

Star Trek: The Motion Picture Calendar 1980.
  $10   **$15**

Star Trek Stardate Calendar 1979, Ballantine Books, 1978.

BALLANTINE BOOKS, 1978

Star Trek Stardate Calendar 1979:

Boxed.
  $15   **$25**
Loose.
  $5   **$10**

Cloth Hanging Calendar, Franco, 1977.

STAR TREK ENTERPRISES, 1968

1968 Your Star Trek Pictorial Calendar.
  $75   **$100**

LINCOLN ENTERPRISES, 1973

1973 Star Trek Calendar.
  $55   **$65**

Star Trek Stardate Calendar 1994, Pocket Books, 1993.

1985 *Star Trek III: The Search for Spock* Calendar, Pocket Books, 1984.

1986 Star Trek Stardate Calendar, Pocket Books, 1985.

1987 Star Trek Stardate Calendar, Pocket Books, 1986.

1988 Star Trek Stardate Calendar, Pocket Books, 1987.

1989 Star Trek Celebration Calendar, Pocket Books, 1988.

1991 Star Trek Stardate Calendar, Pocket Books, 1990.

1992 Star Trek 25th Anniversary Calendar, Pocket Books, 1991.

LINCOLN ENTERPRISES, 1975

1975 Star Trek Animated Calendar.
$65   **$75**

LINCOLN ENTERPRISES, 1976

Star Trektennial Calendar 1976-1978.
$50   **$75**

POCKET BOOKS, 1980

Star Trek: The Motion Picture.
$10   **$20**

POCKET BOOKS, 1981

Star Trek: The Motion Picture.
$10   **$20**

POCKET BOOKS, 1982

Star Trek: The Motion Picture.
$10   **$15**

POCKET BOOKS, 1983

Star Trek II: The Wrath of Khan.
$10   **$15**

POCKET BOOKS, 1984

Original Star Trek television series.
$10   **$15**

POCKET BOOKS, 1985

Star Trek III: The Search for Spock.
$10   **$15**

POCKET BOOKS, 1986

Scenes and crew from the first Star Trek movies.
$15   **$20**

POCKET BOOKS, 1987

Original Star Trek television series.
$10   **$15**

POCKET BOOKS, 1988

Original Star Trek television series and movies.
$10   **$15**

POCKET BOOKS, 1989

Star Trek Celebration Calendar featuring classic episodes from the original series.
$15   **$25**

POCKET BOOKS, 1991

Star Trek Original Series and movies calendar.
$10   **$15**

POCKET BOOKS, 1992

Star Trek 25th Anniversary Calendar.
$20   **$25**

1993 *Star Trek VI: The Undiscovered Country* Calendar, Pocket Books, 1992.

POCKET BOOKS, 1993

Star Trek VI: The Undiscovered Country calendar.
$5   **$10**

POCKET BOOKS, 1994

Star Trek original television series calendar.
$5   **$10**

1995 Star Trek Stardate Calendar, Pocket Books, 1994.

Star Trek 30th Anniversary Original TV Series calendar, Pocket Books, 1996.

1997 Star Trek Stardate Calendar, Pocket Books, 1996.

2000 Star Trek Stardate Calendar, Pocket Books, 1999.

2001 Star Trek Stardate Calendar, Pocket Books, 2000.

2002 Star Trek Stardate Calendar, Pocket Books, 2001.

2003 Star Trek Stardate Calendar, Pocket Books, 2002.

2004 Star Trek Stardate Calendar, Pocket Books, 2003.

POCKET BOOKS, 1995

Star Trek original television series calendar.

$5 $10

POCKET BOOKS, 1996

Star Trek 30th Anniversary original television series calendar.

$20 $25

POCKET BOOKS, 1997

Star Trek original television series calendar.

$5 $10

POCKET BOOKS, 1998

Star Trek original television series calendar.

$5 $10

POCKET BOOKS, 1999

Star Trek original television series calendar.

$5 $10

POCKET BOOKS, 2000

Star Trek original television series calendar.

$5 $10

POCKET BOOKS, 2001

Star Trek original television series calendar.

$5 $10

Ships of the Line 2001.

$10 $15

2004 Star Trek Ships of the Line Calendar, Pocket Books, 2003.

POCKET BOOKS, 2002

Star Trek original television series calendar.

$5 $10

Ships of the Line 2002.

$10 $15

POCKET BOOKS, 2003

Star Trek original television series calendar.

$5 $10

Ships of the Line 2003.

$10 $15

2005 Star Trek Stardate Calendar, Pocket Books, 2004.

POCKET BOOKS, 2004

Star Trek original television series calendar.

$5 $10

Ships of the Line 2004.

$10 $15

POCKET BOOKS, 2005

Star Trek original television series calendar.

$5 $10

Ships of the Line 2005.

$10 $15

2006 Star Trek Stardate Calendar, Pocket Books, 2005.

2006 Star Trek Ships of the Line Calendar, Pocket Books, 2005.

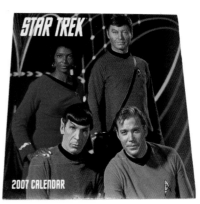

2007 Star Trek Stardate Calendar, Pocket Books, 2006.

2008 Star Trek Stardate Calendar, Pocket Books, 2007.

2008 Ships of the Line Calendar, Pocket Books, 2007.

1980 *Star Trek: The Motion Picture* Calendar, Wallaby, 1979.

POCKET BOOKS, 2006

Star Trek original television series and movies calendar.
$5   **$10**
Ships of the Line 2006.
$10   **$15**

POCKET BOOKS, 2007

Star Trek original television series calendar.
$5   **$10**
Ships of the Line 2007.
$10   **$15**

POCKET BOOKS, 2008

Star Trek original television series calendar.
$5   **$10**
Ships of the Line 2008.
$10   **$15**

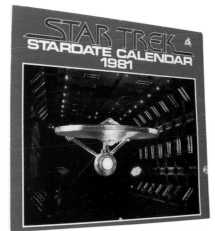

1981 *Star Trek: The Motion Picture* Calendar, Wallaby, 1980.

WALLABY, 1980

The Official U.S.S. Enterprise Officer's Date Book, *Star Trek: The Motion Picture* desk calendar.
$5   **$10**

WALLABY, 1980

Star Trek: The Motion Picture.
$5   **$10**

WALLABY, 1981

Star Trek: The Motion Picture.
$5   **$10**

Clocks

Wall clock, crew, Centric.

Wall clock, Kirk, Centric.

Wall clock, Spock, Centric.

CENTRIC

Wall clocks:

Crew, Kirk, Spock.

   $15 $20 each

Table clocks:

Gravity Base Enterprise.

   $45 $55

Enterprise.

   $25 $35

Mr. Spock.

   $25 $35

Enterprise table clock, Centric.

Enterprise clock, Centric.

Mr. Spock clock, Centric.

Alarm clock, Kirk, McCoy and Spock, Ingraham.

INGRAHAM

Kirk, McCoy, and Spock key-wind alarm clock.

$45   **$55**

Wall clock with 6-face action figure card images.

MEGO

Mego-style face quartz clock wall clock with Mego 6-face action figure card images.

$35   **$45**

Tricorder AM-FM Radio. Full-size Tricorder design features AM/FM radio. Made in Japan. Turn the dial while the lights indicate how strong the reception for each station is; includes leather strap and built-in headphone jack.

$150   **$250**

TOP BANANA

Enterprise talking alarm clock.

$25   **$35**

Tricorder AM-FM Radio, Japan.

Enterprise Talking Alarm Clock, Top Banana.

Enterprise Talking Alarm Clock shown out of its box.

Clothing and Accessories

HATS

It seems that the collectibles market has been flooded over the years with a wide variety of Star Trek-themed baseball caps. I am especially amazed at just how many different ways the command insignia has been used on caps. The brief list of hats here is just a sample of the seemingly limitless variety available.

A & D COMPANY, 1978

Vulcan Ear Cap, features two flesh-colored pointed ears coming out of the sides of the cap.

$45 $55

FANTASTIC FILMS MAGAZINE, DISTRIBUTORS, 1983

Beam Me Up Scotty cap, multi-colored beanie-style cap; a plastic space ship with attached propeller sits on top.

$45 $55

G.T.B. INC., 1987

He's Dead Jim cap, features an image of the Enterprise with "He's Dead Jim" displayed on the saucer section and "Star Trek Forever" on the engine nacelles.

$25 $35

LINCOLN ENTERPRISES, 1984

Star Trek III: The Search for Spock Spock commemorative cap, features an official embroidered commemorative movie logo patch of the Enterprise over planet Genesis; includes gold military-type trim. Cap was made to go with the matching commemorative jackets that used the same embroidered logo patch.

$25 $35

LINCOLN ENTERPRISES, 1986

Star Trek IV: The Voyage Home insignia cap, features an embroidered patch with the movie Enterprise above whales George and Gracie on a logo shield; includes gold military-type trim. Cap was made to go with the matching windbreakers and satin type jackets that used the same embroidered logo patch.

$25 $35

Star Trek IV: The Voyage Home Ultimate Voyagers cap, embroidered patch displays whales George and Gracie with gold military-type trim. Cap was made to go with the matching windbreakers and satin-style jackets that used the same embroidered patch.

$30 $40

LINCOLN ENTERPRISES, 1987

Star Trek IV: The Voyage Home bird of prey cap, features bird of prey and the Golden Gate Bridge with whales George and Gracie below embroidered on a patch; includes gold military-type trim. Cap was made to go with the matching bird of prey windbreakers and satin-style jackets that used the same embroidered logo patch.

$25 $35

Star Trek IV: The Voyage Home two whales visor cap, features the two whales George and Gracie on an arrow head-shaped patch; includes gold military-type trim. Cap was made to go with the matching windbreakers and satin-style jackets that used the same embroidered patch.

$25 $35

Anniversary cap, features the 20th Anniversary logo patch on cap; includes gold military-type trim.

$15 $20

"United Federation of Planets" cap, features embroidered patch on cap and gold military-type trim.

$15 $20

LINCOLN ENTERPRISES, 1988

UFP hat, features the UFP logo screen printed on front of cap.

$5 $10

THE OFFICIAL STAR TREK FAN CLUB, 1987

Star Trek IV: The Voyage Home lettered corduroy logo cap, features red embroidered patch of whales George and Gracie.

$15 $25

OTTO CAP, 1988

Made for Paramount Pictures as an official Paramount crew cap worn on the production set of *Star Trek V: The Final Frontier*.

$45 $55

20th Anniversary cap, Lincoln Enterprises, 1987.

UFP hat, Lincoln Enterprises, 1988.

Starfleet Academy hat.

Starfleet Academy white hat, features the Starfleet Academy logo embroidered on the front.

$10   **$15**

Star Trek rainbow stripe hat, 1979.

Star Trek rainbow stripe hat, 1979. Unique purple-colored hat features the rainbow *Star Trek: The Motion Picture* logo stripes with "TREK" on the bill and on both the sides.

$10   **$15**

STAR TREK CHARACTER HATS

Each hat features an embroidered image of one of the Enterprise crew: Kirk, Spock, McCoy, Scotty, and Uhura.

$25   **$35 each**

Spock character hat; back of hat shown at right.

McCoy character hat; back of hat shown at right.

Scotty character hat; back of hat shown at right.

Uhura character hat; back of hat shown at right.

Star Trek Command Logo hat.

Star Trek 25th Anniversary hat.

Star Trek split-color hat.

Star Trek hat.

Star Trek Goes Country hat.

Star Trek 25th Anniversary hat, features
beautiful screen printed artwork.
$15   **$20**
Star Trek Goes Country hat, unusual
western-themed Star Trek cap.
$10   **$20**

Star Trek Command Logo hat, features
later anniversary version of the command
insignia.
$10   **$15**
Star Trek hat, movie-style gold letters on red
cap.
$5   **$15**
Star Trek split-color hat, features a dark
maroon color on one half and a dark green
on the other, with an embroidered Star Trek
logo on the front.
$15   **$25**
Star Trek 40th Anniversary hat, features
"40th Anniversary" embroidered on front.
$25   **$30**
Star Trek command insignia hat, white with
black rim, features classic gold command
insignia with "Star Trek" in red letters
embroidered on the front.
$25   **$35**

Star Trek 40th Anniversary hat.

Star Trek Command Insignia hat.

Star Trek SFA (Starfleet Academy) hat.

Star Trek Enterprise cap.

Star Trek SFA hat, features "Starfleet Academy SFA" embroidered on front.

$20   **$25**

Star Trek Enterprise cap, "U.S.S. Enterprise" embroidered on front; "To Boldly Go Where No Man Has Before" embroidered on back.

$25   **$35**

THE THINKING CAP COMPANY, 1980

U.S.S. Enterprise gold and red insignia on black cap; available with or without gold military-type trim.

$15   **$20**

THE THINKING CAP COMPANY, 1982

United Federation of Planets/Starfleet Headquarters cap; available with or without gold military-type trim.

$15   **$20**

THE THINKING CAP COMPANY, 1989

Officially licensed cap with the *Star Trek V: The Final Frontier* logo and gold military-type trim.

$10   **$15**

THREE SHIPS PATCH CAP, 1991

Anniversary cap, features the Star Trek 25th Anniversary logo patch on cap, "Star Trek 1966-1991 25th Anniversary" on patch; also has the Enterprise NCC-1701 and NCC-1701-D on cap.

$15   **$25**

U.S.A., 1976

Star Trek fisherman's cap, possibly the first use of the now famous and somewhat still easily obtainable Star Trek Enterprise and K-7 fabric.

$45   **$55**

U.S.S. Kitty Hawk NCC-1903 hat, features embroidered lettering and metal pin insignia.

$10   **$15**

WEST PENN HAT COMPANY, INC., 1976

Official Star Trek television Enterprise cap.

$65   **$85**

Winter pom-pom hat, 1976, with Star Trek Enterprise patch.

$45   **$65**

Star Trek Fisherman's Cap, USA, 1976.

TV Enterprise Cap, West Penn Hat Company, Inc., 1976.

U.S.S. Enterprise hat, The Thinking Cap Company, 1980.

U.S.S. Kitty Hawk NCC-1903 hat.

Pom-Pom hat with Star Trek Enterprise patch, 1976.

Nylon windbreaker, first run, Great Lake Sportswear, 1974.

Nylon windbreaker, second run, Great Lake Sportswear, 1974.

Star Trek 20th Anniversary jacket, Lincoln Enterprises, 1987.

Official Star Trek Adventure jacket, Paramount.

JACKETS

D.D. BEAN & SONS, 1979

Star Trek: The Motion Picture lightweight jacket.
$125   **$150**

Star Trek: The Motion Picture deluxe L.E.D. jacket.
$150   **$200**

GREAT LAKE SPORTSWEAR, 1974

Light blue nylon windbreaker with black collar and cuffs, two white stripes on sleeves w/leatherette science emblem. This was a promotional item sold through AMT.

First run.
$75   **$125**

Second run.
$55   **$75**

United Federation of Planets design windbreaker, silver nylon with embroidered UFP design.
$65   **$85**

LINCOLN ENTERPRISES, 1984

U.S.S. Enterprise design jacket.
$45   **$55**

LINCOLN ENTERPRISES, 1987

Star Trek 20th Anniversary jacket, United Federation of Planets design jacket.
$45   **$55**

OFFICIAL STAR TREK FAN CLUB, 1986

Star Trek 20th Anniversary jacket.
$65   **$75**

Star Trek vintage jacket, 1970s.

Lettermen style, Top Line, 1991.

Denim Star Trek 25th Anniversary Logo, Top Line, 1991.

Black satin 25th Anniversary jacket, Top Line, 1991.

PARAMOUNT, ADVENTURE

Official Star Trek Adventure jacket.

$45   **$55**

Star Trek-themed printed jacket from the early 1970s, rare and unique vintage jacket.

$55   **$75**

TOP LINE, 1991

Original television series Enterprise:

Denim.

$75   **$85**

Wool.

$95   **$125**

Letterman style with Enterprise embroidered on back.

$95   **$125**

Star Trek 25th Anniversary logo:

Denim.

$75   **$100**

Red satin 25th Anniversary jacket, 1991.

Black satin.

$75   **$95**

Red satin.

$75   **$95**

Wool.

$85   **$100**

RALPH MARLIN

Neck ties, various designs.

$25   **$45**

Neck ties, Ralph Marlin.

PATCHES

A wide variety of patches have been created over the years. Due to the large number of patches that now exist, many being either fan created, one offs or custom made and due to their relatively low value, I have chosen to list a small sample selection of the many patches that can be found.

IRON-ON

A small selection of the many patches that can be found.

Star Trek: The Motion Picture iron-on patches, first style, Aviva, 1979.

Star Trek: The Motion Picture iron-on patches, second style, Aviva, 1979

AVIVA, 1979

Aviva made two different styles of iron-on patches.

First style, *Star Trek: The Motion Picture*:

Kirk in hallway.

Mr. Spock.

$5   **$10 each**

Second style, *Star Trek: The Motion Picture*:

Vulcan salute.

Kirk.

$10   **$15 each**

EMBROIDERY, 1976

Iron-on patch of Enterprise.

$5   **$10**

Iron-on Enterprise patch, Embroidery, 1976.

Star Trek command
insignia patch, Roth,
1975.

Alpha Centauri patch,
Roth, 1975.

ROTH, 1975

Some patches were actually based on the designs from Franz Joseph's Technical Manual:

Star Trek command insignia.

Alpha Centauri.

UFP.

U.S.S. Enterprise.

Spock, Live Long and Prosper.

$5   **$10 each**

SHIRTS AND JERSEYS

Hundreds of licensed and non-licensed Star Trek shirts have flooded the market over the years.

Creation Entertainment, the company behind the majority of the Star Trek conventions through the years, has been responsible for the production of a large number of Star Trek-related shirts. Other companies also worth noting are: Huk-a-Poo Clothing, Lincoln Enterprises, GEM (see hockey jerseys), Great Southern, Official Star Trek Fan Club, Paramount, Ralph Marlin, Stanley Desantis, and TAG.

Due to the overwhelming volume of shirts, I have chosen to list only a few examples here.

SWEATSHIRTS

Sweatshirt version of Captain Kirk's shirt.

A sweatshirt version of Captain Kirk's shirt, this could be a replica of an early version episode of the command shirt.

$25   **$45**

HOCKEY JERSEYS

GEM, 1995-1996

Starfleet Academy, black mesh with yellow and red stripes.

$75   **$100**

Command insignia, blue mesh with tan and red stripes.

$75   **$100**

Command insignia, black mesh with yellow and blue stripes.

$75   **$100**

Klingon Empire, black mesh with red, gray, and orange stripes.

$100   **$150**

Starfleet Academy hockey jersey, GEM, 1996.

Blue command insignia hockey jersey, GEM, 1996.

Black command insignia hockey jersey, GEM, 1996.

Klingon Empire hockey jersey, GEM, 1996.

T-SHIRTS

"Space…The Final Frontier"; has Enterprise on shirt and a unique reversed image on back.

    $25   **$35**

Spock as disc jockey.

    $20   **$30**

"Star Trek: To Boldly Go…"

    $15   **$20**

Star Trek Universe design shirt.

    $10   **$15**

"20 Years…and the Adventure Continues."

    $10   **$15**

"Beam Me Up Scotty."

    $15   **$25**

United Federation of Planets.

    $25   **$35**

Star Fleet Academy.

    $25   **$30**

"All I Need to Know About Life I Learned From Star Trek," features unique ideas of how to live life based on Star Trek. A poster of this was also released.

    $25   **$35**

Enterprise firing Photon Torpedo.

    $25   **$35**

Space… The Final Frontier…T-shirt.

Spock as disc jockey T-shirt.

Star Trek: To Boldly Go…T-shirt.

Star Trek Universe design T-shirt.

20 Years..and the Adventure Continues T-shirt.

Beam Me Up Scotty T-shirt.

United Federation of Planets T-shirt.

Star Fleet Academy T-shirt.

All I need to know about life…T-shirt.

Enterprise firing Photon Torpedo T-shirt.

Spock with Vulcan salute T-shirt.

I Am A Trekkie, personal T-shirt made in the '70s.

Enterprise orbiting planet T-shirt.

Enterprise and Klingon fly-by T-shirt.

Warp Factor Two Mr. Sulu shirt.

Uhura, McCoy, Spock and Kirk T-shirt.

Gorn, "Arena" episode T-shirt.

Spock "Live Long and Prosper" T-shirt front and back.

Star Trek: The Arcade Game T-shirt.

Spock with Vulcan salute, vintage Lincoln Enterprises transfer.

$55   **$65**

"I Am a Trekkie" (heat transfer letters). I had this made at a store in Portland, Maine, in the 1970s.

Value unknown

Enterprise orbiting planet.

$10   **$20**

Enterprise fly by to the right on front; Klingon fly by to the right on back.

$25   **$35**

Warp Factor Two Mr. Sulu (muscle shirt).

$15   **$20**

Uhura, McCoy, Spock, and Kirk.

$15   **$25**

Gorn, humanoid reptile "Arena," episode shirt from "Star Trek The Experience."

$45   **$65**

Spock with Vulcan salute (on front); "Live Long and Prosper" on back.

$15   **$20**

Star Trek: The Arcade Game (Sega).

$35   **$45**

Starfleet and Klingon T-shirt front and back.

Star Trek Command Insignia T-shirt front and back.

Multi-print T-shirt.

"Dammit Jim, I'm A Doctor!" T-shirt.

Kirk and Spock publicity photo T-shirt.

Special Effects Apogee Inc. T-shirt.

Ciao, Baby! T-shirt.

Kirk and Spock, Leadership for the Future.

Command Insignia anniversary logo T-shirt.

Starfleet with crew from Undiscovered Country on front; Klingons on back.
   $10   **$15**
Star Trek command insignia on front; Enterprise on back.
   $15   **$25**
Multi-print shirt that includes K-7 Space Station logo among other unique logos; rare.
   $55   **$75**

"Dammit Jim, I'm A Doctor!," classic Dr. McCoy line with image of the doctor.
   $25   **$35**
Star Trek classic publicity photo of Kirk (with Phaser rifle) and Spock.
   $20   **$25**
Special Effects Apogee incorporated crew shirt. The Motion Picture Klingon ship on front; special effects Apogee crew logo on back.
   $45   **$65**

Ciao, Baby (Spock with Vulcan salute).
   $10   **$15**
Kirk and Spock, leadership for the future.
   $25   **$45**
Command Insignia Anniversary logo.
   $10   **$15**

Kirk, Spock and Enterprise montage T-shirt.

Kirk, Spock, and Enterprise in space montage.

$15   **$25**

Five-Year Mission: The Tour T-shirt.

Five-Year Mission: The Tour shirt back lists planets visited with star dates.

$25   **$45**

Kirk, Spock and McCoy discover a cat T-shirt.

Kirk, Spock, and McCoy discover a cat on a planet surface; comical drawing of the landing party encountering a feline entity.

$10   **$15**

Kirk and crew montage T-shirt.

Kirk and crew montage.

$10   **$15**

Command Insignia with sport stripes T-shirt.

Command insignia with sport stripes.

$25   **$35**

"Smell My Fingers" T-shirt.

"Smell My Fingers," Spock with smelly? Vulcan salute.

$20   **$25**

SHOES AND LACES

J.P.N. (JAPAN), 1979

Star Trek: The Motion Picture sandals. These are blue with white foot straps and feature a holographic image disc in the center of the straps with a changing image between artwork of Kirk, Spock, and McCoy and an image of the command insignia.

$150   **$200**

ENTERPRISE SHOELACES, 1991

Pair of 40" white shoelaces with "U.S.S. Enterprise" and "NCC-1701" in black lettering; laces also have a drawing of the Enterprise.

$15   **$25**

Early promotional T-shirt for the latest movie, *Star Trek XI*.

"Star Trek: Stardate 12-25-08," early promotional T-shirt design advertising the release date of *Star Trek XI* as Dec. 25, 2008.

$15   **$25**

SLEEPWEAR

NAZARETH MILLS, 1976

Two-piece children's pajamas; Enterprise artwork with logo.

$55   **$75**

NAZARETH MILLS, 1979

Two-piece *Star Trek: The Motion Picture* toddlers pajamas:

Enterprise.
$40   **$50**
Kirk.
$40   **$50**
Spock.
$40   **$50**

PAJAMA CORP. OF AMERICA, 1979

Star Trek: The Motion Picture children's pajamas:

Enterprise.
$45   **$55**
Kirk.
$45   **$55**
Kirk, Spock, and McCoy.
$45   **$55**
Spock.
$45   **$55**

Children's pajamas, Star Trek sleepwear, 1979.

STAR TREK SLEEPWEAR, 1979

Classic command patch on children's pajamas.

$45   **$55**

SOCKS

BATTS CO. INC., 1976

White cotton crew socks feature appliqués of Kirk and Spock wearing a Phaser while standing on the Transporter pad:

"Captain Kirk" in black letters.
$25   **$45**
"Mr. Spock" in black letters.
$25   **$45**

CHARLESTON HOSIERY, INC, 1979

White polyester/cotton crew socks with different colored tops with characters from *Star Trek: The Motion Picture*:

Enterprise.

Kirk.

Kirk and Spock.

Spock.

Decker.

Ilia.
$20   **$40 each**

Star Trek socks.

FILMWELL-BERLIN, 1997

Star Trek-themed socks made in Germany, with Starfleet logo.

$15   **$20**

Star Trek socks.

HYP, 1998

The original series-themed socks, "Where No Man Has Gone Before."

$20   **$30**

NO-COMMENT INTERNATIONAL, 1995

Original television series-themed socks:

Enterprise.

Enterprise (three views).

Spock.

Starfleet logo.

Transporter Room.

$20   **$40 each**

TRANSFERS, IRON-ON

AMT, 1968

Iron-on color transfers were offered as a promotion through some of the AMT Star Trek models:

Command Insignia, USS Enterprise, Hows Your Tribble and Vulcan Power iron-ons, AMT, 1968.

Keep On Trekkin' iron-on, AMT, 1968.

Klingon Power iron-on, AMT, 1968.

Star Trek Lives iron-on, AMT, 1968.

Command Insignia, U.S.S. Enterprise (text), How's Your Tribble (with image) and Vulcan Power (with Vulcan salute).

$45   **$65**

Keep on Trekkin' (with image of Enterprise).

$25   **$35**

Klingon Power (with Klingon ship).

$25   **$35**

Star Trek Lives.

$35   **$45**

BEAM ME DOWN IRON-ON, 1975

Image of original series' Enterprise with two figures beaming down.

$25   **$35**

GENERAL MILLS, 1979

Star Trek: The Motion Picture promotional iron-on transfers; five different transfers originally made available as a set:

Enterprise iron-on, General Mills, 1979.

Blank transfer (create your own design).

Enterprise (with logo).

Kirk (with logo).

Kirk and Spock (with logo).

Spock (with logo).

$20   **$40 each**

LINCOLN ENTERPRISES, 1980

Spock with Vulcan salute iron-on, Lincoln Enterprises, 1980.

Reproduced color pictures from the original series, these were inexpensively produced and suffer from poor quality.

Enterprise (firing Phasers).

Kirk (in dress uniform).

Kirk (with Phaser).

Kirk and Spock (Patterns of Force).

Kirk and Spock (Spock's Brain).

Kirk and Spock (looking at floor).

Kirk and Spock (holding Phaser).

Kirk, Spock and McCoy (Patterns of Force).

Spock (with lyre).

Spock (Vulcan salute).

$10   **$15 each**

LINCOLN ENTERPRISES, 1984

The Search for Spock logo transfer.
$10   **$15**
Enterprise, in sky seen out a bedroom window.
$25   **$35**

Scotty, Kirk, McCoy, Spock and Enterprise iron-on.

Artwork of Scotty, Kirk, McCoy, and Spock with the Enterprise overhead.
$25   **$45**

MCDONALDS, 1979

Star Trek: The Motion Picture promotional transfers; colorful transfers with glitter, came two transfers to a sheet and were included in Happy Meals.

Spock (standing with logo).
$15   **$20**

MR. HAPPINESS, FEASTERVILLE, PA

Spock with Vulcan salute iron-on, Mr. Happiness.

Enterprise over planet iron-on, Mr. Happiness.

Transfers came packaged with header card:

Spock with Vulcan salute
$45   **$55**
Enterprise over planet; same artwork used on the Enterprise AMT Model
$65   **$75**

PACIFIC TRANSFER, 1982

The Wrath of Khan color photo transfers:

Khan.

Kirk.

Spock.

The Wrath of Khan logo.
$10   **$15**

PARAMOUNT PICTURES, 1989

Star Trek: The Final Frontier transfers, with logo.
$10   **$15**

ROACH, 1979

Star Trek: The Motion Picture color transfers; some feature glitter. These were mass-produced and available in stores and catalogs. They were sold already transferred onto different colored shirts and mostly in kid's sizes. Some un-applied transfers, however, have been found selling on auction sites and in collector catalogs over the years.

Enterprise, Kirk, Spock (with logo).

Enterprise (with logo).

Enterprise (with glitter and logo).

Ilia and Enterprise.

Kirk and Enterprise (with logo).

Spock (with glitter and logo).
$5   **$10**

UMBRELLA

SHAW CREATIONS, 1993

Black umbrella.
$25   **$45**

Star Trek umbrella, Shaw Creations.

UNDERWEAR
FUNDY-UNDIES, 1979

Boy's underwear, Fundy-Undies, 1979.

Boy's underwear with *Star Trek: The Motion Picture* theme.

$25   **$35**

VESTS

Fan-made airbrushed Star Trek jean vest.

Airbrushed Star Trek blue-jean vest, fan-produced, features command insignia logo on the front and U.S.S. Enterprise on the back.

$75   **$125**

WALLET
LARAMIE, 1977

Zippered wallet, Laramie, 1977.

Enterprise and Romulan bird of prey on zippered wallet.

$45   **$55**

Comic Books

The first *Star Trek* comics published by Gold Key bear little resemblance to the original television series. Gold Key published 61 comics on a semi-regular schedule from July 1967 to February 1979. The first nine issues have colorful photo covers, while issues #10-29 and #31-44 have painted artwork covers with a small inset photo of Kirk and Spock. Starting in August 1976, 35 of the Gold Key issues were reprinted in four oversized paperback volumes called *The Enterprise Logs*.

Paramount ended its license with Gold Key right before *Star Trek: The Motion Picture* was released in theaters. Marvel Comics was granted the license in 1979, and produced the official comic adaptation of the movie.

DAN CURTIS GIVEAWAYS, 1974

Western Publishing produced a set of *Star Trek* Dan Curtis Giveaway mini-comics in 1974 which measured only 6" x 3". A total of nine mini-comics was produced, but only two featured *Star Trek*:

#2 Star Trek – Enterprise Mutiny (an abridged reprint-Gold Key #14).

$10   **$20**

#6 Star Trek – Dark Traveler (an abridged reprint-Gold Key #13).

$10   **$20**

Western Publishing, *Star Trek – Dark Traveler #6*, Dan Curtis Giveaways, 1974.

DYNABRITE COMICS, 1978-1979

Dynabrite Comics was a division of Western Publishing. These comics typically had cardboard covers and each issue was a 7-1/8" x 10" reprint of two different Gold Key/Whitman comics.

Star Trek #11357, Dynabrite Comics, 1978-1979.

Star Trek #11357, reprint of Gold Key #33 and #41.

$15 **$25**

Star Trek #11358, Dynabrite Comics, 1978-1979.

Star Trek #11358, reprint of Gold Key #34 and #36.

$15 **$25**

GOLD KEY COMICS, 1967-1979

Star Trek #1, Gold Key Comics, 1967-1979.

Star Trek #2, Gold Key Comics, 1967-1979.

Star Trek #3, Gold Key Comics, 1967-1979.

Star Trek #4, Gold Key Comics, 1967-1979.

Star Trek #5, Gold Key Comics, 1967-1979.

Star Trek:

#1.
$75 **$350**

#2-#5.
$55 **$250**

Star Trek #6, Gold Key Comics, 1967-1979.

Star Trek #7, Gold Key Comics, 1967-1979.

Star Trek #8, Gold Key Comics, 1967-1979.

Star Trek #9, Gold Key Comics, 1967-1979.

#6-#9.
$30 **$125**

#10-#30.

$10   **$30**

Star Trek #10-#30,
Gold Key Comics,
1967-1979.

Star Trek #10-#30, Gold Key Comics, 1967-1979.

Star Trek #10-#30, Gold Key Comics, 1967-1979.

Star Trek #10-#30,
Gold Key Comics,
1967-1979.

Star Trek #10-#30,
Gold Key Comics,
1967-1979.

Star Trek #31-#61,
Gold Key Comics,
1967-1979.

Star Trek #31-#61,
Gold Key Comics,
1967-1979.

Star Trek #31-#61,
Gold Key Comics,
1967-1979.

#31-#61.

$10   **$30**

Star Trek #31-#61,
Gold Key Comics,
1967-1979.

Star Trek #31-#61,
Gold Key Comics,
1967-1979.

Star Trek #31-#61,
Gold Key Comics,
1967-1979.

Star Trek #31-#61, Gold Key Comics, 1967-1979.

FOREIGN PUBLISHERS

Foreign Comic divisions have produced quite a few *Star Trek* issues including these vintage examples:

Foreign Comics divisions.

Foreign Comics divisions.

$25   **$30**

Foreign Comics divisions.

Foreign Comics divisions.

$35   **$40**

VALIANT & TELEVISION 21 COMICS, 1971-1976

This was a weekly newspaper started in 1965 in the UK by Alan Fennell and Gerry Anderson for *City Magazines.* Later issues featured comics of many popular British television shows, including *Star Trek.*

Valiant & TV 21 Comics, UK, 1971-1976.

Valiant & TV 21 Comics, UK, 1971-1976.

$15   **$25**

Reprints of TV 21, UK.

Reprints of *TV-21* in hard back-style book.

$20   **$30**

STRIP 81, FOREIGN COMIC

The Original Series, *Strip 81*, Foreign Comic.

The Original Series.

$15   **$25**

The Motion Picture.

$10   **$20**

GOLDEN PRESS, ENTERPRISE LOGS, 1976-1977

Four-volume set reprints eight of the Gold Key Comics:

 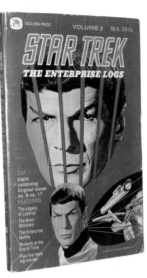  

Enterprise Logs, Volume One, Golden Press, 1976-1977.

Volume One (reprint comics issues 1-8).

$20   **$30**

Enterprise Logs, Volume Two, Golden Press, 1976-1977.

Volume Two (reprint comics issues 9-17).

$20   **$30**

Enterprise Logs, Volume Three, Golden Press, 1976-1977.

Volume Three (reprint comics issues 18-26).

$25   **$35**

Enterprise Logs, Volume Four, Golden Press, 1967-1977.

Volume Four (reprint comics issues 27-28, 30-34, 36 and 38).

$30   **$40**

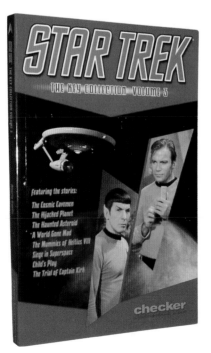

The Key Collection, Volume Three, Checker Publishing, 2005.

CHECKER PUBLISHING, THE KEY COLLECTION, 2004-PRESENT

Ongoing volumes that reprint vintage Gold Key *Star Trek* Comics:

Volume One, 2004 (reprints comics 1-8).

Volume Two, 2004 (reprints comics 9-16).

Volume Three, 2005 (reprints comics 17-24).

Volume Four, 2005 (reprints comics 25-28 and 30-33).

Volume Five, 2006 (reprints comics 34-36 and 38-43).

Special-edition box set, 2006.

Five-volume set of The Key Collection books in an open top slip case that includes a free T-shirt.

Volume Six, 2007 (reprints comics 44 and 46-52).

$20   **$35 each**

MCDONALDS HAPPY MEALS COMICS, 1979

(See Toys)

VOYAGES OF THE ENTERPRISE, NOSTALGIA WORLD, 1979-1983

These are reprints of a newspaper comic strip based on Star Trek that ran in the *Los Angeles Times Syndicate* for only four years due to poor distribution. It consisted of 20 story arcs running from December 1979 through December 1983. Authorized by Paramount Pictures and syndicated in the United States, the strips appeared in newspapers daily in black and white and in color on Sundays. It is interesting to note that number 4 and 5 were apparently never published. The Sunday color strips are not included in the reprints.

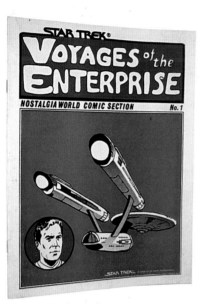

Voyages of the Enterprise, Number 2, Nostalgia World, 1979-1983.

Voyages of the Enterprise, Number 3, Nostalgia World, 1979-1983.

Voyages of the Enterprise, Number 6, Nostalgia World, 1979-1983.

Voyages of the Enterprise, Number 7, Nostalgia World, 1979-1983.

Number 2.
$25 **$35**

Number 3.
$25 **$35**

Number 6.
$45 **$55**

Number 7.
$55 **$65**

Voyages of the Enterprise, Number 1, Nostalgia World, 1979-1983.

Number 1.
$15 **$25**

RARE CARDBOARD STORE DISPLAY
$25 **$45**

TOKYOPOP, SEPTEMBER 2006 TO PRESENT

Unique paperback-book comics in the style of Japanese manga.

Star Trek: The Manga Volume 1: Shinsei/Shinsei by Chris Dows and Jeong-mo Yang (Sept. 5, 2006).

Star Trek: The Manga Volume 2: Kakan ni Shinkou by Bettina Kurkoski, Christine Boylan, and Wil Wheaton (Sept. 11, 2007).

Star Trek: The Manga Volume 3: Uchu by David Gerrold and Ej Su (due out July 15, 2008).

Values are still at the cover price of $10 each

Cardboard store display.

STAR TREK (NEW COMICS)

IDW Publishing, January 2007 to present. *Star Trek* comics are back, thanks to IDW Publishing. What was old is new again as IDW Publishing has issued a variety of new comics based on the classic characters from the original television show.

Star Trek Klingons: Blood Will Tell, IDW Publishing, January 2007 to present.

Star Trek: Year Four #1, IDW Publishing, January 2007 to present.

Star Trek: Year Four #2, IDW Publishing, January 2007 to present.

Star Trek: Year Four #3, IDW Publishing, January 2007 to present.

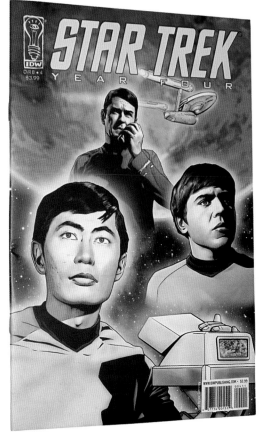

Star Trek: Year Four #4, IDW Publishing, January 2007 to present.

Star Trek: Alien Spotlight The Vulcans, IDW Publishing, January 2007 to present.

Star Trek: Alien Spotlight The Gorn, IDW Publishing, January 2007 to present.

Star Trek Klingons: Blood Will Tell.

Star Trek: Year Four #1.

Star Trek: Year Four #2.

Star Trek: Year Four #3.

Star Trek: Year Four #4.

Star Trek: Alien Spotlight The Vulcans.

Star Trek: Alien Spotlight The Gorn.

Star Trek comics on the shelf at a local comics specialty shop.
Values are still at the cover price of $3.99 each.

Costumes and Patterns

Halloween is one of my favorite holidays and for me, the fancier and more deluxe the mask or costume, the better. That is probably why I like the Don Post masks so much. The detail and realism present in the products is spectacular.

Of course, these days you can find just about any costume you want, either fan-made or professionally done. The more money you have to spend, the more realistic and detailed it can be. I have seen fans dressed up like Klingons who looked as realistic as those seen on any of the television shows or in the movies.

Several years ago, I found a local alterations place that could not only mend and repair garments, but could also take existing patterns and create entire outfits. Since I owned a set of *Star Trek II: The Wrath of Khan* uniform patterns, I took them to Stitches Fine Alterations and found a seamstress who, after talking with the owner, agreed to create my uniform. Her skill was amazing and her attention to detail in making sure that everything was as accurate as possible is clearly seen in the final product.

I still have that costume today. It is truly an amazing piece of workmanship.

COSTUMES/MASKS

AVIVA, 1979

Spock ears, Aviva, 1979.

Spock ears.

$25   **$35**

BEN COOPER, 1972

Early Halloween costumes by Ben Cooper usually came in their standard generic box and can be more desired by collectors.

Box artwork, Mr. Spock, Ben Cooper, 1972.

Captain Kirk.
$55   **$75**

Mr. Spock, Ben Cooper, 1972.

Mr. Spock.
$55   **$75**

BEN COOPER, 1973

Halloween costume:

Captain Kirk.
$35   **$65**
Mr. Spock.
$35   **$65**

BEN COOPER, 1975

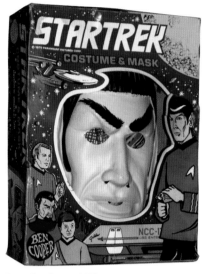

Spock, Ben Cooper, 1975.

Halloween costume of Kirk, Spock, or Klingon.

$35   **$45 each**

DON POST, 1978

Full-head masks:

Kirk.

$75   **$100**

Gorn, Don Post, 1978.

Gorn.

$150   **$175**

COLLEGEVILLE, 1967

Halloween costumes of Kirk and Spock.

$45   **$75 each**

COLLEGEVILLE, 1979

Halloween costumes of a few of the main characters from the movie, *Star Trek: The Motion Picture*:

Ilia, Collegeville, 1979.   Kirk, Collegeville, 1979.   Klingon, Collegeville, 1979.

Ilia.

$30   **$40**

Kirk.

$30   **$40**

Klingon.

$30   **$40**

Spock.

$30   **$40**

Spock.

$100   **$125**

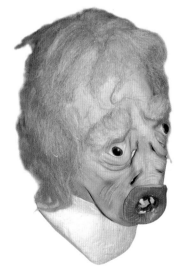

Salt Vampire, Don Post, 1978.

Salt Vampire.

$125   **$150**

DON POST, 1979

Full-head, soft plastic masks:

Kirk.

$50   **$75**

Klingon.

$50   **$75**

Spock.

$75   **$100**

Vulcan Master.

$50   **$75**

FRANCO, 1976

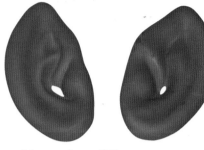

Vulcan ears, Franco, 1976.

Vulcan ears.
$20   **$30**

LINCOLN ENTERPRISES, 1976

Vulcan ears.
$25   **$35**

RUBIES, 1988

Pointed ears, Rubies, 1988.

Pointed ears.
$5   **$10**

RUBIES, 1988

Red mini-dress, Uhura, Rubies, 1988.

Crew outfits:

Yellow–Captain Kirk's shirt.

Blue–Mr. Spock's shirt.

Red–Scotty's shirt.

Red–Uhura's mini dress.
$25   **$55 each**

RUBIES, 1990

Full-head masks: Kirk, Spock, Gorn, Klingon.
$20   **$30**

Klingon, Rubies, 1990.

Spock, Rubies, 1990.

Gorn, Rubies, 1990.

UNIFORM, 2007 TO PRESENT

Mass-produced movie uniform, *Star Trek II* through *Star Trek VI,* Asia, 2007.

Mass-produced movie uniform for *Star Trek II* through *Star Trek VI.* Brand new complete uniform in unopened package; uniform pins sold separately.

$65 **$85**

UNIFORMS AND PATTERNS

LINCOLN ENTERPRISES, 1976

Original television series patterns for man's and woman's uniform shirt.

$10 **$15 each**

LINCOLN ENTERPRISES, 1983

Star Trek II: The Wrath of Khan patterns: man's jacket, pants, turtleneck undershirt and woman's jacket.

$10 **$15 each**

RUBIES, 1990

Original television series uniforms: man's shirt and woman's dress.

$30 **$45 each**

SIMPLICITY, 1990

Original television series patterns: man's shirt and woman's dress.

$10 **$15 each**

Crafts

AVALON, 1979

Star Trek: The Motion Picture Space Design Center Craft Kit; features blue plastic tray, cut-outs of crew members, pens, crayons, paints, and a project instruction book.

$150 **$200**

AVIVA, 1979

Star Trek: The Motion Picture Pen and Poster Kit; includes paintable 14" x 20" poster and five pens.

$25 **$35**

CATALOG SHOPPE, 1975

Each set includes plaster casting set character molds, molding compound, paint, brush, and instructions. Mix 'n Mold:

Kirk.

$60 **$80**

McCoy.

$50 **$70**

Spock.

$50 **$70**

Spock Mix 'n Mold, Catalog Shoppe, 1975.

McCoy Mix 'n Mold, Catalog Shoppe, 1975.

CLIVEDON PRESS, 1985

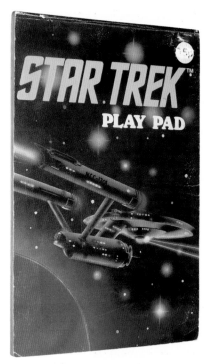

Star Trek Play Pad, Clivedon Press, 1985.

Star Trek: Play Pad; blank pages on one side and art to color on the other. British publication.

$25   **$45**

CRAFTS BY WHITING, 1979

Star Trek: The Motion Picture figurine painting:

Kirk.

$35   **$50**

Spock.

$35   **$50**

HASBRO, 1972

Paint By Numbers Set; includes canvas board, brush and paints.

Large box set of Kirk, Spock and Enterprise Paint By Numbers, Hasbro, 1972.

Kirk, Spock and Enterprise in large box set.

$80   **$85**

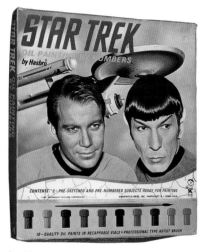

Small box set of Kirk, Spock and Enterprise Paint By Numbers, Hasbro, 1972.

Kirk, Spock and Enterprise in small box set.

$50   **$65**

MAGIC PAINTING, 1979

Kirk and Spock Magic Painting, 1979.

Enterprise Crew and Enterprise Magic Painting, 1979.

British set with two different artwork cover versions: Kirk and Spock on an alien planet and the Enterprise crew with Enterprise under attack.

$100   **$150 each**

MYSTIC DRAWING, 1979

Art pad, Mystic Drawing, 1979.

Art pad with drawings of crew and ships.

$50   **$65**

OPEN DOOR, 1976

String Art Kit, Open Door, 1976.

String Art Kit; includes an 18" x 24" backboard, black background, pins, colored thread, silver metallic string and step-by-step instructions.

$100   **$200**

OPEN DOOR, 1976

Pen a Poster Kit, Open Door, 1976.

Pen a Poster Kit; includes four 14" x 22" posters: "Star Trek Lives," "Tour of the Enterprise," "Enemies of the Federation," and "Journeys of the Enterprise." Also comes with colored felt-tip pens.

$55   **$75**

OPEN DOOR, 1977

Pen a Poster Kit, "How Do You Doodle" poster set; includes two posters and colored pens.

$25   **$35**

PARKES RUN PUBLISHING CO., 1978

Star Trek: The Unchartered World (misprint of "Uncharted") Giant Story 17" x 22" coloring book by Liza Hamill and Dan Dyen.

$25   **$45**

PLACO-FUN-ART, 1984

Star Trek III: The Search For Spock 3-D Poster set, 1984.

Star Trek III: The Search for Spock 3-D poster; "Star Trek III" 3-D pen and poster set; includes poster, unique 3-D overlay, 3-D glasses, and four felt-tip pens.

$25   **$45**

SCRAPBOOKING

THE SCRAPPIN GOOD TIME STORE

Star Trek-themed scrapbook characters, Scrappin Good Time Store.

Star Trek The Original Series scrapbook characters, set of three.

$1   **$5**

WRITING PAD

Writing Pad.

Ten-cent writing pad with Captain Kirk on the cover.

$10   **$15**

WORLD DISTRIBUTORS, 1974

As seen on BBC-TV, *Star Trek* coloring book; includes artwork and a story.

$45   **$65**

WORLD DISTRIBUTORS, 1975

Ready-to-assemble *Star Trek* Press-Out Book.

$55   **$65**

Star Trek Press-Out Book, World Distributors, 1975.

Food and Beverages

Catalog Shop must have read our minds when it decided to produce the Star Trek Freezicles. I don't know exactly what it was about this one. Maybe it was the colorful artwork on the box, or maybe it was the fact that you could make popsicles of three of your favorite Star Trek characters. At any rate, I must have bugged my mother every other day to help me make Star Trek Freezicles and when the fruit concentrate had quickly been used up, my mother had to find a replacement so we could make more. I did open the package *very* carefully, and made sure my mother carefully opened the Heinz fruit concentrate can in a way so I could put it back in the box afterward, even if it was empty.

CATALOG SHOP, 1975

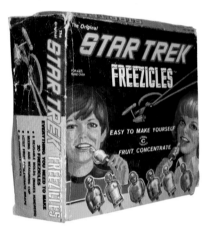

Freezicles, Catalog Shop, 1975.

Freezicles. Contains 6 reusable molds of the crew, mixing and measuring cup, can of Heinz fruit concentrate and 20 freezicle sticks.

$55   **$75**

COFFEE

Star Trek coffee.

For those die-hard fans that must have their morning coffee, there are now *Star Trek*-themed versions for your coffee pot: Wake up to the smell of freshly brewed "Federation Supremo" or if you need decaf, try the delicious "Vulcan Decaffeinated."

Shore Leave, Federation Supremo, Vulcan Decaffeinated.

$5   **$10 each**

GENERAL MILLS

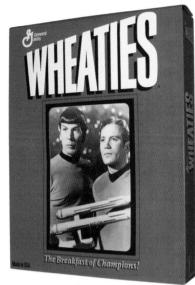

Wheaties, General Mills.

The "Breakfast of Champions" is now also the breakfast of Trekkies and available in the standard-size box only.

Wheaties cereal box (empty).

$25   **$35**

KELLOGG'S, 1996

Corn Flakes box front, Kellogg's, 1996.

Raisin Bran box front, Kellogg's, 1996.

Raisin Bran cereal box (empty).

$20   **$25**

Corn Flakes box back, Kellogg's, 1996.

KEEBLER, 1989-1990

Tribbles bite-size cookie snacks. Four different cookie styles were packaged in small wrapper-type bags. Two different package year variations:

Chocolate Chip Mint.

Malted.

Mint.

Peanut.

$10   **$15 each**

KELLOGG'S, 1969

Sugar Smacks cereal box with Spock and Phaser:

Standard-size cereal box (empty).

$75   **$100**

Single serving-size cereal box (empty).

$65   **$85**

Star Trek cereal is ...Grrrreat! OK, so these aren't frosted flakes, but still...

Available in standard-size box only.

Corn Flakes cereal box (empty)

$15   **$20**

LIQUOR DECANTERS, WINE BOTTLES, AND ROMULAN ALE

TENNESSEE WHISKEY BOTTLES, GEORGE DICKEL, 1964-1969

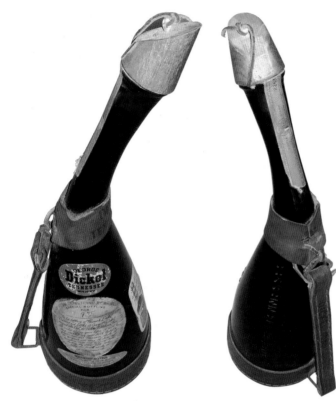

These commemorative "brandy" bottles feature a leather strap holder and were used in *The Original Series* because of their "fantasy" look. They were then used again much later in the sixth movie, *Star Trek VI: The Undiscovered Country*. (Note: Paramount has been obtaining as many George Dickel bottles as it can find for use in the new *Star Trek XI* movie scheduled for release in 2009.) Comes in six versions:

750 ml bottle in box.
  $65   **$95**
Miniature bottle.
  $35   **$55**
One fifth bottle.
  $65   **$85**
One quart bottle.
  $85   **$100**
Gallon bottle (very rare).
  $250   **$350**
Clear bottle (extremely rare).
  $350   **$550**

Commemorative brandy bottle, George Dickel, 1964-1969.

GRENADIER SPIRITS COMPANY, 1979

Porcelain liquor decanter bust of Mr. Spock, 1979.

Porcelain decanter bust of Mr. Spock from *Star Trek: The Motion Picture*. Originally came filled with 25.4 ounces of 49-proof Ceilo liqueur and comes in a square display window box.

  $45   **$65**

GRENADIER/ CEILO, 1979

Limited-edition figural decanter of a metallic gold statue of Mr. Spock from *Star Trek: The Motion Picture*, giving the Vulcan salute molded on display base. Decanters were sold empty and came packaged in a blue satin box. Only 1,200 were produced and each decanter was individually numbered and included a certificate of authenticity. This is an extremely rare piece desired by many collectors, myself included.

  $1,000   **$2,000**

WEIBEL VINEYARDS – WOODBRIDGE, 2002

Collectible bottled Star Trek California Champagne, Chateau Du Trek Wine.

  $20   **$25**

Chateau Du Trek Wine, Weibel Vineyards – Woodbridge, 2002.

STAR TREK THE EXPERIENCE, ROMULAN ALE

Romulan Ale, The Experience.

Romulan Ale bottle opener, The Experience.

Individual bottle (I wonder if there is a no open bottle law when you are in a shuttle craft?).

$10   **$20**

Full six pack (Commander, can you swing by the corner asteroid on your way home and pick up a six pack?).

$60   **$120**

Romulan Ale bottle opener (no self-respecting Romulan would be caught dead without one of these).

$10   **$20**

KRAFT

Kraft marshmallows and mail-away dispenser, 1989.

Marshmallows; the bags featured a *Star Trek V: The Final Frontier* promotional mail-away limited-time offer for a marshmallow dispenser. This is an odd and certainly unique piece.

Marshmallow bag (empty) with *Star Trek V: The Final Frontier* advertisement.

$5   **$10 each**

Mail-away dispenser.

$25   **$35**

MCDONALD'S HAPPY MEALS, 1979

Star Trek: The Motion Picture Happy Meals; each box included a comic printed on it and had a toy inside. (Also see Toys.)

$10   **$20**

NESTLE, 1975

Sulu candy bar; blue wrapper with image of Enterprise with a black panel stating "Star Trek Cream Flavour Candy" and image of Sulu on the bridge at the helm from the animated TV show.

$55   **$75**

PARAMOUNT SPECIAL EFFECTS, 1989

Chocolate candy bars; two-pound chocolate bars feature relief of U.S.S. Enterprise with the words, "Live Long and Prosper." These were available Christmas 1989 only.

$45   **$55**

Happy Meals, McDonald's, 1979.

PAUL'S ICE CREAM, 1979

Striped Popsicles, Paul's Ice Cream, 1979.

Striped Popsicles with *Star Trek: The Motion Picture*-themed wrapper.

Wrapper.

$25   **$35**

Store poster for Paul's Star Trek Popsicles.

$35   **$45**

PHOENIX CANDY, 1976

Star Trek Candy, Phoenix Candy, 1976.

This candy included two prizes per box, with various *Star Trek* images on each box:

#1: Kirk (closer image).

#2: Spock.

#3: McCoy.

#4: Bridge Crew.

#5: Uhura.

#6: Transporter.

#7: Kirk.

#6: Enterprise.

$25   **$45 each**

PRIMROSE CONFECTIONERY, 1970

Candy Cigarettes, Primrose Confectionery, 1970.

Sweet Cigarettes (candy) in a small box; extremely rare.

$50   **$75**

"Warp 4" high-energy soft drink, Warner Trade Ltd, 1995.

SOFT DRINKS/ENERGY DRINKS

WARNER TRADE LTD, 1995

"Warp 4" high-energy soft drink; has image of Enterprise on blue space background. Product information is listed in both English and German on the side of the can.

$25   **$35**

TUTTLE PRESS, 1978

Edible birthday cake candy toppers, in two different styles.

10-piece rosebud candy cake set with cardboard center

$25   **$35**

22-piece candy set with 8 rosebuds and 13 confectionery letters of "Happy Birthday" making up the 22 candy pieces, with smaller cardboard center.

$35   **$45**

Frisbees

AZRAK/HAMWAY (AHI), 1974

Flying U.S.S. Enterprise Frisbee, Remco, 1967.

Zing Wing Saucer Frisbee, red, has artwork of Kirk, Spock and the Enterprise, 9".

$75   **$100**

HUMPHREY FLYER, 1976

Zing Wing saucer Frisbee, Azrak/Hamway, 1974.

Inside Star Trek album promo Frisbee for Columbia Records, light blue, 9".

$30   **$45**

REMCO, 1967

Inside Star Trek album promo Frisbee, Humphrey Flyer, 1976.

"Flying U.S.S. Enterprise" Frisbee, yellow, has Star Trek theme decal that says "Throw it...it flies like a real spaceship," 8-1/2".

$85   **$125**

SAUCER FRISBEE, 1993

Star Trek Enterprise hull Frisbee, 1993.

Star Trek Enterprise Saucer Frisbee, white, has detailed Enterprise Saucer Section design.

$35   **$50**

WHAM-O, 1973

Flying disc with Star Trek Enterprise theme.

$35   **$50**

Games

The first Star Trek board game was released by Ideal in late 1966 and is another one of those cross-collectibles that both Star Trek and board game collectors compete for when one shows up at auction. Because *Star Trek's* popularity didn't really take off until after its cancellation and subsequent syndication, fans and collectors had to wait eight years until Hasbro released its board game in 1974.

The Palitoy (UK) board game version from 1975, like the Ideal board game from 1966, can be hard to find.

Star Trek board game, Ideal, 1966.

BOARD GAMES

IDEAL, 1966

The first Star Trek board game; includes board, four game cards and a variety of playing pieces.

$100   **$150**

HASBRO, 1974

Action and Adventure in Outer Space board game, Hasbro, 1974.

"Action and Adventure in Outer Space"; includes foldout board with colorful plastic pieces and action spinners.

$55   **$65**

MILTON BRADLEY, 1979

Star Trek board game, Milton Bradley, 1979.

Star Trek board game, game includes *Star Trek: The Motion Picture* artwork on the cover, a board, markers, playing pieces and playing cards.

$25   **$30**

Star Trek Trivia Game, Golden, 1985.

GOLDEN, 1985

Star Trek Trivia Game, includes a four-sided plastic card tray, 216 trivia cards and die.

$15   **$20**

PALITOY (UK), 1975

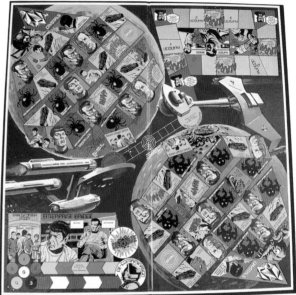

Star Trek Game, Palitoy, 1975.

This Star Trek board game uses some of the Mego action figure card artwork and includes a foldout board and playing pieces. Palitoy was the British division of Mego.

$95   **$125**

FRANKLIN MINT, 1991

Star Trek Franklin Mint 25th Anniversary Chess Set. Commemorative set is a standard one with TOS-themed pieces.

Gold pieces: King: Captain James T. Kirk; Queen: Lt. Uhura; Bishops: Commander Spock/Dr. Leonard McCoy; Knights: Lt. Cmdr. Montgomery Scott/Lt. Hikaru Sulu; Rooks: The U.S.S. Enterprise; Pawns: Starfleet Security Officers.

Silver pieces: King: Khan Noonien Singh; Queen: Romulan Commander from the Enterprise Incident; Bishops: A Vian and a Gorgan; Knights: Romulan Officer and Gorn Commander; Rooks: Klingon Battle Cruiser; Pawns: Klingon Foot Soldiers.

$300   **$400**

BMI, 1992

Star Trek The Final Frontier, first version, BMI, 1992.

Star Trek The Final Frontier has two artwork box styles. This first version by BMI has a few errors on game cards like "Ohora," "Scottie," and "Romulons."

$45   **$50**

Star Trek The Final Frontier, second version, BMI, 1992.

Star Trek The Final Frontier, second box version. Mistakes on game cards are now corrected to "Uhura," "Scotty," and "Romulans." Though box versions of the game play the same, the mistakes make the first version more desirable to collectors.

$25   **$30**

CLASSIC GAMES, 1992

Star Trek: The Game, Classic Games, 1992.

Star Trek: The Game, a strategic board game of logic, trivia, and chance that will engage the senses; for 2-6 players. This same box artwork was used again in 1993 on the puzzle by Golden.

$25   **$35**

FASA

Star Trek: The Role Playing Game:

2001 Deluxe Limited Edition.

Star Trek Basic Set 2004.

Star Trek III Combat Game 2006.

Set of 3 adventures and deck plans for Constitution Cruiser and Klingon D-7 battle cruiser.

$55   **$75 each**

Special autographed editions, signed by James Doohan or Walter Koenig.

$100   **$120**

Enterprise deck plans for 2001 game.

$20   **$25**

Klingon deck plans for 2001 game.

$15   **$20**

Star Trek: The Role-Playing Game, second deluxe edition.

$35   **$40**

Star Trek: The Role-Playing Game 2004 basic set, complete rules in 3 books.

$20   **$25**

Star Trek: The Role-Playing Game, second deluxe edition, FASA.

Star Trek: The Role-Playing Game supplements: The Klingons: A Sourcebook and Character Generation Supplement 2002, in book or boxed set form.

$25 $30

Ship Construction Manual 2004, Build Your Own Starship, sold in two editions.

$15 $25

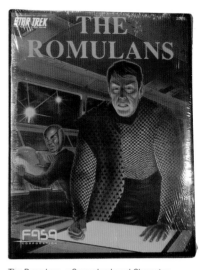

The Romulans, a Sourcebook and Character Generation supplement 2005, FASA.

The Romulans, a Sourcebook and Character Generation supplement 2005.

$15 $25

The Orion, a Sourcebook and Character Generation Supplement 2008.

$15 $20

The Romulan Way: Game Operations Manual, FASA.

The Romulan Way: Game Operations Manual.

$15 $20

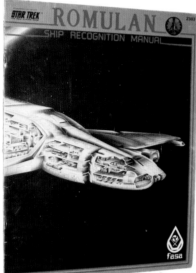

Romulan Ship Recognition Manual 2303, FASA.

Romulan Ship Recognition Manual 2303.

$10 $15

The White Flame, Starship Combat Scenario Pack 2225, FASA.

The White Flame: Starship Combat Scenario Pack 2225.

$15 $20

The Mines of Selka 2213, FASA.

The Mines of Selka 2213.

$15 $20

A Matter of Priorities 2211, FASA.

A Matter of Priorities 2211.

$15 $20

Graduation Exercise 2216, FASA.

Graduation Exercise 2216.
$15   **$20**

Margin of Profit 2209, FASA.

Margin of Profit 2209.
$15   **$20**

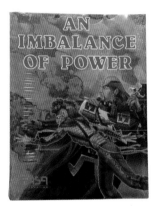

An Imbalance of Power, FASA.

An Imbalance of Power.
$15   **$20**

Orion Ruse 2208, FASA.

Orion Ruse 2208.
$15   **$20**

Tricoer/Starship Sensors Interactive
Display 2803, FASA.

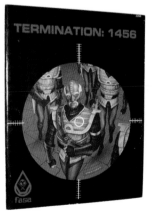

Termination: 1456, FASA.

Decision at Midnight 2219, FASA.

Decision at Midnight 2219.
$15   **$20**

Trader Captains and Merchant Princes 2203; two versions of
supplement allowing creation of traders, merchants, and riff-raff.
$15   **$18**

The Triangle 2007.
$15   **$20**

The Federation 2011.
$15   **$20**

Starfleet Intelligence Manual 2014; details spies and covert
operatives.
$15   **$20**

Starfleet Intelligence Agent Orientation Manual 2014A.
$5   **$10**

Starfleet Intelligence Operations Manual 2014B.
$5   **$10**

Tricorder/Starship Sensors Interactive Display 2803.
$25   **$30**

Termination: 1456.
$15   **$20**

FRANKLIN MINT, 1993

Standard checkers set, produced in pewter and plated in either 24k gold or sterling silver. The gold checkers depict the U.S.S. Enterprise on one side and the Enterprise Command Insignia on the other. The silver checkers depict the Klingon D7 Battlecruiser on one side and the Klingon insignia on the other. Includes a beautiful blue and silver playing field.

$300   **$400**

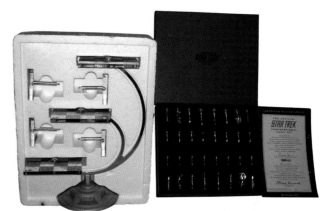

FRANKLIN MINT, 1994

Tri-dimensional chess set has a three-level playing field comprised of three main playing grids (shelves) and four smaller attack grids; the arched stand is 24k gold-plated.

$250   **$450**

Tri-dimensional chess set, Franklin Mint, 1994.

PARKER BROTHERS, 1998

Star Trek Monopoly.

$65   **$100**

Star Trek Monopoly, Parker Brothers, 1998.

ARCADE GAMES

BALLY, 1979

Star Trek Pinball Machine. It is said that two different playfield designs exist, but the one pictured here is the only one I have ever seen other than an early picture of a Bally prototype playfield. Note: A good back glass for this pin alone can sell for well over $500.

$1,000   **$2,500**

Bally Star Trek Pinball Brochure.

$20   **$25**

SEGA, 1979

Star Trek: The Arcade Game. Sega produced three versions:

Stand up.

$1,000   **$1,500**

Sit-down cockpit; has a unique captain's chair design with view screen.

$2,000   **$2,500**

Kit (converts a different arcade game to Star Trek: The Arcade Game).

$500   **$750**

Sega Star Trek arcade game brochures.

$20   **$30**

Star Trek pinball machine, Bally, 1979.

HOME-BASED GAMES AND CARTRIDGES

Quite a few Star Trek games were produced for the home-based gaming systems created over the years, but for the most part, their values have yet to reach any real collectible level. Much of this is due to the ever-changing home game systems market, where games become old or obsolete as soon as a new and better game system is released. Listed here are just some of the many games and cartridges available.

ACTIVISION

Invasion, Playstation, Activision.

Star Trek Invasion:

Playstation.

$20   **$25**

BETHESDA SOFTWARE

Tactical Assault, Nintendo DS,
Bethesda Software.

Star Trek Tactical Assault-UMD:

Playstation Portable (PSP).

$25   **$30**

Star Trek Tactical Assault:

Nintendo DS.

$25   **$30**

Tactical Assault, PSP, Bethesda
Software.

INTERCEPTOR SOFTWARE, 1983

Star Trek for the Commodore 64,
Interceptor Software, 1983.

Rare Star Trek cassette game
cartridge for the Commodore 64.

$20   **$35**

MILTON BRADLEY, 1979

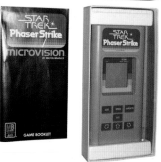

Phaser Strike Game cartridge and overlay,
Milton Bradley, 1979.

Phaser Strike Game Cartridge and Overlay: Cartridge works with Milton Bradley's Microvision hand-held game system that was released by the Milton Bradley Company in 1979. The package included the game cartridge control overlay for the hand-held unit and an instruction manual. Microvision was designed by Jay Smith, who designed the Vectrex gaming system as well.

$25   **$35**

SEGA, 1983

Strategic Operations Simulator, Atari 2600, Sega, 1983.

Strategic Operations Simulator, patterned after the Sega arcade game, Texas Instruments, Sega, 1983.

Star Trek: Strategic Operations Simulator. The arcade game comes home for the Atari 2600.

Cartridge.

$15   **$20**

Star Trek: Strategic Operations Simulator.

Texas Instruments cartridge.

$10   **$15**

SEGA, 32X

Starfleet Academy for the 32X, Sega.

Star Trek: Starfleet Academy cartridge.

$5   **$15**

VECTREX, 1979

Vectrex cartridge, Vectrex, 1979.

Vectrex is a small table-top stand-alone game system with a built-in black and white screen. It offered different game cartridges including Star Trek and a colored overlay for the screen.

Star Trek Vectrex Cartridge.

$25   **$35**

COMPUTER SOFTWARE AND GAMES

Quite a bit of Star Trek computer software and games are currently on the market, but for the most part, their values have yet to reach any real collectible level. It is common for computer software to be purchased in two types of packaging: in a regular cereal box-sized store display box, or shrink-wrapped in just its jewel case. Most games were released for both PC and Mac platforms. Here is a sample of just some of the software that can be obtained for your computer.

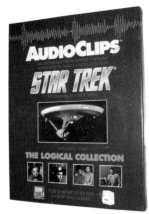

Audio clips; sound clips for your computer.

$5   **$10**

Sound clips for your computer.

Star Trek 25th Anniversary game.

Star Trek 25th Anniversary game.

$5   **$15**

Star Trek 25th Anniversary game.

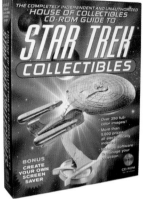

Star Trek: Judgment Rites.

Star Trek: Starship Creator.

Star Trek: Collectibles software.

Case of Star Trek software by Lil Bits.

Star Trek: Judgment Rites.
$5   **$10**

Star Trek: Starship Creator.
$10   **$15**

Star Trek: Collectibles software
to help organize and catalog
your collection.
$5   **$10**

Case of Star Trek Font software
by Lil Bits; the box breaks down
into a cardboard store display.
$25   **$35**

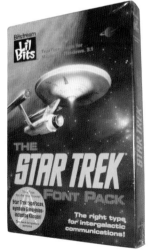

The Star Trek Font Pack.

Star Trek Screen Saver bundle.

Star Trek the Screen Saver.

Star Trek Screen Posters.

The Star Trek Font Pack.
$5   **$10**

Star Trek screen saver bundle.
The set included both the *Star
Trek: The Original Series* screen
saver and the *Star Trek* movies
screen posters screen saver.
$25   **$45**

Star Trek the Screen Saver. *The
Original Series* screen saver by
After Dark.
$5   **$15**

Star Trek Screen Saver: Screen
Posters; images from the
various motion pictures.
$5   **$15**

Starfleet Academy in jewel case.

Captain's Chair in jewel case.

Starfleet Command: Neutral Zone in jewel case.

Starfleet Academy:		Captain's Chair:		Starfleet Command: Neutral Zone:	
Boxed.		Boxed.		Boxed.	
$15	$35	$15	$35	$15	$35
Jewel case.		Jewel case.		Jewel case.	
$5	$15	$5	$15	$5	$25

CARD GAMES

AVIVA, 1979

Star Trek: The Motion Picture Enterprise card deck. Basic deck of playing cards with the *Motion Picture* movie Enterprise on blue space background with movie title.

$10 $25

MATTEL, 1999

UNO, Mattel, 1999.

UNO, Star Trek Special Edition. Card game comes packaged in a collector's tin. Features a photo of one of the characters or ships from the original *Star Trek* television show on each card, each with a unique card value. Also features unique differences to traditional UNO, like the "Beam Me Up, Scotty" Wild and Stop Cards and the "Double Tribble Card."

$10 $15

MOVIE PLAYERS, LTD., 1982

The Wrath of Khan card deck; basic deck of playing cards with the movie logo. Two editions were released with a very slight logo change on the second.

First edition, "Star Trek Wrath of Khan" in blue on black background:

$50 $75

Second edition, "Star Trek II Wrath of Khan" on black background:

$40 $65

"Mirror, Mirror" customizable card game.

Star Trek "Mirror, Mirror" customizable card game.

$15 $25 per box

TWA, 1986

Give-away premium card deck with movie logo.

$10 $25

"Tribbles" customizable card game.

Tribbles customizable card game.

$10 $15 per box

ZOLKE AND DAVIS, 1976

Fizzbin. Cards feature collage of four images from *The Original Series* episode. Fizzbin was first introduced to the public by Captain James T. Kirk in *The Original Series* episode, "A Piece of the Action." Game includes playing rules, which is good because anyone who wanted to try and learn how to play the game simply from listening to Kirk explain it on the episode would have a hard time for sure.

$65 $85

Greeting Cards and Postcards

GREETING CARDS

CALIFORNIA DREAMERS, 1985-1987

There were a total of three series in this set.

Chekov – Inhuman Cossacks! Pigs! They've destroyed everything. You'll never be 29 again. Happy Birthday.

Enterprise – Space is not the final frontier…You are!

Gorn attacks Kirk – Beam me up, Scotty…It's been one of those days.

Kirk and Spock – Fire all phasers…Fire all photon torpedoes…What the heck. It's your Birthday!

Kirk – This is Captain James T. Kirk of the Starship Enterprise. Our mission is a peaceful one. We mean no harm…Sure the check's in the mail and you're 29. Happy Birthday.

Kirk – Sometimes I just to say to hell with Starfleet, to hell with regulations and responsibility, to hell with everything. Except you!

Kirk, McCoy, Uhura – Phasers charged and ready. Photon torpedoes fully armed…Here comes Monday!

Kirk, Spock, McCoy from "Piece of the Action" – You've got to dress for success!

Kirk – The landing party is expendable. The ship is not. If we're not back by 0500, contact Starfleet Command, get the Enterprise out of here, and whatever you do…Have a good time on your Birthday!

Kirk – I was going to shoot you with a Phaser…But it seemed so unromantic.

Kirk with the Providers from Gamesters of Triskelion – Who am I? Where am I? Why do I have on these strange clothes…Why do I have such strange friends?

McCoy – I've run every test, checked every medical reference in the galaxy, and damn it. I can't find a cure for what you've got…Old Age…Happy Birthday.

McCoy – Listen to me. I'm a doctor. I know…Birthdays are hell.

Planet on Bridge Screen – To boldly go where no man has gone before…or woman either. Congratulations.

Scotty – Three dilithium crystals, a tablespoon of kironide, a pinch of antimatter, and just a dash of phaser…I'm going to make you a birthday cake that will light up the universe…Happy Birthday.

Spock – You were born on this day. It is therefore quite logical to wish you a happy birthday…Live long and prosper.

Spock – There are 3 billion worlds in the known universe, with a combined population of approximately 6,307,000,000,000 composed of carbon- and non-carbon-based life forms…But there is only 1 of you. Happy Birthday.

A Christmas holiday card I received in 2007.

Spock Happy Birthday card, California Dreamers, 1985-1987.

Spock – The heat here is extreme. Far beyond normal ranges…How many candles were on that cake, anyway? Happy Birthday!

Spock – History banks indicate that inhabitants of 20th century Earth would oftentimes undergo a strange suicide-like ritual on many of their post-30th birthdays…Death by chocolate. Happy Birthday.

Spock – Readings indicate an unparalleled cosmic phenomena occurred on this day. It was in a time so ancient, the year cannot be ascertained by ship's computers…I guess we'll just have to look at the cake and count all those candles! Happy Birthday.

Spock – It is not logical. It makes no sense. …It must be Love!

Spock – You make me smile!

Spock – Just because one is logical…does not mean that one cannot be cool. You're cool. Happy Birthday.

Spock – I fail to understand the inexplicable human need to so primitively celebrate the anniversary of one's birth. Nevertheless, I offer you the words of Surak, the most revered of all Vulcan philosophers. "Krut Toba Grig-Toba Grig." If you party, party BIG! Happy Birthday.

$5 $10 each

CAMBRIDGE, 1979 GREETING CARDS

Enterprise front view.

Enterprise head on view.

Enterprise side view.

Kirk, Spock, and Enterprise.

Kirk with Communicator.

Kirk, Spock, McCoy on Bridge.

Spock at Science station.

Star Trek: The Motion Picture Crew and Enterprise.

$5 $10 each

HALLMARK HOLIDAY CARDS, SHOEBOX GREETINGS

Spock Easter card, Hallmark Holiday Cards, Shoebox Greetings.

Kirk and Spock Christmas card, Hallmark Holiday Cards, Shoebox Greetings.

Christmas card, Hallmark Holiday Cards, Shoebox Greetings.

Christmas card, Hallmark Holiday Cards, Shoebox Greetings.

Christmas card, Hallmark Holiday Cards, Shoebox Greetings.

Spock and Easter Bunny: "Hmm, what's with those ears?" "Happy Easter."

$10   **$15**

Kirk and Spock w/Phasers: "There it is again…up on the 'B' deck…click…click…"

Drawing of Santa and Elves on bridge.

Kirk and Spock (w/odd color editing) "Oh, Christmas tree…"

Spock w/Lirpa and Santa hat: "These humans…"

$5   **$10 each**

STAY TUNED

Akuta greeting card, Stay Tuned.

Chekov, Kirk and Uhura birthday card, Stay Tuned.

McCoy, Kirk and Spock birthday card, Stay Tuned.

Enterprise firing phasers greeting card, Stay Tuned.

Kirk greeting card, Stay Tuned.

Spock with visor greeting card, Stay Tuned.

Landing party beaming down greeting card, Stay Tuned.

Crew on the bridge greeting card, Stay Tuned.

These greeting cards feature classic scenes and publicity stills from *The Original Series*. Envelopes have image of the Enterprise firing Phasers in the bottom left corner and a command symbol where postage stamp would be placed. The back of the envelope has an image of the crew on the bridge:

Akuta of Gamma Trianguli VI from "The Apple."

Chekov, Kirk and Uhura: Another year older, and you look younger than ever!

McCoy, Kirk and Spock: It's your birthday!

Enterprise firing Phasers.

Kirk yelling from "The Enemy Within."

Spock w/visor from "Is There In Truth No Beauty."

Landing party beaming down.

Crew on the bridge (publicity photo).

$5   **$10 each**

RANDOM HOUSE, 1976 ORIGINAL TELEVISION SERIES CARDS

Kirk – Star light, star bright, first star I see tonight…I wished on a star for your birthday.

Kirk – This is your Captain speaking…Have a far-out Birthday!

Kirk holding rose – The Captain and I both wish you a very happy birthday.

Kirk on viewer – COURAGE!

Kirk, Spock, Scott, Uhura, and McCoy – Happy Birthday to a great human being!

Kirk standing on planet – There's so much space between us.

Kirk with medals – Congratulations.

Kirk with communicator – Let's Communicate.

McCoy and Kirk – Don't worry – You'll feel better soon.

McCoy and Kirk – Happy Birthday from one big shot…to another.

McCoy, Scott, Chekov, and Uhura – Happy Birthday!

Scotty, Spock, Kirk, McCoy, Uhura, and Chekov – Happy Birthday from the whole spaced out crew.

Spock – Know what I like about you?

Spock – Sorry I blew it…

Spock in uniform – It is illogical not to wish a Happy Birthday to someone so charming.

Spock and headset – I must be hard of hearing.

Spock by door – Let's keep in touch.

Spock with visor – Having a Birthday?

Uhura – I hear it's your Birthday…Opening all hailing frequencies!

Uhura and Kirk on Bridge – Off course… Hope you're back on the right trek soon.

U.S.S. Enterprise – For your Birthday I'd like to take you on a trip to Venus.

U.S.S. Enterprise orbiting orange planet – I'm sending you something from outer space…

U.S.S. Enterprise orbiting planet – One of the nicest earthlings in the universe…just opened this card. Happy Birthday!

U.S.S. Enterprise over planet – The world's a better place because of you.

$5 $10 each

Birthday card, Random House, 1976.

Greeting card, Random House, 1976.

Birthday card, Random House, 1976.

Greeting card, Random House, 1976.

Greeting card, Random House, 1976.

Birthday card, Random House, 1976.

Greeting card, Random House, 1976.

Greeting card, Random House, 1976.

Greeting card, Random House, 1976.

Birthday card, Random House, 1976.

Greeting card, Random House, 1976.

Birthday card, Random House, 1976.

Birthday card, Random House, 1976.

Birthday card, Random House, 1976.

Birthday card, Random House, 1976.

Greeting card, Random House, 1976.

POPSHOTS, 1993

3-D pop-up card, Popshots, 1993.

3-D pop-up artwork:

City on the Edge of Forever.
Jumping through guardian.

Kirk buried in Tribbles.

Kirk, Spock, McCoy, and
Enterprise.

$5   **$15 each**

City on the Edge of Forever, Popshots, 1993.

Kirk buried in Tribbles, Popshots, 1993.

Kirk, Spock, McCoy and Enterprise, Popshots, 1993.

POSTCARDS

A.H. PRISMATIC, 1993 LASERGRAMS

Enterprise.

Spock.

Kirk, McCoy, Spock, and Uhura.

$5   **$10 each**

ANABAS, 1987 STAR TREK ORIGINAL TELEVISION SERIES

Enterprise.

$10   **$15**

Kirk, McCoy, Uhura.

$5   **10**

APPLIED HOLOGRAPHICS, 1991

25th Anniversary logo on silver.

$10   **$15**

CALIFORNIA DREAMERS, INC., 1987

Greeting postcards:

Spock with Horta.

Kirk and Tellurite.

Enterprise.

Kirk with communicator.

Kirk in command chair.

Spock with mind-control headset.

Sulu.

$5   **$10 each**

CHRONICLE BOOKS, 2006

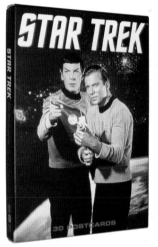

Box set of 30 postcards.

$10   **$15**

Box set of Star Trek postcards, Chronicle Books, 2006.

ENGALE MARKETING, 1989

Postcard, Engale Marketing, 1989.

Signed postcard, Walter Koenig, May 5, 1990, Engale Marketing, 1989.

Series of 16 postcards.

$5   **$10**

EXETER PRESS, 1977

Image of Enterprise on postcard.
$5   **$7**

LINCOLN ENTERPRISES, 1983

Star Trek: The Motion Picture postcards:

Kirk.   Chekov.

Spock.   Chapel.

McCoy.   Rand.

Scotty.   Ilia.

Sulu.   Decker.

Uhura.   Enterprise.
$1   **$5 each**

Set of all 12 cards.
$5   **$10**

LUDLOW SALES, 1986

Sepia fotocards:

Bridge scene.
$5   **$15**

Mr. Spock w/phaser.
$5   **$10**

MONSTER TIMES, 1976

Enterprise Crew postcards, set of six.
$5   **$10**

PARAMOUNT PICTURES, DATE UNKNOWN

Postcard-style publicity photos.
$15   **$20**

T-K GRAPHICS, 1984

Starfleet Headquarters Official Mail Postcards, set of 8.
$5   **$10**

Starfleet Headquarters Tactical Operations Center, set of 8.
$5   **$10**

STARFLEET IMPORTS, 1982

Fantasy Card Set of three:

Star Trek: The Motion Picture, Kirk.
$5   **$10**

Female Romulan commander.
$5   **$10**

LINCOLN ENTERPRISES, 1967

Star Trek postcards, Lincoln Enterprises, 1967.

Enterprise Crew postcards, set of 7.
$25   **$50**

Postcard-style publicity photos, Paramount Pictures.

POSTCARD BOOK
PRIME PRESS, 1977

Book of photo postcards, Prime Press, 1977.

Inside pages of book of photo postcards, Prime Press, 1977.

Star Trek Postcard Book, original television series, has 48 photo postcards.

$25   **$55**

Housewares

Raise your hand if you ever drank milk or ate cereal using the Deka plastic mug and bowl set from 1975!

The Cheinco wastepaper basket from 1977 is another great collectible not only because of the incredible artwork on the sides, but because it is one of those rare pieces you can actually use and display at the same time.

AIR FRESHENERS

U.S.S. Enterprise Air Freshener; "Freshens the air at the speed of light"; for use in house or car.

$15   **$20**

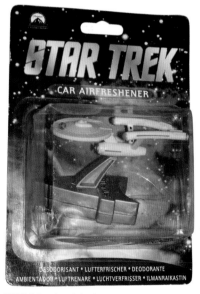

U.S.S. Enterprise air freshener.

BULLETIN BOARD
MILTON BRADLEY/ WHITING, 1979

3-D "The Motion Picture" poster bulletin board that includes pre-printed die-cut board and four color pens.

$55   **$75**

CAR HANGERS
H & L ENTERPRISES, 1986

"Beam Me Up" in black lettering car hanger. Sign is similar to "Baby on board" signs. Square plastic sign includes a clear suction cup.

Large sign.

$10   **$15**

Small sign, 1987.

$5   **$10**

STARPOOL INC., 1982

Star Trek II Kinetic Passengers characters:

Busts of Kirk or Spock attach to the rear window of your car. Hands are spring-loaded and "wave" as you drive.

$50 $75

STRAVINA, 1985

"Beam Me Up" in red lettering on yellow caution sign style car hanger. Includes suction cup.

$5 $10

WEAVER, 1986

"Beam Me Up" in black lettering on square yellow car hanger. Includes suction cup.

$5 $10

VISION AERIES, 1988

Yellow caution-style signs with black lettering. Include suction cup:

"Tribble On Board."

"Spock You!"

"Shuttle Craft"

$15 $25

CELL PHONE BELT HOLDER, 2003

Pouch designed to fit most cell phones.

Features classic command insignia stitched type patch on front flap in yellow, blue, or red.

$25 $35 each

COMB AND BRUSH SET

GABIL, 1977

Blue oval brush with blue comb featuring color decal-style transfer images. Sold in clear plastic package.

$55 $75

COOKIE JARS

STAR JARS, 1996

30th Anniversary ceramic cookie jars. Each 14" to 16" tall cookie jar was a limited edition to only 1,000 pieces. Jars feature colorful artwork finished off with metallic glaze and cloisonné inset pieces—another "holy grail" piece for many collectors. Cookie jars are also a cross collectible, which means that Star Trek collectors are competing against cookie jar collectors to own one. These are rare and truly spectacular though extremely hard to find and complete as a set.

Enterprise and UFP logo: "Space the Final Frontier."
$250 $350
Spock and Kirk: "These are the Voyages of the Starship Enterprise."
$400 $500
Enterprise and crew members: "It's Five Year Mission…To Explore New Worlds."
$400 $500
Alien Ships and Starfleet insignia: "To Seek Out New Life and New Civilizations."
$300 $400
Vulcan salute: "To Boldly Go Where No Man Has Gone Before."
$300 $400

DIORAMAS

APPLAUSE, 1996

Arena diorama display, Applause, 1996.

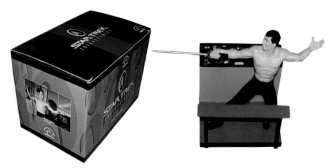

Man Trap M-113 diorama display, Applause, 1996.

Resin diorama displays: These diorama displays re-create a famous scene from a popular episode. These are not toys and are specifically advertised as for adult collectors only:

The Man Trap with Kirk, M-113 creature and McCoy.

Arena with Kirk and the Gorn.

The Naked Time with Sulu and a sword.

The Menagerie (The Cage) with Kirk, Spock, and Pike.

Space Seed with Kirk and Khan.

$15 $20 each

DOORHANGERS

ANTIOCH, 1992

"Beam Me Up…"

   $5   **$10**

"Beam Me Up" doorhanger, Antioch, 1992.

GLASSES AND TUMBLERS

7-11 STORES

Limited-edition Slurpee-Star Trek cups, 7-11 stores.

Limited-edition anniversary Slurpee cups: In 1991, *Star Trek* was celebrating its 25th anniversary, and so was the Slurpee, so 7-11 joined the two together and released a set of anniversary Slurpee-Star Trek cups.

   $5   **$10**

COCA-COLA, 1979

Star Trek: The Motion Picture glasses:

Kirk, Spock, McCoy, Decker, Ilia.

   $25   **$45**

Enterprise.

   $35   **$65**

Star Trek: The Motion Picture plastic tumblers:

Kirk, Spock, McCoy, Decker, Ilia.

   $25   **$35**

FIGURINES

WESTLAND GIFTWARE, 2007

Mr. Weiner, Hot Diggity figurine, Westland Giftware, 2007.

Hot Diggity ceramic figurine:

Mr. Weiner No. 16554.

Mr. Spock-themed Dachshund figurine.

   $25   **$35**

DEKA, 1975

Bowl and two mugs, *The Original Series*, Deka, 1975.

Plastic mug and matching bowl with colorful images of Kirk, Spock, McCoy, Enterprise, and Klingon ships on the sides.

Mug.

   $25   **$45**

Bowl.

   $35   **$55**

DEKA, 1979

Star Trek: The Motion Picture mug and bowl set, Deka, 1979.

Star Trek: The Motion Picture mugs, tumbler, and plate set, Deka, 1979.

Star Trek: The Motion Picture set:

Plastic tumbler, 11 oz.
   $10   **$15**
Plastic three-section snack tray.
   $35   **$45**
Plastic mug.
   $10   **$20**
Plastic bowl.
   $25   **$35**

DR. PEPPER. 1976

Set of four glasses, *Star Trek: The Animated Series*, Dr. Pepper, 1976.

Star Trek: The Animated Series glasses:

Captain Kirk, Doctor McCoy, Mr. Spock.
   $25   **$35**
U.S.S. Enterprise.
   $55   **$65**

DR. PEPPER, 1978

Set of four glasses, *The Original Series* Dr. Pepper, 1978.

Star Trek: The Original Series glasses:

Captain Kirk, Doctor McCoy, Mr. Spock.
   $35   **$45**
U.S.S. Enterprise.
   $65   **$75**

FIRST AID KIT

ADAM JOSEPH, 1979

Star Trek: The Motion Picture-themed small complete first aid kit.
   $50   **$65**

LAMPS AND LIGHTS

FRANKLIN MINT, 1995

Enterprise replica lights up under saucer section and sits on curved black base.

$150 **$250**

PRESTIGELINE, INC.

Swag-style hanging lamp shaped similar to the Enterprise with three light-up globed bulbs, one on the front of each engine tube and one in front on the larger bottom body tube. Very rare.

$150 **$250**

TV LIGHTS

TV lights, Edition 1: Light string that features small TV screen lights that display a different scene from *The Original Series*.

$15 **$25**

Hanging neon light sign.

Hanging neon light sign, flat panel style plastic neon sign.

$10 **$25**

FUNATIK PRODUCTS, INC.

Enterprise desk lamp, Funatik Products, Inc.

Enterprise-shaped desk lamp: Enterprise body attached on a spring-loaded arm with large base. Two-way switch lets you either use the lamp under the saucer as a reading light or light up the windows in the body of the ship for use as a night-light.

$75 **$150**

Night light style display sign.

Night-light style light up sign: light up display has "Star Trek" on top with an image of *The Original Series*. Enterprise displayed in the center followed by "U.S.S. Enterprise" underneath.

$10 **$15**

LICENSE PLATES/FRAMES

U.S.S. Enterprise NCC-1701 license plate frame.

U.S.S. Enterprise NCC-1701 license plate.

U.S.S. Enterprise NCC-1701 license plate frame; blue with raised white letters and command insignia.

$20 **$25**

U.S.S. Enterprise NCC-1701 license plate; black painted metal tin plate with raised imprint lettering and border.

$25 **$30**

LIGHT SWITCH PLATES

AMERICAN TACK AND HARDWARE, 1985

Plastic single wall switch plates.

#1 Yellowish Enterprise over planet.

#2 Greenish Enterprise over planet.

$15   **$25 each**

AVIVA, 1979

Set of four different stick on color single switch decals from *Star Trek: The Motion Picture*: Enterprise; Enterprise, Kirk and Spock; Phaser Control; Spock.

$15   **$25 each**

LOTTERY TICKETS

Through the years, quite a few *Star Trek*-themed lottery tickets were released in a variety of different states across the country as well as overseas. Sadly, there is no current way to track what tickets were issued and where. Lottery tickets I have seen have been averaging only a few dollars at best due to their small collectible value.

Virginia lottery ticket.

MAILBOXES

BACOVA GUILD, 1990

Paramount Pictures and Bacova Guild released this exclusive unique steel mailbox with a scratch proof vinyl type outer cover featuring artwork of the U.S.S. Enterprise with "Captain Kirk"; printed on the side in white letters. Artwork looks to be inspired by the animated series' Enterprise.

$100   **$200**

MATCHES

D.D. BEAN CO., 1979

Star Trek: The Motion Picture promotional matches.

$1   **$5**

PARAMOUNT PICTURES CORP., 1982

Star Trek II: The Wrath of Khan promotional matches.

$5   **$10**

Star Trek matches, 1979.

MONEY CLIP

RARITIES MINT, 1989

22k gold-plated silver commemorative coin hinged money clip of Mr. Spock with Vulcan salute. Came packaged in a maroon velvet lined gift box.

$75   **$100**

MARSHMALLOW DISPENSER

KRAFT, 1989

Marshmallow dispenser and marshmallow bag, Kraft foods, 1989.

Unique marshmallow dispenser based on the camping scene in *Star Trek V: The Final Frontier* with Kirk, Spock, and McCoy.

Dispenser.

$25   **$35**

Empty marshmallow bag with *Star Trek V* advertisement.

$5   **$15 each**

MOUSE PADS

Mouse pads have been both mass produced by licensed manufacturers as well as fan made in smaller quantities. The fan made mouse pads will vary in quality.

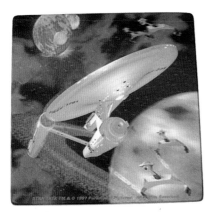

Lenticular Enterprise mouse pad.

Generations mouse pad.

Star Trek XI teaser art mouse pad.

Lenticular mouse pad of the Enterprise firing photon torpedoes while under attack by two Klingon Battle cruisers.

$20   **$25**

Star Trek: Generations mouse pad.

$5   **$10**

Star Trek XI teaser artwork mouse pad. I figured this mouse pad would be very appropriate for this book.

$10   **$15**

MUGS AND STEINS

APPLAUSE, INC., 1994

Figural bust-style mugs: Kirk, Spock, McCoy, Gorn.

$20   **$40**

BEE INTERNATIONAL, 1993

Ceramic mugs using the first six movie posters for artwork. Mugs were originally sold filled with candy:

Star Trek: The Motion Picture.

Star Trek II: The Wrath of Khan.

Star Trek III: The Search for Spock.

Star Trek IV: The Voyage Home.

Star Trek V: The Final Frontier.

Star Trek VI: The Undiscovered Country.

$20   **$35**

Star Trek figural mugs, Applause, Inc., 1994.

CERAMARTE/CATCH-A-STAR, 1994

"Star Trek the Original Cast" lidded stein.

$55   **$75**

Two views of Star Trek relief ceramic mug.

Ceramic relief mug; detailed relief of *Star Trek* ships.

$25   **$50**

DRAM TREE, 1996

30th Anniversary lidded stein, Dram Tree, 1996.

30th Anniversary lidded stein series:

"To Boldly Go" featuring pewter-plated Enterprise and lid.

$125   **$155**

"To Boldly Go" featuring 22k gold-plated pewter Enterprise and lid.

$155   **$175**

"Final Frontier" featuring pewter-plated Enterprise and lid.

$125   **$155**

"Balance of Terror" featuring pewter-plated Romulan ship and lid.

$125   **$155**

"Balance of Terror" featuring 22k gold-plated pewter Romulan ship and lid.

$155   **$175**

"Errand of Mercy" featuring pewter-plated Klingon ship and lid.

$125   **$155**

"Errand of Mercy" featuring 22k gold-plated pewter Klingon ship and lid.

$155   **$175**

ERNST, 1986

Kirk and Spock ceramic steins, artwork by Susie Morton, Ernst, 1986.

Ceramic stein. Artwork by Susie Morton includes Kirk and Spock.

$20   **$35**

LIMITED EDITION CERAMIC STEINS, DRAM TREE

"The Crew of Star Trek" stein, Dram Tree, 1996.

Limited edition of only 3,000. Sold through Spencer Gifts:

"The Crew of Star Trek"; features a variety of different images of the crew.

$20   **$25**

"New Life and New Civilizations": features a variety of different images of the Aliens.

$20   **$25**

"Anniversary Episode: The Man Trap"; features images from *The Original Series* episode, "The Man Trap."

$10   **$15**

ENESCO

"The Crew" and "U.S.S. Enterprise NCC-1701" ceramic mugs, Enesco.

Enesco released a set of commemorative collectors mugs using the same artwork from its commemorative plate collection:

"The Crew" and "U.S.S. Enterprise NCC-1701."

$25   **$45**

FRANKLIN MINT, 1991

Two different views of the 25th anniversary pewter tankard, Franklin Mint, 1991.

25th Anniversary pewter tankard.

$100   **$150**

FRANKLIN MINT, 2000

"U.S.S. Enterprise" porcelain stein with pewter top.

$175   **$225**

Enterprise porcelain stein, Franklin Mint, 2000.

LONGTON CROWN, 1997

These are the Voyages lidded stein series. First in the series, "The Doomsday Machine."

$65   **$85**

"The Doomsday Machine" lidded stein, Longton Crown, 1997.

IMAGE DESIGN CONCEPTS/PRESENTS, 1989

Heat sensitive mug, Image Design Concepts/Presents, 1989.

Heat sensitive printing on mugs create disappearing images when hot liquid is added:

Kirk, Spock, and McCoy in the Transporter.

$15   **$20**

Klingon Bird of Prey decloaking.

$20   **$25**

IMAGE PRODUCTS/RUMPH, 1982

Kirk and Spock ceramic steins from the movie *Star Trek II: The Wrath of Khan.* (The holy grail of Star Trek steins.) Features raised relief image on front and *Star Trek II: The Wrath of Khan* text in raised relief on back with character name at the bottom. Steins were sold shrink-wrapped on cardboard. These are extremely rare, especially the white uniform Kirk version.

Adm. Kirk (red uniform).
    $200   **$300**
Adm. Kirk (white uniform).
    $550   **$750**
Mr. Spock (red uniform).
    $200   **$300**

HAMILTON/ERNST, 1986

Set of eight ceramic crew mugs, Hamilton/Ernst, 1986.

The set of eight mugs were created jointly by Hamilton and Ernst and used the same artwork as their first series blue-bordered plates. Mugs were sold individually or boxed in sets of four. Mugs were reissued by Hamilton in 1991 to celebrate the 25th anniversary but under the "Presents" name.

Includes: Kirk; Spock; McCoy; Scotty; Uhura; Sulu; Chekov; "Beam Us Down Scotty" (crew in transporter).
    $25   **$55**

HAMILTON COLLECTION, 1994

Tankard collection:

"U.S.S. Enterprise NCC-1701" ceramic tankard.
    $75   **$100**
"Captain Kirk" ceramic tankard.
    $75   **$100**
"Mr. Spock" ceramic tankard.
    $75   **$100**

"U.S.S. Enterprise NCC-1701" ceramic tankard, Hamilton Collection, 1994.

PARAMOUNT, 1993

Spinner Mug. Unique ceramic mug with spinning Enterprise built into the handle.
    $25   **$45**

Spinner Mug, Paramount, 1993.

NOTEBOOKS
CAPTAIN'S LOG, 2001

Notebook with built-in calculator.
    $25   **$35**

Captain's Log notebook with built-in calculator.

PLATES, PORCELAIN

All plates included Certificates of Authenticity.

ENESCO, 1993

Commemorative plates, set of three, artwork by Todd Treadway.

"The Crew"; "U.S.S. Enterprise NCC-1701"; "Captain Kirk."

$45   **$65**

"The Crew" commemorative plate, Enesco, 1993.

U.S.S. Enterprise NCC-1701 commemorative plate, Enesco, 1994.

HAMILTON/ERNST, 1983-89

Kirk, First Series blue bordered plate, Hamilton/Ernst, 1983.

Spock, First Series blue bordered plate, Hamilton/Ernst, 1983.

McCoy, First Series blue bordered plate, front and back, Hamilton/Ernst, 1983.

Scotty, First Series blue bordered plate, Hamilton/Ernst, 1983.

Uhura, First Series blue bordered plate, Hamilton/Ernst, 1983.

Sulu, First Series blue bordered plate, Hamilton/Ernst, 1983.

Chekov, First Series blue bordered plate, Hamilton/Ernst, 1983.

First Series plates: blue bordered, artwork by Susie Morton:

Includes Kirk; Spock; McCoy; Scotty; Uhura; Sulu; Chekov; "Beam Us Down Scotty" (crew in transporter).

$45   **$55 each**

Amok Time, Second Series episode plate, Hamilton/
Ernst, 1986.

City on the Edge of Forever, Second Series episode
plate, Hamilton/Ernst, 1986.

Devil in the Dark, Second Series episode plate,
Hamilton/Ernst, 1986.

Journey to Babel, Second Series episode plate, front and back, Hamilton/Ernst, 1986.

Piece of the Action, Second Series episode plate,
Hamilton/Ernst, 1986.

Second Series: episode plates, gold bordered, artwork by Susie Morton,
part of the 20th Anniversary Collection:

Includes Amok Time; City on the Edge of Forever; Devil in the Dark; Journey to Babel;
Menagerie; Mirror, Mirror; Piece of the Action; Trouble with Tribbles.

    $75   **$125 each**

The Menagerie (rare).

    $100   **$150**

Third Series: episode plates, blue bordered:

The Tholian Web.

    $75   **$125**

Platinum Edition plates, 20th Anniversary series: Has the same artwork as the blue-bordered
First Series plates, but with a platinum border. It is a 9-piece special 20th anniversary plate
set of the crew and Enterprise. Each plate features a platinum border with most plates also
displaying a gold embossed simulated autograph of the actor for the corresponding character
plate. Only 1701 sets of each plate were produced, making this one of the rarest of the many
plate sets Hamilton released until the company closed.

Includes Kirk, Spock, McCoy, Scotty, Uhura, Sulu, Chekov.

    $100   **$150**

The Tholian Web, Third Series episode plate, blue
border, Hamilton/Ernst, 1996.

U.S.S. Enterprise NCC-1701, 25th Anniversary plate, Hamilton/Ernst, 1991.

Kirk, 25th Anniversary plate, gold border, Hamilton/Ernst, 1991.

Spock, 25th Anniversary plate, gold border, Hamilton/Ernst, 1991.

McCoy, 25th Anniversary plate, gold border, Hamilton/Ernst, 1991.

Scotty, 25th Anniversary plate, gold border, Hamilton/Ernst, 1991.

Uhura, 25th Anniversary plate, gold border, Hamilton/Ernst, 1991.

Crew and Enterprise, 25th Anniversary plate, gold border, Hamilton/Ernst, 1991.

25th Anniversary Commemorative plate collection, with artwork by Thomas Blackshear II. Gold border:

Includes U.S.S. Enterprise NCC-1701; Kirk; Spock; McCoy; Scotty; Uhura; Sulu; Chekov; Crew and Enterprise.

$25   **$45**

STAR TREK 30TH ANNIVERSARY COMMEMORATIVE PLATES

U.S.S. Enterprise and crew, gold border, Hamilton/Ernst, 1983.

Captain's Tribute: artwork features Captain Kirk, Picard, Sisko, and Janeway.

$55   **$75**

Second in Command: artwork features first officers Spock, Riker, Kira, and Chacotay.

$75   **$100**

U.S.S. Enterprise (with crew along bottom edge): artwork by Susie Morton. Plates are gold bordered.

$55   **$75**

STAR TREK: GENERATIONS PLATES

Gold bordered edge; rare set.

"Kirk's Final Voyage."

$55   **$75**

"Act Of Courage."

$155   **$225**

"SPACE, THE FINAL FRONTIER" PLATE COLLECTION

Flyer for "Second Star from the Right" plate, Hamilton/Ernst, 1996.

"To Boldly Go," Space The Final Frontier Collection, Hamilton/Ernst, 1996.

Oval plates feature various ships in very colorful space scenes.

"Second Star from the Right."

"Cataloging Gaseous Anomalies."

"Where Not Man Has Gone Before."

"We are Borg."

"Beyond the Neutral Zone."

"To Boldly Go."

"Preparing To Cloak."

"Distant Worlds."

"Signs of Intelligence."

"Searching The Galaxy."

$55   **$75 each**

THE MOVIES COMMEMORATIVE PLATES

Star Trek: The Motion Picture, Movie series plate, Hamilton/Ernst, 1995.

Plates feature scenes from the first six *Star Trek* movies. Each plate has an edged border.

The Motion Picture.

Destruction of the Reliant.

The Search for Spock.

Triumphant Return.

The Final Frontier.

The Undiscovered Country.

$65   **$125 each**

THE POWER OF COMMAND PLATE SET

Each plate features a ship and the character that was in command.

Captain Kirk and The U.S.S. Enterprise.

$65   **$75**

Admiral Kirk and the U.S.S. Enterprise-A.

$45   **$65**

Khan and The U.S.S. Reliant NCC-1864.

$45   **$65**

Captain Sulu and The U.S.S. Excelsior.

$45   **$55**

General Chang and The Klingon Bird of Prey.

$35   **$45**

THE VOYAGERS COMMEMORATIVE SERIES

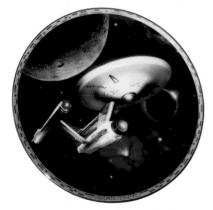

U.S.S. Enterprise, The Voyagers Series, Hamilton/
Ernst, 1995.

Klingon Battle Cruiser, The Voyagers Series,
Hamilton/Ernst, 1994.

U.S.S. Enterprise-A, The Voyagers Series, Hamilton/
Ernst, 1994.

U.S.S. Excelsior, The Voyagers Series, Hamilton/
Ernst, 1994.

Klingon Bird of Prey, The Voyagers Series, Hamilton/
Ernst, 1994.

Featuring the ships of *Star Trek*.
Gold bordered.

Including: U.S.S. Enterprise NCC-1701;
Klingon Battle Cruiser; U.S.S. Enterprise
NCC-1701-A; U.S.S. Excelsior; Klingon
Bird of Prey.

$45   **$55**

HAMILTON COLLECTION, 1991

Mini-Plates, Hamilton Collection, 1991.

Set of mini-plates: Mini-character plates
are the same as the first series plates
and mini-ship plates are the same as the
Voyagers plate series. Most mini-plates
were originally shipped as a set of two, ie.,
Kirk and Spock, etc.

Mini-character plates:

"Beam Us Down, Scotty" (crew
in transporter).

Enterprise (animated version).

Kirk.

Spock.

McCoy.

Scotty.

Uhura.

Sulu.

Chekov.

$10   **$15**

Mini-ship plates:

U.S.S. Enterprise.

Klingon Battle Cruiser.

U.S.S. Enterprise-A.

U.S.S. Excelsior.

Klingon Bird of Prey.

$15   **$20**

Hanging display shelf for
mini-plates.

$20   **$25**

MUSIC BOXES
HAMILTON GIFTS, 1991

Crew Music Box, No. 931284, wooden box featuring artwork from the first series of Hamilton ceramic plates. Music box plays the theme from Star Trek. Limited edition of 25,000. Includes certificate of authenticity.

$65   **$75**

Music Box, Hamilton Gifts, 1991.

PAPERWEIGHTS
DILITHIUM CRYSTALS, 1974

Solid semi clear plastic "crystal" displayed on a revolving base.

$25   **$45**

Domed paperweights.

GTB, INC

Dilithium Crystal quartz-style rock advertised as a "spare" Dilithium Crystal and used as a paperweight. Came packaged with a "Star Trek Forever" header card.

$45   **$55**

Domed paperweights featuring different Star Trek-themed images under glass. Appear to be fan made, sold individually: Starfleet Command United Federation of Planets; Starfleet Academy Red Squadron.

$5   **$15**

PFALTZGRAFF, 1993

U.S.S. Enterprise NCC-1701-A. Released at the same time as the film, *Star Trek VI: The Undiscovered Country*.

Stoneware Buffet Set:

The inscription on the back of the plate in the *Star Trek VI: The Undiscovered Country* Stoneware Buffet Set, Pfaltzgraff, 1993. Also shown is the original box.

USS Enterprise NCC-1701-A Tankard, Pfaltzgraff, 1993.

Dinner plate.		Saucer and cup.		Cookie jar.	
$65	**$75**	**$40**	**$50**	**$75**	**$100**
Mug.		Complete boxed set.		Tankard.	
$45	**$55**	**$200**	**$250**	**$55**	**$75**

Plate, cup and saucer from *Star Trek VI: The Undiscovered Country* Stoneware Buffet Set, Pfaltzgraff, 1993.

Stoneware serving dishes:

Candy dish.
$22 $24
Four coasters.
$24 $26
Chip 'n dip set.
$35 $37

Limited Edition Bone China Set:

Dinner plate.
$275 $350
Saucer and cup.
$150 $250

Bone China Set:

Dinner plate.
$65 $75
Saucer and cup.
$35 $40
Complete boxed set.
$100 $150

U.S.S. Enterprise NCC-2000
Bone China Buffet Dinner Set:

Dinner plate.
$150 $165
Saucer and cup.
$100 $125
Complete boxed set.
$250 $300

U.S.S. Enterprise NCC-1701-B Bone China Buffet Dinner Set:

U.S.S. Enterprise NCC-1701-B Bone China Buffet Dinner Set, Pfaltzgraff, 1993. Front of the plate and the inscription on the back are shown.

Star Trek: Generations Set:

Dinner plate.
$150 $175
Saucer and cup.
$100 $150
Complete boxed set.
$250 $300

The original box the set came in.

SHOWER CURTAINS

JCPENNEY, 1986

Shower curtain, JCPenney, 1986.

Black vinyl curtain with movie versions of the Enterprise and Klingon ships orbiting a planet.

$45   **$55**

"Parking for Star Trek Fans Only" metal sign.

SIGNS

"Parking for Star Trek Fans Only" metal sign.

"U.S.S. Enterprise Parking Only" metal sign.

"Shuttlecraft Parking Only" metal sign.

"Klingon Parking Only" metal sign.

$15   **$25**

SNOW GLOBES AND DOMES

Enterprise Star Globe and unused store display, Willett's Designs, 1992.

Photo frame snow globe of *The Original Series* crew.

Mini snow globe of the original series Enterprise.

WILLETT'S DESIGNS, 1992

The Original Series Enterprise Star Globe Halodome, removable hood.

$25   **$75**

Willett's Star Globe Store Display.

$55   **$65**

Snow Globe Photo Frame of *The Original Series* crew, manufacturer and date unknown.

$15   **$20**

Mini Snow Globe, Enterprise in small water globe with sparkles.

$10   **$15**

FRANKLIN MINT, 1993

Tholian Web Galaxy Globe: Pewter globe sculpture featuring 24k gold accents and a tempered glass globe with unique light up "web" effect.

$150   **$250**

FRANKLIN MINT, 1995

U.S.S. Enterprise mini-globe, Franklin Mint, 1995.

Galileo II mini-globe with orangish planet variation, Franklin Mint, 1995.

Galileo II mini-globe with brownish blue planet variation, Franklin Mint, 1995.

Romulan Bird of Prey mini-globe, Franklin Mint, 1995.

K-7 Space Station mini-globe, Franklin Mint, 1995.

Klingon Encounter mini-globe, Franklin Mint, 1995.

SS Botany Bay mini-globe, Franklin Mint, 1995.

The Motion Picture mini-globe, Franklin Mint, 1995.

The Search for Spock mini-globe, Franklin Mint, 1995.

The Voyage Home mini-globe, Franklin Mint, 1995.

The Final Frontier mini-globe, Franklin Mint, 1995.

The Undiscovered Country mini-globe, Franklin Mint, 1995.

Limited Edition Mini-Globes; various highly detailed scenes from *The Original Series* and the movies displayed under a small glass dome:

U.S.S. Enterprise; Romulan Bird Of Prey, Galileo II Shuttlecraft variation with orange Saturn in background; Space Station K-7; Klingon Encounter; S.S. Botany Bay.

$25   **$35**

Galileo II Shuttlecraft variation with brown/blue Saturn in background.

$45   **$55**

The Motion Picture; The Wrath Of Khan; The Search For Spock; The Voyage Home; The Final Frontier; The Undiscovered Country.

$35   **$45**

SOFT DRINKS

WARNER TRADE LTD, 1995

"Warp 4" high energy soft drink. Image of Enterprise on blue space background. Product information listed in both English and German on side of can.

$25   **$35**

Warp 4 high energy drink, Warner Trade Ltd, 1995.

STATIONERY

CHRONICLE BOOKS, 2006

Star Trek stationery featuring 40 sheets with 5 different designs repeating throughout. No envelopes needed as the unique design allows the stationery to be moistened, folded, and sealed.

$10   **$15**

Star Trek stationery, Chronicle Books, 2006.

SPOONS

TALLY-HO, 1974

Collector set of 4 spoons featuring original Mego figures artwork in custom display case, Tally-Ho, 1974.

Collector spoons with Mego artwork: Kirk, Spock, McCoy, Scotty.

$15   **$20 each**

Set of 4 spoons.

$45   **$55**

PARAMOUNT PARKS, 1988

Collector pewter spoons:

Star Trek logo at top of plain spoon.

$15   **$25**

Star Trek logo at top of Enterprise spoon.

$35   **$55**

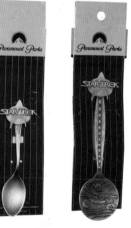

Collector pewter spoons by Paramount Parks, 1988.

STOVE BURNER COVERS

STOVE BURNER COVERS, 1995

White round steel burner covers with image of U.S.S. Enterprise-A.

Small 8" covers.

$35   **$45**

Large 10" covers.

$25   **$35**

UNIVERSAL STUDIOS, FLORIDA

Enterprise collector pewter spoon. Same spoon as Paramount Parks Enterprise spoon but packaged in a Universal Studios pouch.

$35   **$55**

STREET SIGN

Thick black metal street sign measures 30" x 6" with white painted raised "STAR TREK DR." letters. Turn your street from a boring name like Maple St. or Vista Dr. into something much more unique.

$15   **$25**

"Star Trek Dr." metal street sign.

THIMBLES

Ceramic thimbles with the Enterprise crew.

Ceramic thimbles with images of the original series crew.

$5   **$10**

TELEPHONES
TELEMANIA

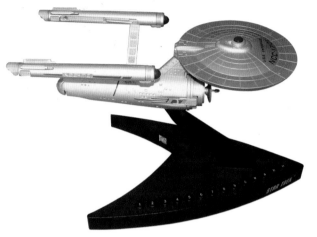

Enterprise telephone, Telemania.

Enterprise-shaped push button telephone with command insignia-shaped base.

$75   **$125**

TOTE BAGS

AVIVA, 1979

Star Trek: The Motion Picture-themed blue canvas tote bag. Featured Kirk or Spock.

$50   **$75 each**

SEARS, 1975

Black and gray with zipper: Kirk, Spock, Enterprise.

$85   **$100 each**

"Starfleet Space Shuttle" decal on white canvas tote bag with command insignia, 1976.

$45   **$55**

TWA PROMOTIONAL TOTE BAG

"Star Trek to the Bahamas."

$55   **$75**

U.S.S. Enterprise-shaped large tote duffle bag.

Take it to the gym, on a picnic or even to Starfleet Academy.

$150   **$350**

Enterprise-shaped large tote duffle bag.

TRAYS

AVIVA, 1979

Mr. Spock metal tray, *Star Trek: The Motion Picture*, Aviva, 1979.

Star Trek: The Motion Picture, Spock metal tray table with foldout legs.

$35   **$45**

TELEVISION REMOTE CONTROL

KASH N' GOLD LTD/TELEMANIA, 2000

Universal Remote Control Type 2 phaser, Kash N' Gold/Telemania, 2000.

Universal Remote Control Original Series Type 2 hand phaser. Features authentic sound effects provided by Paramount Pictures that are activated with the use of the control keys. Includes standard universal remote control features.

$55   **$75**

WALLPAPER

IMPERIAL WALLCOVERINGS, 1981

Enterprise and K-7 Space Station with other spaceships on blue space background. Sold per roll.

$65   **$85**

WASTEPAPER BASKETS

CHEINCO, 1977

Oval metal trash can with artwork of Enterprise and Galileo on one side and starship statistics on the other.

$55   **$100**

CHEINCO, 1979

Oval metal trash can with rainbow poster artwork from *Star Trek: The Motion Picture.*

$45   **$75**

Front and back of the Star Trek metal trash can, Cheinco, 1977.

Metal trash can, *Star Trek: The Motion Picture*, Cheinco, 1979.

JEWELRY

AMERICAN MISS, 1974

Flat gold-plated necklaces: "Star Trek"; Enterprise orbiting ringed planet; Spock.

$25 $35

AVIVA, 1979

Two-sided picture key chains: Enterprise; Kirk, Spock and Enterprise; Spock; Spock and Uniform Insignia; Spock: *Star Trek: The Motion Picture*; Mr. Spock with Vulcan Salute.

$10 $15

Poly pins: Enterprise; Kirk; McCoy; Spock; Uniform Insignia; Vulcan Salute.

$10 $15

Enamel pins: Kirk, McCoy.

$10 $15

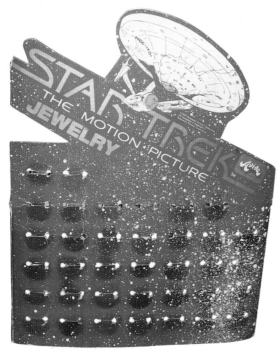

Cardboard display for jewelry line, Aviva, 1979.

Jewelry display: cardboard display for *Star Trek: The Motion Picture* jewelry line.

$45 $55

Tie clasps: Enterprise; Mr. Spock; Original television Series Uniform Insignia; Vulcan Salute.

$10 $15

BUTTON UP, 1980

"Beam Me Up Scotty" key chain.

$25 $35

CALIFORNIA DREAMERS, 1987

Photo key chain, California Dreamers, 1987.

Two-sided photo key chains:

Chekov – I hate Mondays.

Kirk – Beam Me Up Scotty.

Kirk – The Captain.

Kirk, Spock, McCoy – Fire All Phaser Weapons.

Kirk, Spock, Uhura – Keep Your Shields Up.

Kirk, Spock, Uhura – Seek Out Strange New Worlds.

Spock – Hang In There.

Spock – I Need Space.

Spock – Spock For President.

Spock – Live Long and Prosper.

Spock – Superior Being.

$10 $15

CLAIRE MASON, 1973

Fan Club-Issued key holder; picture of Leonard Nimoy.

$50 $75

GOODTIME JEWELRY, 1976

Kirk and Spock pewter jewelry, Goodtime Jewelry, 1976.

Enterprise pewter jewelry, Goodtime Jewelry, 1976.

Spock and Kirk pewter jewelry, Goodtime Jewelry, 1976.

Enterprise pewter medallion, Goodtime Jewelry, 1976.

Display header card, Goodtime Jewelry, 1976.

Pewter necklaces and medallions: Kirk and Spock; Enterprise; Spock and Kirk; Enterprise circling planet medallion.

$20   **$25**

Header card for display.

$10   **$15**

HOLLYWOOD COMMEMORATIVE PIN, 1985

Standing crew cut-out enamel pins: Kirk, Spock, McCoy, Scotty, Uhura, Sulu, Chekov.

$10   **$15 each**

Enamel character pins, Hollywood Commemorative Pin, 1985.

HOLLYWOOD COMMEMORATIVE PIN, 1990

Selection of episode and other pins, Hollywood Commemorative Pin, 1990.

Star Trek episode pins (more than 60 individual pins).
   $10 $20 each pin

HOLLYWOOD COMMEMORATIVE PIN, 1991 TO PRESENT

Selection of pins including later versions from Hollywood Commemorative Pin.

Hollywood Commemorative Pin has produced a wide variety of pins since the 1980s. The additional selections are too numerous to attempt a faithful list. The company does a good job of marking its pins with its logo so you can easily tell if the pin you are looking at is a Hollywood Pin. Most Hollywood pins sell for **$1 to $5**.

INTERSTELLAR PRODUCTION, INC, 1984

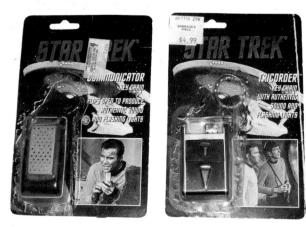

Communicator with working lights and sounds, Interstellar Production, Inc., 1984.

Tricorder with working lights and sounds, Interstellar Production inc., 1984.

Electronic key chains with working lights and sound: Classic Communicator; Classic Tricorder; Classic Phaser; SFX is a small square unit that plays eight classic sound effects.
   $25 $50

LINCOLN ENTERPRISES, 1975 (MAJEL BARRETT RODDENBERRY'S COMPANY)

Tribble Key Guard.
   $25 $50

LINCOLN ENTERPRISES, 1975, 1980

IDIC necklace.
$15 $25

IDIC necklace, Lincoln Enterprises, 1975.

LINCOLN ENTERPRISES, 1977

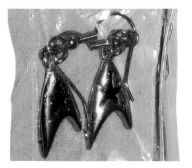

Enterprise earrings, Lincoln enterprises, 1977.

Command chevron earrings, Lincoln Enterprises, 1977.

Earrings: Enterprise; Command Chevron.
$10 $15

LINCOLN ENTERPRISES, 1976

Filigree pendants: Enterprise; Rigel Castle; Try Trekkin'; Where No Man Has Gone Before.
$10 $15

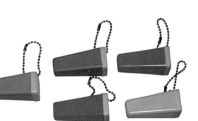

Key chain viewers, Lincoln Enterprises, 1976.

Kirk key chain viewer, Lincoln Enterprises, 1976.

Spock key chain viewer, Lincoln Enterprises, 1976.

Scotty key chain viewer, Lincoln Enterprises, 1976.

Uhura key chain viewer, Lincoln Enterprises, 1976.

Sulu key chain viewer, Lincoln enterprises, 1976.

Key chain picture viewers: Five different viewers each displaying a different image including Kirk (yellow); Spock (blue); Scotty (orangish red); Uhura (orangish red); Sulu (light green).
$5 $10 each

LINCOLN ENTERPRISES, 1982

Star Trek II: The Wrath of Khan movie uniform pins (also see Clothing):

Uniform chest command pin.
$25 $45

Uniform sleeve pips.
$5 $10 (set)

Uniform rank pin.
$10 $20

Uniform shoulder strap back pin.
$20 $25

Belt buckle.
$25 $35

Star Trek II uniform pins, Lincoln Enterprises, 1982.

REED PRODUCTIONS, 1989

Original TV Series key chains: Kirk, Spock in Transporter; Kirk, Spock with Enterprise; Kirk, Spock, and McCoy.
$15 $20

STAR TREK GALORE, 1976

Key chains: Phaser—Three Dimensional; Vulcan Hand; Vulcan Hand—Three Dimensional.
$10 $15

Tribble key chain: Furry Tribble shakes and makes noise when string is pulled.
$25 $35

STAR TREK ANNIVERSARY COMMAND INSIGNIA EARRINGS, 1996

Gold command chevron.
$10 $15

Anniversary command chevron earrings, 1996.

GENERAL MILLS, 1979

Star Trek: The Motion Picture identification bracelet.
$10 $15

HOLLYWOOD PINS, 1994

Original Enterprise cut-out enamel key chain.
$5 $10

Enterprise key chain, Hollywood Pins, 1994.

Tribble key chain.

RINGS

Starfleet Academy class ring, various sizes/stone colors.
$25 $50 each

Starfleet Academy class ring.

WATCHES

ASA, 1974

Enterprise firing phasers watch.

$50   **$75**

BRADLEY, 1979

Star Trek: The Motion Picture analog watch. Spock artwork with Enterprise and Shuttlecraft on second hand.

$150   **$200**

BRADLEY, 1980

Star Trek: The Motion Picture Enterprise analog watch. Dark blue Enterprise with "Star Trek" in yellow; busts of Kirk and Spock.

$85   **$100**

Star Trek: The Motion Picture Enterprise digital watch. Enterprise in light blue. Black dial with white hands.

$125   **$150**

FOSSIL, 1995-96

Spock watch, Fossil, 1995-1996.

Various watches in metal tins: U.S.S. Enterprise Analog Watch; Spock with IDIC; Klingon Analog Watch; Klingon Analog Watch in Gold; Thirty-Year Commemorative Analog Pocket Watch; Thirty-Year Commemorative Analog Pocket Watch in Gold.

$100   **$200**

FRANKLIN MINT, 1991

Twenty-fifth Anniversary Analog Watch.

$100   **$230**

FRANKLIN MINT, 1999

Pocket watch, Franklin Mint, 1999.

Pocket watch flyer from Franklin Mint, 1999.

Pocket watch flyer from Franklin Mint, 1999.

Pocket watch; features sculpted watch face minted in solid sterling silver, accented in 24k gold. Includes pouch and chain.

$125   **$350**

Pocket watch flyer.

$5   **$9**

FAN-MADE CUSTOM WATCH, DATE UNKNOWN

Star Trek logo.

$15   **$20**

GAMAZONE, 1999

Gorn watch, green with Gorn image.

$35   **$50**

Gorn Watch, Gamazone, 1999.

Fan-made custom watch.

HOPE INDUSTRIES, 1996

Barbie and Ken watch, Hope Industries, 1996.

Barbie and Ken watch:

Based on the Mattel Special Edition 30th Anniversary Barbie and Ken figure set, this matching analog wristwatch with storage case was packaged as a "collector timepiece."

$25 $30

LEADER TOYS, 1976

Tenth Anniversary Commemorative Star Trektennial Watch designed by Uri Geller.

$150 $200

LEADER TOYS, 1977

Enterprise watch with swinging pendulum and viewable internal workings.

$200 $250

Children's analog watch.

$100 $150

LEWCO, 1987

Spock watch by Lewco, 1987.

Spock portrait watch with Enterprise.

$20 $30

LINCOLN ENTERPRISES, 1976

Enterprise watch 1966-1976.

$200 $250

MALIBU, 1989

Analog watches: Klingon Bird of Prey and movie ship; Original Ship – side view; Original Ship – front view; Original Ship orbiting planet.

$45 $75

RARITIES MINT, 1989

Analog coin watch:

Original Enterprise.

$75 $100

Original Enterprise Variation Prototype.

$500 $750

STAR TREK CLASSIC WATCH

U.S.S. Enterprise watch.

U.S.S. Enterprise on white background.

$45 $50

STAR TREK: THE MOTION PICTURE WRISTWATCH, 1980

Design by Doug Little. Analog watch with starship and starburst design.

$25 $45

TIMEX, 1993

Watch by Timex, 1993.

Store display case for Star Trek Timex watches, Timex, 1993.

Various Timex watches:

Chronoscanner digital watch; Disappearing Warbird analog watch; Enterprise Indiglow analog watch; Klingon Chronometer digital watch; Rotating Enterprise analog watch.

$55 $75 each

Star Trek watch store display case.

$50 $75

VALUECENTER, 1998

Classic logo insignia with Enterprise on second hand orbiting around watch face. Plays original theme song at the touch of a button. Includes bonus nostalgic tin case and certificate of authenticity.

$20 $25

Watch by Valuecenter, 1998.

Lunch Boxes

Lunch boxes are considered cross-collectible items, because both Star Trek collectors and lunch box collectors compete for them.

The dome lunch box by Aladdin is a rare piece and considered a "must have" by many Star Trek collectors. Obtaining one in mint condition is especially difficult because time and use have left many boxes with scratches, dents, and rust. The beautiful artwork was created by Robert O. Burton and Elmer Lehnhardt, and the box makes a great display piece even in good condition. Released in 1968, Aladdin made 250,000 units that sold for $3.50 in stores.

Note: *The Next Generation* and *Deep Space Nine* lunch box/bags are included in this category due to the very small number of original series/movie-themed lunch boxes that have been released to date.

ALADDIN INDUSTRIES, 1968

Very rare metal domed lunch box and thermos, Aladdin Industries, 1968.

Metal Domed Lunch Box with thermos, extremely rare in collectible condition. A mint-condition thermos can easily fetch half or more of what a mint box alone can fetch.

$550   **$1,500**

KING-SEELEY THERMOS CO., 1979

Metal lunch box from *Star Trek: The Motion Picture*, King-Seeley Thermos Co., 1979.

Star Trek: The Motion Picture Metal Lunch Box; thermos can easily fetch $25 or more in mint condition.

$45   **$150**

HALSEY TAYLOR/THERMOS, 1988.

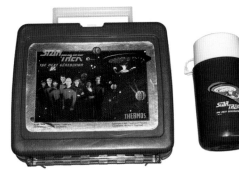

The Next Generation first season blue lunch box, Halsey Taylor/Thermos, 1988.

The Next Generation Lunch Box; first season blue plastic with image of cast of nine.

$10   **$25**

The Next Generation third season blue lunch box, Halsey Taylor/Thermos, 1988.

The Next Generation Lunch Box; third season blue plastic with image of Wesley, Picard and Data. An unknown number of blue versions were also shipped with red thermos. It's unknown if this error changes its value since it would be easy to swap the thermos from two normal sets.

$15   **$30**

The Next Generation third season red lunch box, Halsey Taylor/Thermos, 1988.

The Next Generation Lunch Box; third season red plastic version with image of Wesley, Picard, and Data. This is the rarest of the three TNG lunch boxes.

$25   **$45**

PAM & FRANK IND. CO. LTD., 1993

Star Trek: The Next Generation talking Borg head lunch box, Pam & Frank Ind. Co. LTD., 1993.

Star Trek: The Next Generation talking Klingon head lunch box, Pam & Frank Ind. Co. LTD., 1993.

Star Trek: The Next Generation talking Ferengi head lunch box, Pam & Frank Ind. Co. LTD., 1993.

Star Trek: The Next Generation Borg talking head lunch box; lunch box has different sayings when opened.

$20   **$40**

Star Trek: The Next Generation Klingon talking head lunch box; lunch box has different sayings when opened.

$15   **$25**

Star Trek: The Next Generation Ferengi talking head lunch box; lunch box has different sayings when opened.

$10   **$20**

Vinyl Deep Space Nine lunch bag, 1994.

Deep Space Nine Lunch Bag, 1994; vinyl lunch bag w/DS9 station on front.

$10   **$25**

HALLMARK, 1999

Original Series mini lunch box, Hallmark, 1999.

The Original Series Mini Lunch Box; part of Hallmark's Retro School Days Mini Lunch Box Series.

$10   **$20**

NECA, 2001

Original Series retro metal lunch box, NECA, 2001.

NECA's Original Series Classic Retro Metal Lunch Box.

$15   **$35**

Magazines

In the summer of 1976, while in a small bookstore in Lebanon, New Hampshire, I spotted a new magazine called *Starlog*. (Its cover, depicting Kirk, Spock, and the Enterprise, is still considered one of the best pieces of *Star Trek* artwork ever created.) I must have read the whole magazine twice right there in the store before finally going up to the counter to purchase it. I read that first issue from front to back so many times that the cover started to fall off. Since then I've obtained another copy in mint condition. I still have a special place in my heart for that memorable issue.

16 MAGAZINE

September Star Trekkers "The Things We Hate & the Things We Love."

$15 $20

AMA NEWS

December 1986, Vol. 29, No. 45, article and photos from *Star Trek IV: The Voyage Home.*

$5 $10

AMERICAN CINEMATOGRAPHER – ASC HOLDING CORPORATION

October 1967, *Star Trek* special effects.

$25 $35

February 1980, Vol. 61, No. 2, *Star Trek: The Motion Picture.*

$15 $30

October 1982, Vol. 63, No. 10, *Star Trek II: The Wrath of Khan* special effects.

$10 $15

September 1984, Vol. 65, No. 8, *Star Trek III: The Search for Spock.*

$15 $20

December 1986, Vol. 67, No. 12, cover and article on S*tar Trek IV: The Voyage Home.*

$10 $15

Vol. 73, No. 1, *Star Trek* Special Issue.

$10 $15

BANANAS

1976, No. 7, Star Trek: Conventions.

$25 $30

1979, No. 33, preview of *Star Trek: The Motion Picture.*

$15 $20

Cover of September issue, *16 Magazine.*

Inside of September issue, *16 Magazine.*

Cover of Star Trek: Conventions, *Bananas,* 1976, No. 7.

Inside of Star Trek: Conventions, *Bananas,* 1976, No.7.

Inside of Star Trek: Conventions, *Bananas,* 1976, No.7.

Preview of *Star Trek The Motion Picture, Bananas,* 1979, No. 33.

CASTLE OF FRANKENSTEIN – GOTHIC CASTLE PUBLISHERS

1967, #11, *Star Trek*/Spock cover.
$15   **$25**
1969, #14, Kirk and Spock cover.
$10   **$15**

CINEFANTASTIQUE – F.S. CLARK PUBLISHERS 1979-90

Vol. 8, No. 2/3, Interview with Gene Roddenberry on *Star Trek: The Motion Picture.*

Vol. 9, No. 1, *Star Trek: The Motion Picture* report.

Vol. 9, No. 2, Article on *Star Trek: The Motion Picture.*

Vol. 9, No. 3/4, *Star Trek: The Motion Picture* review and photos comparing movie to television series.
$5   **$15 each**

CINEFEX – DAN SHAY PUBLISHING

March 1980, No. 1, *Star Trek: The Motion Picture.*
$10   **$20**
August 1980, No. 2, Star Trek Special Effects.
$5   **$15**
August 1984, No. 18, Special Effects.
$5   **$15**

CO-ED MAGAZINE

January 1969, Leonard Nimoy/Mr. Spock.
$25   **$30**

CORONET MAGAZINE

May 1969, Leonard Nimoy - Mr. Spock.
$25   **$30**

CRACKED – GLOBE COMMUNICATIONS

September 1975, No. 129, Star Tracks parody.

July 1980, No. 169, Star Drek parody.

November 1981, No. 170, Star Trek article.

October 1984, No. 207, Spock/Michael Jackson parody.

January 1985, No. 209, Star Drek III parody.

February 1986, No. 65, reprint Star Drek: The Moving Picture parody.

March 1986, No. 43, Two Trek specials.

April 1987, No. 3, Star Yeech.

July 1987, No. 228, Star Drek IV Parody.
$10   **$15 each**

CRAWDADDY MAGAZINE

Dec. 1976, Ed Naha, producer of "Inside Star Trek" is interviewed.
$5   **$10**

Cover of *Dynamite*, 1976, #20.

DYNAMITE, 1976

#20, Cher on cover. Article inside, "Star Trek: The show that wouldn't die."
$15   **$20**

EBONY – JOHNSON PUBLICATIONS

January 1967, Vol. 22, No. 3, Nichelle Nichols.
$45   **$55**

Ebony, January 1967, Vol 22 No 3, Johnson Publications.

EGO ENTERPRISES, 1976-1977

Cover of *All About Star Trek Fan Clubs*, Ego Enterprises, 1976-1977.

Cover of *All About Star Trek Fan Clubs*, Ego Enterprises, 1976-1977.

Cover of *All About Star Trek Fan Clubs*, Ego Enterprises, 1976-1977.

All About Star Trek Fan Clubs:

Issue #1.
$10   **$15**
Issue #2-6.
$5   **$10**

ENTERPRISE – HJS PUBLICATIONS

#1 April 1984.
$10   **$20**
#2 (June 1984) through #13.
$5   **$10**

ENTERPRISE INCIDENTS – SCIENCE-FICTION COMIC ASSOC.

#1.
$20   **$30**

#2-3.
$15   **$20**

#4-8.
$10   **$15**

ENTERPRISE INCIDENTS – NEW MEDIA PUBLISHING

#9-12.
$5   **$10**

#13-36.
$5   **$8**

Enterprise Incidents – The Best Of.
$10   **$15**

ENTERTAINMENT WEEKLY - TIME, INC.

Fall 1994, special oversized-edition.
$10   **$20**

FAMOUS MONSTERS – WARREN PUBLICATIONS

1979. No. 145, Review of *Star Trek: The Motion Picture.*

1980. No. 161, *Star Trek: The Motion Picture* special.

1982. No. 185, Review of *Star Trek II: The Wrath of Khan.*

1982. No. 186, *Star Trek II: The Wrath of Khan.*

1982. No. 187, *Star Trek II: The Wrath of Khan.*
$10   **$15**

*Enterprise Incidents –
Science-Fiction Comic
Assoc.*

*Enterprise Incidents –
Science Fiction Comic
Assoc.*

Fighting Stars, April
1974.

Star Trek Treasures,
Franklin Mint Almanac.

FANTASTIC FILMS, BLAKE PUBLISHING COMPANY

1978. Vol. 1, No. 3, Susan Sackett interview.

1978. No. 5, article on Spock.

1979. Vol. 2, No. 10, Robert Wise interview on *Star Trek: The Motion Picture.*

1980. Vol. 2, No. 14, Collector's Issue Costumes and Designs from *Star Trek: The Motion Picture* Part I.

1980. Vol. 2, No. 15, Part II.

1981. No. 22, Special Edition The Very Best of Fantastic Films.
$10   **$20**

FIGHTING STARS, APRIL 1974

Celebrities in the art of self defense

William Shatner…The Fighting Star of "Star Trek."
$10   **$15**

The Best of Enterprise Incidents.

FRANKLIN MINT ALMANAC

Star Trek Treasures.
$20   **$25**

FREE ENTERPRISE, 1976

The Capitalists Reporter,
Free Enterprise, 1976.

Media Spotlight October
Cover.

The Capitalists Reporter.

The *Star Trek* Cult. Bonanza from outer space.
$25   **$35**

Media Spotlight, October.

U.S.S. Enterprise on cover.
$25   **$35**

MAD MAGAZINE – E.C. PUBLICATIONS, INC.

November 1966, Star Bleech parody.

December 1967, No. 115, Star Trek parody.

October 1976, No. 186, The Mad Star Trek Musical parody.

September 1979, No. 209, *Star Trek: The Motion Picture* parody.

July 1980, No. 216, *Star Trek: The Motion Picture* parody.

$10   **$20**

MONSTER TIMES – MONSTER TIMES PUBLISHING COMPANY

February 1972, Vol. 1, No. 2, Star Trek Special Edition.

March 1973, No. 25, Trouble with Star Trek.

September 1973, No. 26, Star Trek returns.

1973, Collector's Issue #1, Star Trek articles and interviews.

June 1974, No. 34, Star Trek Convention and Shatner interview.

October 1974, No. 36, Leonard Nimoy article.

1974, No. 42, Star Trek returns.

1974, No. 43, Star Trek's Captain Kirk.

1974, People of Star Trek Collector's Issue.

1976, No. 45, Star Trek Shatner article.

March, 1976 No. 46, The Final Frontier.

May, 1976 No. 47, Star Trek review.

$15   **$25 each**

MOVIE LIFE, FEBRUARY 1974

Inside features a bonus collectors photo album.

$15   **$20**

MOVIE LIFE, AUGUST 1974

Inside features a bonus collectors photo album.

$15   **$20**

MOVIE MONSTERS NO. 1, DECEMBER

Star Trek article.

$10   **$25**

NEWSWEEK – NEWSWEEK INC.

1984, June No. 24, Star Trek article.

$15   **$20**

1986, December Star Trek article.

$10   **$15**

NEW YORKER – NEW YORKER MAGAZINE, INC.

1982, Vol. 58, No. 19, Star Trek.

$5   **$10**

1984, No. 21, Star Trek.

$5   **$10**

QUASIMODO'S MONSTER MAGAZINE

Star Trek Biographies.

$5   **$15**

Quasimodo's Monster Magazine.

Movie Life, February 1974.

Movie Life, August 1974.

Movie Monsters, No 1, December.

SCANNER, OCT. 6-12, 1996

A weekly guide to Television; Trek Meet article.

$5   **$8**

Scanner, Oct. 6-12, 1996.

Sc-Fi Monthly, No. 5.

SCI-FI MONTHLY, NO. 5

Star Trek, The Enterprise Crew.

$10   **$15**

Screen Stories, September.

SCREEN STORIES SEPTEMBER

Gossip-TV-Movies. Leonard Nimoy and Bill Shatner, their topsy-turvy lives.

$5   **$10**

SPACE TREK, 1978

Special with preview of "Star Trek The Movie."
$10 $15

Space Trek, 1978.

STARBURST #341

Article on New 2008 Star Trek movie.
$1 $5

Starburst #341.

STARLOG, 1976

Starlog, premier first issue, August 1976.   *Starlog* #3.

#1 Premier first issue; featured article on classic Star Trek.
$35 $50

#3 Star Trek Conventions; featured a story about Star Trek Conventions.
$20 $35

STAR TREK FILES MAGAZINES – NEW MEDIA PUBLISHING

#1 Where No Man Has Gone Before.

#1 Reprint Part 1.

#1 Reprint Part 2.

The Early Voyages.

The Early Voyages reprint Part 1.

The Early Voyages reprint Part 2.

#2 Time Passages.

#3 A Taste of Paradise.

#4 On The Edge of Forever.

#5 Mission Year Two.

#6 Journey to Eternity.

#7 The Deadly Years.

#8 Return to Tomorrow.

#9 Assignment Earth.

#10 Enterprise Incident.

#11 Tholian Web.

#12 Whom Gods Destroy.

#13 All Our Yesterdays.

#15 The Animated Voyages Begin.

#16 The Animated Voyages End.

Star Trek: The Motion Picture Vol. 1.

Star Trek: The Motion Picture Vol. 2.

Star Trek: 20th Anniversary Tribute.

Complete Guide to Star Trek Vol. 1.

Complete Guide to Star Trek Vol. 2.

Complete Guide to Star Trek Vol. 3.

Complete Guide to Star Trek Vol. 4.

Complete Guide to Star Trek Vol. 5.
$15 $20 each

Enterprise Command Book.
$10 $20

Star Trek Encyclopedia.
$20 $25

Enterprise Incidents Vol. 1.
$5 $10

Enterprise Incidents Vol. 2.
$5 $10

Enterprise Incidents 1989 Tribute.
$15 $25

Federation and Empire.
$15 $25

Interviews Aboard the Enterprise.
$20 $25

Lost Years.
$12 $15

Monsters and Aliens Vol. 1.
$10 $15

Monsters and Aliens Vol. 2.
$15 $25

Star Trek Year One.
$15 $20

Star Trek Year Two.
$15 $20

Star Trek Year Three.
$15 $20

The Early Voyages, *Star Trek Files Magazines,* New Media Publishing.

Enterprise Incident #10, *Star Trek Files Magazines,* New Media Publishing.

Captain Kirk.

Spock.

McCoy.

Scotty.

Chekov.

Uhura.

Sulu.

Crew File Finale.

Harry Mudd.

Vulcans.

Romulans.

Klingons.

Spock and Vulcans.

The Captains Before Kirk.

Character Guide Vol. 1 A-D.

Character Guide Vol. 2 M–R.

Character Guide Vol. 3 S-Z.

Star Trek Comics Vol. 1.

Star Trek Comics Vol. 2.

Reflections of the '60s.

Special Effects.

Starship Enterprise.

Super Villains.

Tech Files—Star Trek Devices.

Tribute Book Vol. 1.

Tribute Book Vol. 2.

Star Trek That Almost Was.

Star Trek That Never Was.

Star Trek Universe.

Time Travel.

Undiscovered Star Trek Vol. 1.

Undiscovered Star Trek Vol. 2.

Undiscovered Star Trek Vol. 3.

Undiscovered Star Trek Vol. 4.

Undiscovered Star Trek Vol. 5.

Undiscovered Star Trek Vol. 6.

Dagger of the Mind.
$15 $25 each

Villains Vol. 1.

Villains Vol. 2.

Villains Vol. 3.
$10 $15 each

TEEN SCREEN, APRIL 1968

Star Trek Bonus Super Color Poster.

$15 $20

TELEVISION, SEPTEMBER 1996

German television magazine.

$15 $20

TIGER BEAT

Leonard Nimoy talks about Mr. Spock.

$10 $15

TREK, 1978

#1: First Issue Special.

$55 $65

#2.

$20 $25

TREK, THE MAGAZINE FOR STAR TREK FANS

#1-5.

$20 $25

#6-10.

$15 $20

Special Spock issue.

$20 $25

Motion Picture issue.

$20 $25

Teen Screen, April 1968.   *Teen Screen,* April 1968.   *TeleVision,* September 1996.

Tiger Beat.   #1 First issue special, *Trek,* 1978.   #2, *Trek,* 1978.   *Trek,* 1978.

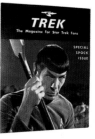

Trek, 1978.   *Trek,* 1978.   *Trek,* November 1978.   *Trek,* Spring 1981.

TV CHANNELS, AUG. 19, 1973

The News American Weekly Magazine. "Star Trek's 3000 Fan Clubs Are Finally Getting Wish – In Animated Form."

$15 $20

The News American Weekly Magazine, TV Channels, Aug. 19, 1973.

TV GUIDE

Fall preview issue, *TV Guide*, Sept. 10, 1966.

First Star Trek Cover, *TV Guide*, March 4, 1967.

Fall preview issue, *TV Guide*, Sept. 15, 1967.

TV Guide, Nov. 18, 1967.

TV Guide, Aug. 24, 1968.

Because *TV Guides* are a cross-collectible, prices can surge due to demand coming from more than one collectible market.

9/10/66, fall preview issue.
   $100   **$150**
3/4/67, first Star Trek cover.
   $175   **$275**
3/24/67, first Star Trek review.
   $25   **$50**

7/15/67, Nichelle Nichols interview.
   $25   **$45**
9/15/67, Fall Preview issue with Star Trek listing.
   $50   **$75**
10/14/67, photos from "I, Mudd."
   $25   **$50**

11/18/67, Star Trek cover.
   $100   **$175**
6/22/68, William Shatner interview.
   $25   **$50**
8/24/68, Star Trek cover.
   $75   **$110**
3/25/72, Star Trek article.
   $25   **$45**

10/14/76, Star Trek article.
   $20   **$30**
9/4/93, Kirk cover.
   $10   **$25**
2/17/96, 30th Anniversary with 4 different covers.
   $5   **$10**

12/05/04, 100 Most Memorable TV Moments: Kirk and Uhura kiss.
   $5   **$10**
05/30/04, 25 Top Cult Shows Ever: Kirk and Spock cover.
   $5   **$10**
04/17/05, Star Trek: Ultimate Tribute.
   $5   **$10**

TV GUIDE CROSSWORDS

June 2002, Women of Outer Space.
   $5   **$10**

TV MIRROR, AUGUST

A salute to Star Trek.
   $10   **$20**

TV STAR ANNUAL

1967 #23, Spock.

1968 #24, Stories of Crew.

1969 #25, Star Trek.
   $25   **$35 each**

TV Mirror, August issue.

TV Mirror, August issue.

TV Star Parade,
September 1967.

TV Star Parade, September 1967.

TV Star Parade, August
1968.

TV Star Parade, August 1968.

TV STAR PARADE

July 1967, Spock/Behind the Scenes at Star Trek.

August 1967, Photos of Nimoy/Shatner.

September 1967, Inside scoops from Star Trek.

October and November 1967, Leonard Nimoy and Mike Barrier.

December 1967, Star Trek set.

January 1968, Nimoy.

February 1968, Star Trek cast Kelley, Nichols, Nimoy, Shatner.

April 1968, Shatner and his family.

June 1968, Shatner, Nimoy, Doohan.

July 1968, Nimoy and Nichols.

August 1968, Star Trek special effects.

September 1968, Shatner and Nimoy.

November 1968, Shatner, Nimoy, Doohan.

January 1969, Nichelle Nichols and DeForest Kelley.

$10   **$15 each**

TV TIMES, MAY 28-JUNE 3, 1967

The *Bay City Times* with Nichelle Nichols article.
$10   **$15**

TV ZONE 1990-91

April #5, *Star Trek* article.
$15   **$25**
August #9, *Star Trek* article.
$10   **$20**

TWILIGHT ZONE – TZ PUBLICATIONS

June 1984, Vol. 4, No. 2, TV episode "Nightmare at 20,000 Feet" script starring William Shatner.

August 1984, Vol. 3, Leonard Nimoy and Cathie Sheriff Star Trek II.

June 1987 Vol. 7, No. 2, Star Trek IV review.
$10   **$15**

US MAGAZINE

Dec. 25, 1979, "Star Trek The Motion Picture."
$10   **$15**
Jan. 8, 1980, Khambatta of "Star Trek: The Motion Picture" interview.
$10   **$15**
June 22, 1982, *Star Trek* article.
$5   **$10**

TV Times, May 28-June
3, 1967.

TV Times, May 28-June 3, 1967.

US, December 25, 1979.   US, January 8, 1980.

WOMAN'S DAY – CBS MAGAZINES, INC.

October 1970, article on Mr. and Mrs. Leonard Nimoy.

$10   **$20**

WORLD OF HORROR – DALRUTH PUBLISHING COMPANY, 1974

Issue with Spock on cover and Star Trek article.

$10   **$15**

NEWSLETTERS, NEWSZINES, AND FANZINES

Newsletters/newszines are usually created by and for clubs and/or fan groups.

Fanzines, or "zines," are fan-made magazines that consist of individual original stories or compilations of original stories and usually fan created artwork as well. Fanzines can also include fan dedications, commentaries, editorials, poetry, songs, short stories, drawings, and more. Quite a few news flyers and newsletters were created specifically for conventions.

The first and most well known of the early fanzines is "Spockanalia." This speculative fiction fanzine first appeared in New York in 1967, and placed Mr. Spock in a wide variety of perilous or humorous situations, and also included fan poetry. It established the format for science fiction-based fanzines.

It would be an impossible task to document the many newsletters, newszines, and fanzines created over the years, so a sample is provided here.

The Granite Viewscreen newsletter.

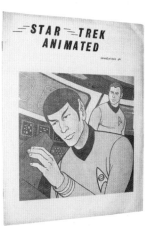

Star Trek Animated newsletter #4.

Star Trek Animated newsletter #5.

Spock Enslaved.

The Granite Viewscreen.

$5   **$10**

Star Trek Animated Newsletter #4.

$10   **$15**

Star Trek Animated Newsletter #5.

$15   **$20**

Spock Enslaved.

$25   **$30**

The Sensuous Vulcan.

T-Negative.

Leonard Nimoy Association of Fans.

The Star Trek Scene #1.

Star Trek '74 Convention handout.

Star Trek August '76, Space...The Final Frontier No. 2, official convention souvenir program.

$10   **$20**

The Sensuous Vulcan.

$25   **$35**

T-Negative.

$25   **$30**

LNAF: Leonard Nimoy Association of Fans.

$35   **$45**

The Star Trek Scene #1.

$5   **$10**

Star Trek '74 Convention handout.

$15   **$25**

Magnets

AT-A-BOY, 1993

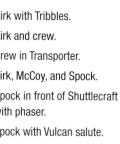

Movie magnets, At-a-Boy, 1993.

Star Trek: The Original Series:

Crew, artwork.

Crew, promotional photo.

Crew in Spacesuits.

Enterprise.

Kirk on Bridge.

Kirk with Enterprise.

Kirk with Tribbles.

Kirk and McCoy.

Kirk, McCoy, and Spock.

Klingon Cruiser.

McCoy.

Spock.

Spock, Kirk, Scotty.

Spock with Phaser.

Spock with Visor.

Spock – Vulcan Salute.

Sulu and Chekov.

$1 $5 each

Star Trek movies:

Enterprise.

Kirk, Spock, McCoy, Scotty.

Spock.

Star Trek: The Motion Picture poster.

Star Trek II: The Wrath of Khan poster.

Star Trek III: The Search for Spock poster.

Star Trek IV: The Voyage Home poster.

Star Trek V: The Final Frontier poster.

$1 $5

CREATION CONVENTION, 1988

Special convention "Scotty Magnets": "Beam Me Up," "What a glorious thing, transwarp 10."

$5 $10 each

HAMILTON, 1991

Collection magnets, Hamilton, 1991.

TV Guide covers:

Crew with Enterprise, artwork.

Kirk, Spock, McCoy, and Uhura, promotional photo.

Enterprise firing phasers.

Kirk on bridge.

Kirk, Spock, and Scotty with phasers.

Kirk with Tribbles.

Kirk and crew.

Crew in Transporter.

Kirk, McCoy, and Spock.

Spock in front of Shuttlecraft with phaser.

Spock with Vulcan salute.

$5 $10 each

MAGNETIC COLLECTIBLES, 1992

Star Trek: The Original Series:

Beam me up, Scotty.

Enterprise.

Galileo Shuttlecraft.

Kirk.

McCoy.

Scotty.

Spock.

Star Trek Insignia.

Sulu.

Uhura.

Vulcan Salute.

$1 $5

Close-up of a *Star Trek* Insignia magnet, Magnetic Collectibles.

PRESENTS

Command Insignia with Enterprise in center.

$1 $5

Magnetic Counter Display for Magnets.

$25 $50

Magnet Counter Display, Presents, 1991.

Model Kits

The Starship Enterprise is one of the most recognizable icons in television history, and the Enterprise model kit by AMT is one of the longest running and highest selling model kits in the company's history. AMT acquired the license to make model kits soon after *Star Trek's* premier in 1966, and the company continued to release vehicle kits through the movie releases.

AMT, 1966

Enterprise with lights, AMT, 1966.

Enterprise:

Large box, features working lights.
  $350   **$550**
Decals and instruction sheet.
  $25   **$35**

Klingon Battle Cruiser with lights, AMT, 1966.

Klingon Battle Cruiser:

Large box, features working lights.
  $300   **$500**
Instruction sheet and mail-away coupon offer.
  $20   **$25**

Mr. Spock, AMT, 1966.

Mr. Spock, large box.
  $250   **$350**

AMT, 1968

Enterprise in large box, AMT, 1968.

Enterprise, large box.
  $100   **$150**

Klingon Battle Cruiser, AMT, 1968.

Klingon Battle Cruiser, large box.
  $100   **$150**

Enterprise in small box, AMT, 1968.

Enterprise, small box.
  $75   **$100**

Mr. Spock in small box, AMT, 1968.

Mr. Spock, small box.
  $100   **$125**

AMT, 1973

AMT brochure, AMT, 1973.

AMT brochure, AMT, 1973.

AMT Brochure. Note that it states that the Mr. Spock model is new for '73.

$20 $35

AMT, 1975

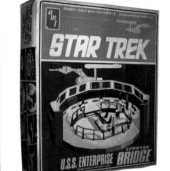

Romulan Bird of Prey in small box, AMT, 1975.

U.S.S. Enterprise Command Bridge, AMT, 1975.

Romulan Bird of Prey, small box.
$75 $100
U.S.S. Enterprise Command Bridge.
$75 $100

AMT, 1977

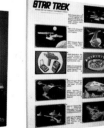

AMT 1977 Catalog.

AMT 1977 Catalog.

AMT 1977 Catalog.
$20 $30

AMT, 1974

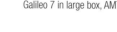

Exploration Set in large box, AMT, 1974.

Galileo 7 in large box, AMT, 1974.

Exploration Set in small box, AMT, 1974.

Galileo 7 in small box, AMT, 1974.

Exploration Set, large box.
$125 $175
Exploration Set, small box.
$75 $100

Galileo 7, large box.
$100 $125
Galileo 7, small box.
$75 $100

AMT, 1976

K-7 Space station in small box, AMT, 1976.

Klingon battle Cruiser in small box, AMT, 1976.

K-7 Space Station, small box.
$75 $125
Enterprise, small box.
$45 $55

Klingon Battle Cruiser, small box.
$35 $45

AMT, 1979

Enterprise with *Star Trek: The Motion Picture* artwork/images on box; features lights in the saucer section.

$75   **$125**

Klingon Cruiser with *Star Trek: The Motion Picture* artwork/images on box.

$75   **$125**

Mr. Spock, AMT, 1979.

Mr. Spock. Reworked AMT model now features Spock in movie uniform and no longer has the three-headed Snake.

$75   **$125**

Vulcan Shuttle, AMT, 1979.

Vulcan Shuttle with *Star Trek: The Motion Picture* artwork/images on box; features removable sled.

$65   **$85**

AMT, 1983

Enterprise with *Star Trek II: The Wrath of Khan* artwork/images on box.

$25   **$35**

AMT, 1984

Enterprise with *Star Trek III: The Search for Spock* artwork/images box.

$15   **$25**

Klingon Cruiser with *Star Trek III: The Search for Spock* artwork/images on box.

$8   **$10**

Vulcan Shuttle; features detachable sled with *Star Trek: The Motion Picture* artwork/images on box.

$30   **$40**

AMT, 1986

Enterprise with *Star Trek IV: The Voyage Home* artwork/images on box.

$15   **$20**

AMT, 1989

Enterprise with *Star Trek V: The Final Frontier* artwork/images on box.

$15   **$20**

AMT, 1991

Enterprise Special Edition, same model as the other movie versions but with added lights and sounds.

$45   **$65**

Klingon Cruiser with *Star Trek V: The Voyage Home* artwork/images on box.

$8   **$10**

Reliant. Box displays basic *Star Trek* design/logo.

$15   **$20**

AMT, 1995

Enterprise B with *Star Trek: Generations* artwork/images on box.

$15   **$20**

Excelsior. Box displays basic *Star Trek* design/logo.

$15   **$20**

Klingon Bird of Prey with *Star Trek: Generations* artwork/images on box.

$15   **$20**

AURORA, 1966

Enterprise; same model as AMT but with different artwork.

$350   **$600**

AURORA, 1972

Mr. Spock, Aurora, 1972.

Mr. Spock; same AMT model with different artwork.

$125   **$275**

Replica of the Type 2 hand Phaser, 23rd Century Pistol.

23rd Century Pistol; replica of the Type 2 Hand Phaser.

$50   **$75**

MATCHBOX, 1980

Foreign versions:

Klingon Cruiser.

$55   **$75**

Vulcan shuttle.

$55   **$75**

MEDORI, 1969

U.S.S. Enterprise model kit; Japanese model features added propeller to the front of the ship. Box features color picture of Kirk and Spock.

$150   **$250**

MEGO (GRAND TOYS LTD.), 1979

Star Trek: The Motion Picture Model Ships; these are extremely rare and were limited to Canadian/foreign release only.

Enterprise.
$150   **$250**

Klingon Cruiser.
$150   **$250**

Vulcan Shuttle Sled.
$100   **$175**

MUSASAIYA, 1989

Mr. Spock model kit; Japanese model features color photo of Mr. Spock on the front from *Star Trek II: The Wrath of Khan* with movie logo.

$150   **$200**

POLAR LIGHTS, 2004

Polar Lights was the model kit division of the Playing Mantis Company, and was acquired by Racing Champions/ERTL, which also owned AMT/Ertl. Polar Lights released a series of models in 2004-05.

U.S.S. Enterprise NCC-1701 (*The Original Series*): Kit features the ability to build three versions of *The Original Series* U.S.S. Enterprise: The Enterprise first seen in the pilot "The Cage"; then reworked for the second pilot, "Where No Man Has Gone Before," and what is considered the "standard" version seen in all of the later episodes. Model is 1/1000 scale. Kit #4200.

$10   **$20**

Klingon D7 Battlecruiser (*The Original Series*): Kit features the ability to build two versions of *The Original Series* Klingon D-7 Battlecruiser. The standard Klingon version or the Romulan version seen in "The Enterprise Incident." Model is 1/1000 scale. Kit #4202.

$10   **$15**

POLAR LIGHTS, 2005

U.S.S. Enterprise NCC-1701-A (movie version): Box artwork by Chris White. Considered the best movie version model kit made to date. Very large scale model at 1:350. Kit #4204.

$100   **$150**

SOUTHBEND, 1979

U.S.S. Enterprise, Southbend, 1979.

U.S.S. Enterprise Electronic Toy/Model based on *Star Trek: The Motion Picture*.

$150   **$250**

MODEL ROCKETS

ESTES, 1975 FLYING MODEL ROCKETS

Enterprise Model Rocket, ESTES, 1975.

Klingon Cruiser Model Rocket, ESTES, 1975.

ESTES 1975 catalog.

Enterprise Model Rocket.
$75   **$125**

Klingon Cruiser Model Rocket.
$75   **$125**

ESTES 1975 Catalog.
$35   **$55**

ESTES, 1976

Star Trek Flying Model Rocketry Starter Kit, ESTES, 1976.

ESTES 1976 catalog.

Star Trek Flying Model Rocketry Starter Kit.
$125   **$250**

ESTES 1976 catalog.
$25   **$50**

Ornaments

Since 1991, Hallmark has released at least one Star Trek ornament each year. The following listings represent a sampling of those releases.

HALLMARK, 1991

U.S.S. Enterprise, Hallmark, 1991.

U.S.S. Enterprise with blinking lights.

$150   **$250**

HALLMARK, 1992

Shuttlecraft Galileo, Hallmark, 1992.

Shuttlecraft Galileo with Spock's voice.

$20   **$30**

Hallmark Shuttlecraft store display, 1992.

Hallmark Shuttlecraft store display.

$50   **$150**

HALLMARK, 1995

Captain Kirk, Hallmark, 1995.

Captain Kirk in command chair.

$25   **$30**

HALLMARK, 1996

Commander Spock, Hallmark, 1996.

Commander Spock at science station.

$25   **$30**

30th Anniversary Enterprise with shuttlecraft, Hallmark, 1996.

30th Anniversary die-cast Enterprise with shuttlecraft.

$25   **$30**

HALLMARK, 1997

Dr. Leonard H. McCoy, Hallmark, 1997.

Dr. Leonard H. McCoy on transporter pad.

$20   **$30**

HALLMARK, 1999

Hand blown glass U.S.S. Enterprise, Hallmark, 1999.

U.S.S. Enterprise (blown glass ornament).
$75   **$150**

Hand blown glass U.S.S. Enterprise, Hallmark, 1999.

U.S.S. Enterprise Century stamp, Hallmark, 1999.

U.S.S. Enterprise Century Stamp.
$35   **$45**

HALLMARK, 2004

Kirk and Spock, Hallmark, 2004.

"City on the Edge of Forever" with lights and sounds; Kirk and Spock jumping through Guardian of Forever.
$45   **$65**

HALLMARK, 2005

U.S.S. Enterprise NCC-1701-A, Hallmark, 2005.

U.S.S. Enterprise NCC-1701-A with lights.
$25   **$35**

Khan Noonien Singh, Hallmark, 2005.

Khan Noonien Singh (*The Original Series*: "Space Seed").
$20   **$25**

HALLMARK, 2006

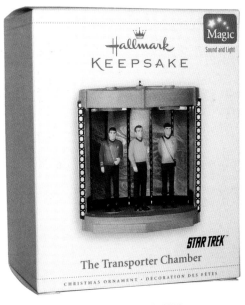

Enterprise Transporter Chamber, Hallmark, 2006.

Enterprise Transporter Chamber with lights and sounds.

$45   **$65**

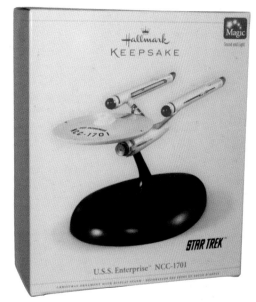

U.S.S. Enterprise NCC-1701, Hallmark, 2006.

U.S.S. Enterprise NCC-1701 (featuring *The Original Series* theme).

$55   **$65**

HALLMARK, 2007

Lieutenant Uhura, Hallmark, 2007.

Lieutenant Uhura at communications station.

$35   **$45**

Star Trek II: The Wrath of Khan Enterprise, Hallmark, 2007.

Star Trek II: The Wrath of Khan Enterprise bridge helm station with Kirk, Spock, and Sulu (U.S.S. Reliant on light-up screen background) with lights and sound.

$45   **$75**

Hallmark store header card.

Hallmark store header card.

$20 $25

Photographs and Other Artwork

Photographs, like posters, can be an inexpensive way to collect images of some of your favorite characters, ships, and scenes, and there is a huge variety available. Plenty of beautiful artwork related to the series and movies has also been done and is highly collectible.

ARTWORK
KELLY FREAS, 1976

Officers of the Decker: Beautiful artwork set of seven star portfolios of individual portraits that were originally commissioned for the first National Star Trek Convention program book have since been on display at the Smithsonian Institution; includes Kirk, Spock, McCoy, Scotty, Uhura, Sulu, Chekov. Each full color print measures a large 12-1/2" x 19".

$15   **$25 each**

Kirk by Kelly Freas, 1976.

Spock by Kelly Freas, 1976.

McCoy by Kelly Freas, 1976.

Scotty by Kelly Freas, 1976.

Uhura by Kelley Freas, 1976.

Sulu by Kelly Freas, 1976.

Chekov by Kelly Freas, 1976.

Artwork for *Star Trek* novels:

Boris Vallejo art print.
$10   **$20**
Kirk, Spock, and McCoy.
$10   **$20**
Framed artwork of two starships.
$15   **$25**

Boris Vallejo Star Trek art print.

Kirk, Spock, and McCoy artwork.

Artwork of two starships.

AUTOGRAPHS: PHOTOS AND CARDS

Autographs can easily become one of the more personal and cherished parts of a collection, especially if you are able to obtain the autographs in person. This also allows you to be sure that the signature obtained is truly authentic. However, when buying autographed memorabilia and photos sold by others, especially off of the Internet, you have to be careful, as signatures can easily be forged. Even the most careful and knowledgeable collectors have been fooled by fakes at times. Stars have admitted that sometimes they cannot tell a fake from their actual signature, especially if their signatures do not stay consistent over the years. Many dealers offer certificates of authenticity, but these can easily be created. Try to buy from a reputable dealer who has a good track record of authenticity.

The values of autographs are much harder to document because values can be based as much on sentimental attachment as on star power. Of course, you can always use the time-tested rule—if the price seems too good to be true, it probably is.

Autographs can be obtained on almost anything. Photos remain the most common, but fans get cast member signatures on magazines, shirts, jackets and other clothing, action figure and toy packaging, CD and DVD jackets and jewel cases, body parts, and even on scrap pieces of paper if nothing else was available.

Here is a small example of some autographed pieces.

William Shatner autograph.

William Shatner. Publicity photo as Captain Kirk with Phaser rifle.
$75   **$200**

Leonard Nimoy autograph.

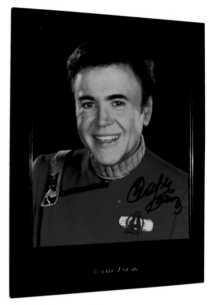

Nichelle Nichols autograph.

Walter Koenig autograph.

Leonard Nimoy. Publicity photo as Mr. Spock with Phaser.

$100   **$250**

Nichelle Nichols. Publicity photo as Lt. Uhura at her communications station.

$75   **$100**

Walter Koenig. Publicity photo as Pavel Chekov in movie uniform.

$50   **$75**

William Shatner, Leonard Nimoy, and DeForest Kelley autographs.

George Takei, James Doohan, Nichelle Nichols, and Walter Koenig autographs.

Star Trek: Crucible trilogy cover artist John Picacio autograph.

William Shatner, Leonard Nimoy, and DeForest Kelley: Publicity photo as Captain Kirk, Mr. Spock, and Dr. McCoy in the transporter. Autographs of stars that have since passed away can quickly double in value.

$350   **$750**

George Takei, James Doohan, Nichelle Nichols, and Walter Koenig: Autographed artwork of the four as Sulu, Scotty, Uhura, and Chekov in red movie uniforms. The value of this piece will certainly increase due to the passing of James Doohan.

$250   **$400**

Star Trek: Crucible trilogy book series advertising card: Autographed by artist John Picacio, who did the book's cover art. Autographs by people who were not main or supporting characters of a show or movie can also be collectible. In this case, the cover artist for an original Trek-related book autographed an advertisement card for the book.

$10   **$25**

ANIMATION CELS

Animation cel of Kirk and Spock, Filmation, 1976.

Animation cel from More Tribbles, More Troubles, Filmation, 1976.

FILMATION, 1977

Hand-drawn cel artwork from the Animated Series that debuted on Saturday, Sept. 8, 1973, on NBC:

These individual cels were first offered through *Starlog* magazine in 1976 and include Kirk and Spock on the Bridge; Scotty and Sulu on the Bridge; Scotty in Engineering; Kirk and Scotty on the Bridge; the Crew of the Enterprise; Kirk and McCoy in More Tribbles, More Troubles; A young Spock on his "pet" in Yesteryear; the large alien ship in Beyond the Farthest Star; The Ambergris Element; Jihad; and many more. Some cels were framed and sold through Starlog and then later through other magazines, mail order outlets, and through dealers at conventions. The framed cels were usually given actual names for the artwork. There are also a large number of unframed cels, most of which can be found for sale at conventions or online auctions like eBay. An unknown number of different scene/cels were released. The more popular cels appear to be those featuring any of the space ships, especially the Enterprise, as well as those that feature the main characters on the Bridge, most notably Captain Kirk in his command chair.

$50   **$150**

PHOTOGRAPHS

LANGLEY AND ASSOCIATES, 1976

Pictures, Langley and Associates, 1976.

Publicity, scenes, ships, and crew pictures including Chekov, portrait; crew on planet; crew on bridge; Dr. McCoy; Enterprise firing phasers; Enterprise following a Federation ship; Enterprise surrounded by aliens' ships; Kirk; Kirk with Tribbles; Kirk in dress uniform; Kirk with communicator; Kirk, Spock, McCoy; Lt. Uhura; Mr. Scott; Spock with beard; Spock portrait; Spock and hand signal; Spock smiling; Spock and Kirk; Sulu.

$5   **$25**

PARAMOUNT PICTURES, 1966-69

Spock and Pike, Paramount Pictures, 1966-1969.

Spock, Paramount Pictures, 1966-1969.

Kirk and Spock playing Tri-Dimensional chess, Paramount Pictures, 1966-1969.

Black and white photographs: Spock and Pike; Spock with tube; Kirk, Spock and Tri-Dimensional Chess; Kirk and Spock; Enterprise Bridge Crew; Enterprise NCC-1701 with stats.

$15   **$25**

PHOTOGRAPH ALBUMS

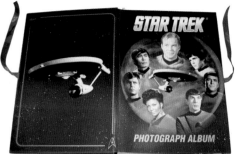

ROBERT FREDERICK LTD., 1998

Star Trek Photograph Album; features different-shaped cardboard photo pages. Includes a ribbon tie to help keep your photos where they belong.

$15   **$25**

Star Trek Photograph Album, Robert Frederick Ltd., 1998.

Star Trek Photograph Album, Robert Frederick Ltd., 1998.

PLAQUES

TEAM METAL, 1996

Plaque with Dilithium Crystal: Photo of Kirk, Spock, McCoy, and Uhura in upper section, Dilithium Crystal prop on Enterprise image in lower section.

$25   **$35**

Star Trek plaque and Dilithium Crystal.

Enterprise and crew plaque, Team Metal, 1996.

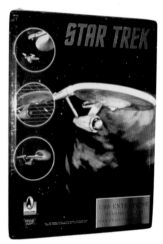

Enterprise, Team Metal, 1996.

Plaque, "Generations": Wooden plaque with "Generations" display showing the release date of 11-18-94.

$20   **$25**

Plaque, "Generations," 11-18-94.

Kirk plaque, Team Metal, 1996.

Spock plaque, Team Metal, 1996.

Set of four metal 30-year commemorative plaques: Enterprise and crew; Enterprise; Kirk; Spock.

$10   **$15 each**

STANDEES

Kirk full-size standable cardboard cutout, Advanced Graphics.

Spock full-size standable cardboard cutout, Advanced Graphics.

ADVANCED GRAPHICS, 1992-1995

Star Trek: original TV series standees: Life-size stand-up cardboard character cutouts. Now you can have Captain Kirk, Mr. Spock, or Dr. McCoy at your house.

$45   **$65**

PARAMOUNT VIDEO, 1989

Store Promotional Cardboard Standees, *Star Trek V: The Final Frontier.*

Kirk: Small version in Starfleet movie uniform pictured holding video. Spock: Small version in Starfleet movie uniform pictured holding video. Small foot-high table top version. Priced as a set.

$20   **$25**

Kirk: Large version in Starfleet movie uniform holding an actual video. Spock: Large version in Starfleet movie uniform holding an actual video. Life-size version.

$45   **$65 each**

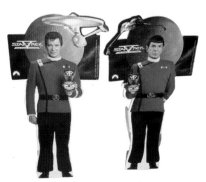

Kirk and Spock, *Star Trek V: The Final Frontier* video tabletop store displays, 1989.

Mr. Spock, rare *Star Trek II: The Wrath of Khan* cardboard standee, 1982.

Mr. Spock in *Star Trek II: The Wrath of Khan* uniform full-size cardboard standee, manufacturer unknown.

$150   **$250**

Posters

Posters remain one of the most popular forms of fandom and a wide variety are available today, many within a reasonable price range.

POSTERS – STAR TREK: THE ORIGINAL SERIES

BOICHOT, 1975

Crew, Boichot, 1975.

Black and white artwork of crew; Klingons, Your Duty Is To Serve the Empire; United Federation Command Wants You.

$35   **$45**

CARSAN, 1977

Collage of crew; Enterprise.

$25   **$35**

COUSINS PUBLISHING, 1977

Collage of crew.

$25   **$45**

DARGIS ASSOCIATES, 1976

Kirk, Dargis Associates, 1976.   Enterprise, Dargis Associates, 1976.   Galileo, Dargis Associates, 1976.   Klingon Battle Cruiser, Dargis Associates, 1976.   Starfleet Headquarters, Dargis Associates, 1975.

Artwork for the Enterprise, Galileo, Klingon Battle Cruiser, and StarFleet Headquarters was created by John Carlance: Kirk in Command Chair; Spock; McCoy; Sulu; collage of pictures; Enterprise; Galileo; Klingon Battle Cruiser; StarFleet Headquarters.

$25   **$45**

DYNAMIC PUBLISHING COMPANY, 1976

Black Light Flocked Posters. These posters are known for getting very brittle over the years, making them harder to find in collectible condition: Enterprise; Kirk; Spock.

$65   **$95**

JIM STERANKO, 1974

Color artwork collage of crew and spaceships.

$20   **$25**

HEINEKEN, 1975

Spock, Heineken, 1975.

Spock drinking Heineken beer.

$25   **$35**

JERI OF HOLLYWOOD, 1967 PROMOTIONAL POSTERS

These are the very first *Star Trek* posters produced and were printed on very thin paper stock, making them hard to find in excellent condition: Kirk; Spock; McCoy.

$65   **$85**

LANGLEY ASSOCIATES, 1976

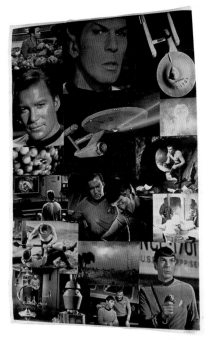

Collage of pictures, Langley Associates, 1976.

Collage of pictures: crew in Transporter; crew on bridge; Enterprise and crew; Enterprise and Klingon; Enterprise firing on a ship; Enterprise firing phasers; Enterprise with an enemy ship; Kirk; Kirk in Transporter, life-size door poster; Klingon Battle Cruiser; Rigel Castle; Spock; Spock in Transporter, life-size door poster.

$25   **$45 each**

Spock in Transporter, Langley Associates, 1976.

Kirk and Spock, Langley Associates, 1976.

Kirk and Spock, Langley Associates, 1976.

Kirk and Spock – Neon looking reverse negative effect image, #P1012.

Kirk and Spock – artwork used for cover of *Starlog Magazine's* premier first issue.

$10   **$20 each**

LINCOLN ENTERPRISES

Crew collage; Kirk as Romulan; Kirk collage; Spock artwork; Spock collage.

$25 **$45**

SCHOLASTIC BOOK, 1978

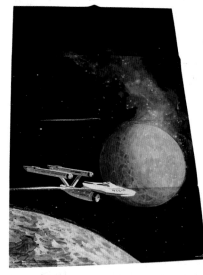

Enterprise foldout, Scholastic Books, 1978.

Enterprise foldout, Scholastic Books, 1978.

Enterprise foldout.

$25 **$35**

PARAMOUNT PICTURES, 1974

Painting by Moak, Paramount Pictures, 1974.

Standard Orbit. Painting by Moak exclusively for Starfleet.

$25 **$40**

Publicity photo, Paramount Pictures, 1974.

Crew in Transporter. Publicity photo of main cast.

$15 **$25**

SAL QUARTIUCCIO, 1976

Artwork by Ken Barr, Sal Quartiuccio, 1976.

Artwork of the Enterprise crew by Ken Barr: The poster was offered as a special promotion through *Starlog* Magazine in 1976.

$50 **$75**

SCI-FI MAGAZINE, '70S

Collage by Allison of Star Trek, *Starburst* magazine, 1978.

Pullout poster from '70s *Sci-Fi* magazine.

$5 **$10**

STARBURST MAGAZINE, 1978

Pullout poster, *Sci-Fi Magazine*, 1970s.

Sci-Fi collage by Allison of Star Trek, This Island Earth, and LaserBlast. Was a pullout poster in *StarBurst* magazine from summer 1978.

$20   **$30**

STAR TREK GALORE, 1976

Kirk and Lirpa, Star Trek Galore, 1976.

Crew collage; crew collage with ship; Enterprise firing phasers; Federation recruiting poster; Kirk; Kirk and Lirpa; Klingon recruiting poster; landing party and Klingons; scene from "A Taste of Armageddon"; scene from "Journey to Babel"; Spock with harp.

$25   **$45 each**

STARCON, 1975

Starship by Kelly Freas, Starcon, 1975.

Starship Battling Planet by Kelly Freas.

$5   **$15**

Landing party and Klingons, Star Trek Galore, 1976.

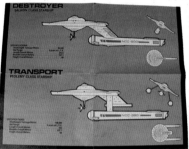

Scene from "A Taste of Armageddon," Star Trek Galore, 1976.

Scene from "Journey to Babel", Star Trek Galore, 1976.

STARSHIP DESIGNS, 1976

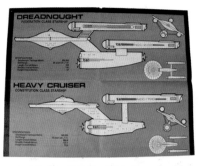

Franz Joseph's Starship designs poster, 1976.

Rare foldup poster featuring Franz Joseph's Starship designs from his *Starfleet Technical Manual* published in 1975 by Ballantine Books.

$45   **$65**

SUPER HERO WALL BUSTERS, 1977

Kirk and Spock, Super Hero Wall Busters, 1977.

Kirk and Spock.

$50   **$75**

POSTERBOOKS

PARADISE PRESS, INC., 1976-78

The Voyages' Posterbook Series. There were a total of 17 different posters that came folded into pages and included articles, facts, stories, behind the scenes, technical specs, and more from selected episodes.

The Posterbooks were also available shrink-wrapped in sets of five. The value for a shrink-wrapped set of five poster books depends on which five posters are in that set.

Voyage One: Special collectors issue! Articles include Spock: The Evolution; U.S.S. Enterprise: A City in Space; The Cage: Star Trek Film We Never Saw; and a poster of the U.S.S. Enterprise caught in the "Tholian Web."

$25   **$35**

Voyage One, Paradise Press, Inc., 1976-1978.

Voyage Two: Articles include Harlan Ellison's "City": A critique; Special Effects: Star Trek Technique; Kirk-Spock-McCoy: The Relationship; a poster of Kirk, Spock, and McCoy in "Spectre of the Gun."

$25   **$35**

Voyage Two, Paradise Press, Inc., 1976-1979.

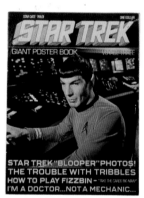

Voyage Three: Articles include Star Trek Blooper Photos!; The Trouble with Tribbles; How to play Fizzbin - "Take the cards big man!"; I'm a Doctor, not a mechanic…; a poster of Spock at the science station.

$25   **$35**

Voyage Three, Paradise Press Inc., 1976-1979.

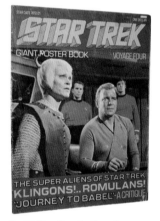

Voyage Four: Articles include The Super Aliens of Star Trek; Klingons!..Romulans!; "Journey to Babel" - A Critique; a poster of Kirk and Kang in "Day of the Dove."

$25   **$35**

Voyage Four, Paradise Press Inc., 1976-1979.

Voyage Five: Articles include Exclusive: Spock Interview!; Inside a Vulcan Mind; Planet Vulcan Revisited; a poster of Spock Playing the Vulcan Lyrette.

$15   **$20**

Voyage Five, Paradise Press, Inc., 1976-1979.

Voyage Six: Articles include "Amok Time" - A Critique; The Art of Star Trek; Phasers!!! Tricorders!!! And More…; a poster of Kirk & Crew on the bridge. Closing scene from "Shore Leave."

$15   **$20**

Voyage Six, Paradise Press, Inc., 1976-1979.

Voyage Seven: Articles include For The Love Of Jim; The Enemy Within: A Critique; Analysis: James T. Kirk; a poster of Captain Kirk wearing dress uniform in "Journey to Babel."

$15   **$20**

Voyage Seven, Paradise Press, Inc., 1976-1979.

Voyage Eight: Articles include Exclusive: Interview with McCoy; McCoy's Medical Miracles; Medical Treknology; a poster of Kirk, McCoy and Yeoman Rand in "Miri."

$15   **$20**

Voyage Eight, Paradise Press, Inc., 1976-1979.

Voyage Nine: Articles include Assignment: Earth - A Critique; The Music of Star Trek; Vulcan Logic - How to Use It; a poster of Uhura from "Mirror, Mirror."

$35   **$40**

Voyage Nine, Paradise Press, Inc., 1976-1979.

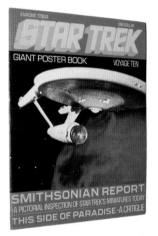

Voyage Ten: Articles include Smithsonian Report - A pictorial inspection of Star Trek's miniatures today; This Side of Paradise - A Critique; a poster of Kang & Company in "Day of the Dove."

$25   **$35**

Voyage Ten, Paradise Press, Inc., 1976-1979.

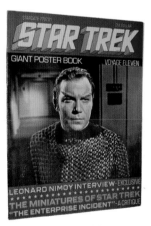

Voyage Eleven: Articles include Leonard Nimoy Interview – Exclusive; The Miniatures of Star Trek; "The Enterprise Incident" - A Critique; a poster of Spock at science station.

$20   **$30**

Voyage Eleven, Paradise Press, Inc., 1976-1979

Voyage Twelve: Articles include Chapel, Rand & Uhura; Heroines of Star Trek; "The Paradise Syndrome" - A Critique; a poster of Yeoman Janice Rand.

$20   **$30**

Voyage Twelve, Paradise Press, Inc. 1976-1979.

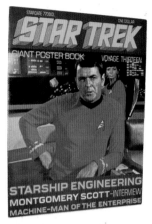

Voyage Thirteen: Articles
include Starship Engineering;
Montgomery Scott – Interview;
Machine - Man of the Enterprise;
a poster of Lt. Commander
Montgomery Scott.

$20   **$30**

Voyage Thirteen, Paradise Press, Inc.,
1976-1979.

Voyage Fourteen: Articles
include Rules for Tri-D Chess;
A History of the Federation;
"Where No Man Has Gone
Before" - A Critique;
a poster of Kirk & Spock on
the bridge.

$20   **$30**

Voyage Fourteen, Paradise Press, Inc.,
1976-1979.

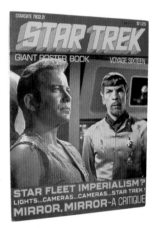

Voyage Fifteen: Articles include
The Nonhumanoid Aliens;
Conscience of the King - A
Critique; Sulu - A Very Human
Helmsman; a poster of Kirk &
Sulu in "The Squire of Gothos."

$20   **$30**

Voyage Fifteen, Paradise Press, Inc.,
1976-1979.

Voyage Sixteen: Articles include
Star Fleet Imperialism?;
Lights…Cameras…Cameras…
Star Trek!; Mirror, Mirror - A
Critique; a poster of Kirk on the
bridge of the I.S.S. Enterprise in
"Mirror, Mirror."

$25   **$35**

Voyage Sixteen, Paradise Press, Inc.,
1976-1979.

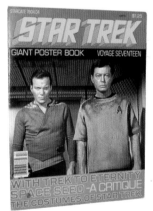

Voyage Seventeen: Articles
include With Trek to Eternity;
Space Seed - A Critique; The
Costumes of Star Trek; Poster:
Behind the scenes photo of the
Enterprise in "Botany Bay."

$45   **$55**

Voyage Seventeen, Paradise Press,
Inc., 1976-1979.

Posterbook, *Star Trek: The
Motion Picture*: Same style and
layout as the voyages' giant
posterbooks. *The Motion Picture*
posterbook includes articles,
facts and, of course, folds out to
a poster.

$15   **$25**

Posterbook, *Star Trek: The Motion
Picture*.

Cutaway poster of the Enterprise, *Star Trek: The Motion Picture*, 1979.

Cutaway poster of the Enterprise, from *Star Trek: The Motion Picture,* 1979.

$20   **$25**

Posterbook, Hawk.

Hawk, Posterbook-
Classic Trek: Eight "Captain's
Log" posters on large thick
card stock.

$25   **$35**

The following is a selection of some of the posters released since those mentioned earlier. These include the official posters from the various movies since *Star Trek: The Motion Picture,* as well as posters based on *The Original Series.*

Unusual *Star Trek II: The
Wrath of Khan* movie poster,
Sat Nam Kaur, 1982.

Sat Nam Kaur, 1982:
Unusual and rare *Star
Trek II: The Wrath of
Khan* movie poster that
seems more fantasy than
movie based.

$50   **$75**

Star Trek II: The Wrath of Khan poster, 1982.

Star Trek II: The Wrath of Khan official movie
poster, 1982.

$10   **$20**

Star Trek V: The Final Frontier
poster, 1989.

*Star Trek V: The Final
Frontier* official movie
poster, 1989.

$10   **$20**

Promotional photo of Kirk
with phaser rifle, 1996.

$20   **$25**

Kirk with Phaser rifle, 1996.

Enterprise with Command bridge and Shuttlecraft cutaway
poster.

U.S.S. Enterprise cutaway poster. Poster also includes
cutaway images of the Command bridge and
Shuttlecraft, plus stats and information.

$25   **$30**

Props

Below is the bottle of Dilithium Crystals that I came across in an auction on eBay, which of course led to James "Scotty" Doohan's son, Chris, writing the foreword for this book.

James Doohan and sons as extras on set.

Dilithium Crystal prop, with signed Certificate of Authenticity from The Doohan family.

Dilithium Crystals prop used on screen during filming of *The Original Series.* Sold through the Doohan family, with a Certificate of Authenticity signed by Chris Doohan, son of James Doohan.

$15   **$25**

The first Phasers, Communicators, Tricorders, etc., that were as close to being realistic in size and accuracy as possible were fan-made props. These are just a very small sampling of the many different and unique props that can be found.

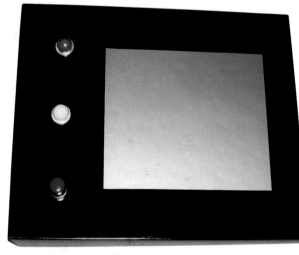

Fan-made electronic bridge tablet prop.

Electronic bridge tablet prop with working lights, fan made.

$25   **$50**

Fan-made Agonizer static prop.

Agonizer static prop from "Mirror, Mirror," fan made.

$15   **$20**

Starfleet Command Certificate prop.

Starfleet Command Certificate of Command prop; personalized certificate of award to the rank of captain.

$10   **$25**

Starfleet Command Certificate of Marriage prop.

Starfleet Command Certificate of Marriage prop; personalized marriage certificate.

$10   **$25**

Starfleet Academy graduation certificate prop.

Starfleet Academy certificate prop; personalized certificate of graduation.

$10   **$25**

Starfleet Academy Graduate certificate prop.

Starfleet Academy Graduate certificate prop; a deluxe personalized certificate inducting me into Starfleet.

$20   **$30**

Horta Creature prop.

Horta Creature, Mego 8" action figured-scaled toy prop. Also see "Toys."

$25   **$35**

Wooden Starfleet Command UFP sign prop.

Wooden carved Starfleet Command UFP sign prop.

$20   **$35**

Puzzles

Collectors often enjoy the artwork and colorful packaging of a toy as much, if not more, than the toy itself. That continues to be true with many of the Star Trek puzzles. The fantasy artwork and exotic scenery created for many of the Whitman puzzles, for example, are truly spectacular. Though many times inaccurate with things like uniform colors (Kirk in red shirt) or planet spellings (Romulon), these "mistakes" simply add to the charm of these now vintage collectibles. Prices are based on puzzle boxes being in good condition and all pieces present.

COMMAND TEAM JIGSAW, BBC-TV, 1972

Kirk, Spock, and McCoy, Command Team Jigsaw, BBC TV, 1972.

Kirk, Spock, McCoy on bridge (Spock with phaser inset), 100 pieces, 11" x 9".

$10   **$20**

HG TOYS, FIRST SERIES, CARTOON STYLE, 1974

Battle on the Planet Klingon, HG Toys, 1974.

Battle on the Planet Klingon, 150 pieces, 10" x 14".

$20   **$30**

Battle on the Planet Romulon, HG Toys, 1974.

Battle on the Planet Romulon (Note the incorrect spelling of Romulan), 150 pieces, 10" x 14".

$20   **$30**

Attempted Hijacking, HG Toys, 1974.

Attempted Hijacking of the U.S.S. Enterprise and Its Officers, 300 pieces, 14" x 18".

$30   **$40**

Kirk and Officers Beaming Down, HG Toys, 1974.

Captain Kirk and Officers Beaming Down, 150 pieces, 10" x 14".

$30   **$40**

Captain Kirk and Officers Beaming Down (in round tube tin), 150 pieces, 10" x 14".

$35   **$45**

Kirk and Officers Beaming Down. Puzzle in round tin, HG Toys, 1974.

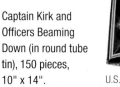

U.S.S. Enterprise and Officers, HG Toys, 1974.

Starship U.S.S. Enterprise and Its Officers, 300 pieces, 14" x 18".

$30   **$40**

WHITMAN, BBC-TV, CARTOON STYLE (NOTE: KIRK HAS RED SHIRT), 1975

Kirk in command chair, Whitman, BBC TV, 1975.

Kirk in command chair looking at Klingon on View Screen with Spock looking in viewer, McCoy standing, and Scotty at helm pointing at the screen, 224 pieces, 18" x 13".

$30   **$40**

Kirk, Spock, and McCoy, Whitman, BBC TV, 1975.

Kirk, Spock, and McCoy pointing phasers at greenish-yellow creatures on alien planet with Enterprise flying by in background, 224 pieces, 18" x 13".

$30   **$40**

Kirk with microphone, Whitman, BBC TV, 1975.

Kirk standing with microphone looking at Spock with McCoy and Uhura standing in the background with spaceship flying by on the screen, 224 pieces, 18" x 13".

$35   **$45**

WHITMAN, BBC-TV, 1973

Kirk, Spock, and Sulu, Whitman, BBC TV, 1973.

Kirk looking in viewer, Spock, Sulu on bridge with spaceship passing by viewscreen, 125 pieces, 15" x 11-1/4".

$10   **$20**

Kirk and Spock, Whitman, BBC TV, 1973.

Kirk, Spock on alien planet firing phasers at green lizard-like creatures in cave, 125 pieces, 15" x 11-1/4".

$10   **$20**

HG TOYS, SERIES II, NON-CARTOON STYLE ART, 1976

   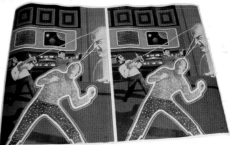

Kirk, Spock, and McCoy, HG Toys, series II, 1976.

Capt. Kirk, Mr. Spock, and Dr. McCoy, 150 pieces, 14" x 10".

$25 $35

Force Field Capture, HG Toys, series II, 1976.

Force Field Capture, 150 pieces, 14" x 10".

$25 $35

The Alien, HG Toys, series II, 1976.

The Alien, 150 pieces, 14" x 10".

$25 $35

The Alien, HG Toys, series II, 1975.

The Alien, extremely rare printer's color separation sheet for box art, 21" x 14-1/2", PZ-16.

$55 $100

WHITMAN, 1978

Interesting artwork depicting Kirk and crew in surreal settings, each puzzle 200 pieces, 14" x 18".

Kirk surrounded by glow, Whitman, 1978.

Red border, Kirk with crew surrounded by glow on misty planet.

$25 $35

Kirk, Spock and shuttlecraft, Whitman, 1978.

Yellow border with Kirk yelling, Spock in background with shuttle craft appearing in a flash.

$25 $35

Kirk, Spock, crew and shuttlecraft on fire, Whitman, 1978.

Purple border with Kirk, Spock, crew, and a shuttlecraft on fire.

$25 $35

Kirk and crew on planet, Whitman, 1978.

Green border with Kirk and crew on planet, shuttlecraft landing with Enterprise in orbit near alien space station.

$25 $35

WHITMAN (MERRIGOLD PRESS), FRAMETRAY, 1978

Crew on bridge, Whitman Frametray, 1978.

In the transporter, Whitman Frametray, 1978.

Kirk, Spock, and Enterprise, Whitman Frametray, 1978.

Kirk in spacesuit, Whitman Frametray, 1978.

12-piece puzzles in cardboard trays, 8-1/2" x 11": Crew on the bridge; in the Transporter ready to beam down; Kirk and Spock with the Enterprise; Kirk outside in space in spacesuit.

$25   **$35**

LARAMI SLIDING PUZZLES, 1979

Unscramble the crew, Whitman Frametray, 1978.

Small white sliding puzzles, 2" x 2": U.S.S. Enterprise; Kirk; Spock; Unscramble the Crew.

$15   **$20**

MILTON BRADLEY, 1979

#1: U.S.S. Enterprise, Milton Bradley, 1978.

#2: Faces of the Future, Milton Bradley, 1978.

#3: Sickbay, Milton Bradley, 1978.

Color photos from the movie, 250 pieces, 19-7/8" x 13-7/8": #1: U.S.S. Enterprise; #2: Faces of the Future; #3: "Sickbay."

$25   **$35**

GOLDEN, 1993

Kirk, Spock, and Enterprise, Golden, 1993.

Kirk, Spock, and Enterprise art from TOS, 300 pieces, 36" x 24".

$15   **$25**

KING INTERNATIONAL (HOLLAND), 1993

U.S.S. Enterprise leaving Space Station K-7, King International, 1993.

U.S.S. Enterprise leaving Space Station K-7 with shuttlecraft flying nearby, 100 pieces, 30-1/2 cm x 21-1/2 cm.

$55   **$65**

Records, Tapes, and Compact Discs

I can remember going into a small record store called The Music Shop in the mall in West Lebanon, New Hampshire in the late 1970s and seeing, on its 8-track wall, the Leonard Nimoy tape, *The Touch of Leonard Nimoy*. The shop also had the soundtrack from *Star Wars* as well. Since the movie had just come out and, like every other kid, I was totally blown away by it, I snatched up the soundtrack in a heartbeat. That is probably the only time I can remember going for a Star Wars piece over a Star Trek one.

The interesting thing and one that diehard fans will probably enjoy knowing is that, the last I checked, *The Touch of Leonard Nimoy* 8-track tape was worth quite a bit more than the *Star Wars* 8-track tape.

8-TRACKS

A selection of some of the Star Trek-related recordings released on 8-track.

COLUMBIA HOUSE

Inside Star Trek, Columbia House.

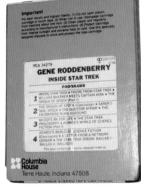

Inside Star Trek program listing.

Inside Star Trek.

$15   **$20**

COLUMBIA RECORDS AND TAPES

Star Trek: The Motion Picture Soundtrack, Columbia Records & Tapes.

Star Trek: The Motion Picture Soundtrack.

$15   **$20**

PARAMOUNT RECORDS AND TAPES

The Touch of Leonard Nimoy, rare 8-track version of his album.

$25   **$45**

CASSETTES

A selection of some of the Star Trek-related recordings released on cassette:

BUENA VISTA RECORDS

Star Trek: The Motion Picture read-along tape and book.
    $10   **$15**

GREAT AMERICAN AUDIO CORP., 1986

Star Wreck: "At the Sound of the Beep" is a collection of 15 *Star Trek* musical satire-styled telephone answering machine messages. Total running time: 8 minutes.
    $25   **$35**

GREAT AMERICAN AUDIO CORP., 1990

Star Wreck Gift Set: Special double cassette set of "At the Sound of the Beep" collection of 32 answering messages from the "Telephone Comedy and TV Classics" and "Star Wreck" telephone answering machine message collection.
    $45   **$55**

VARESE SARABAND

Star Trek Episodes Volume One, Varese Saraband.

Star Trek Episodes Volume Two, Varese Saraband.

Star Trek Episodes Volume Three, Varese Saraband.

Star Trek Tapes, produced by Jack M. Sell.

Spock Rock.

Star Trek Episodes Volume One: "Charlie X," "The Corbomite Maneuver," "Mudd's Women", and "The Doomsday Machine." Performed by Fred Steiner and the Royal Philharmonic Orchestra.
    $10   **$15**

Star Trek Episodes Volume Two: "Mirror Mirror," "By Any Other Name," "The Trouble With Tribbles," and "The Empath." Performed by Fred Steiner and the Royal Philharmonic Orchestra.
    $10   **$15**

Star Trek Episodes Volume Three: Music from the episodes "Shore Leave" and "The Naked Time."
    $10   **$15**

Star Trek Tapes: A compilation of official press recordings with the cast of *The Original Series* from the 1970s. Produced by Jack M. Sell.
    $5   **$10**

Spock Rock: An Unauthorized 25th Anniversary Star Trekker Comedy.
    $10   **$15**

Star Trek: The Motion Picture soundtrack.

Star Trek II: The Wrath of Khan soundtrack.

Star Trek III: The Search of Spock soundtrack.

Star Trek IV: The Voyage Home soundtrack.

Star Trek V: The Final Frontier soundtrack.

Star Trek VI: The Undiscovered Country soundtrack.

Soundtracks on cassette include *Star Trek: The Motion Picture*, *Star Trek II: The Wrath of Khan*, *Star Trek III: The Search of Spock*, *Star Trek IV: The Voyage Home*, *Star Trek V: The Final Frontier*, *Star Trek VI: The Undiscovered Country*.

$5   **$10 each**

AUDIO NOVELS

Audio novels are cassette tapes based on popular *Star Trek* novels and books. The novels are often read by at least one of the actors from the series or by the author. The fascinating thing about most of these audio novels is that when you listen, you are hearing the familiar voices you grew up with while watching the original television series. This list is just a small sampling of some of the great *Star Trek* audio novels available.

DOVE AUDIO

Warped Factors by Walter Koenig, Dove Audio.

Warped Factors, read by the author, Walter Koenig.
$10 $15

HARPER AUDIO

Memories by William Shatner, Harper Audio.

Memories, read by the author, William Shatner.
$10 $15

SIMON AND SCHUSTER, 1986

Star Trek: The Voyage Home, read by Leonard Nimoy and George Takei.
$10 $15

SIMON AND SCHUSTER, 1987

Strangers From the Sky, read by Leonard Nimoy and George Takei.
$10 $15

SIMON AND SCHUSTER, 1988

Enterprise: The First Adventure, read by Leonard Nimoy and George Takei.
$10 $15
Web of the Romulans, read by Leonard Nimoy and George Takei.
$10 $15
Yesterday's Son, read by Leonard Nimoy and James Doohan.
$10 $15

SIMON AND SCHUSTER, 1989

Final Frontier, read by Leonard Nimoy and James Doohan.
$10 $15
Lost Years, read by Leonard Nimoy and James Doohan.
$15 $20

Prime Directive read by James Doohan, Simon and Schuster.

Prime Directive, read by James Doohan.
$15 $20
Spock's World, read by Leonard Nimoy and George Takei.
$15 $20
Star Trek: The Final Frontier, read by Leonard Nimoy and George Takei.
$10 $15

Time For Yesterday, read by Leonard Nimoy and James Doohan.
$10 $15

RECORDS

Power Records probably sold more of its 12" *Star Trek* LP records in 1975 because of the incredible cover artwork than for the audio content. The artwork perfectly captured the feeling of the original television show, making it desirable to today's collectors.

Here is a selection of some of the related recordings released on vinyl.

AR-WAY PRODUCTIONS, 1979

"Beyond Antares/Uhura's Theme," 45 single sung by Nichelle Nichols.

$10 $15

BACKSTAGE PRODUCTIONS, INC

Radio Interview Special LP of *Star Trek: The Motion Picture* Backstage Productions, Inc.

A Radio Interview Special LP of *Star Trek: The Motion Picture.*

$25 $35

BLUE PEAR RECORDS

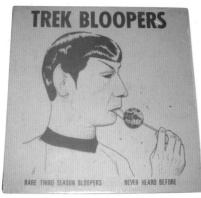

Star Trek Bloopers, Blue Pear Records.

Star Trek Bloopers.

$10 $15

BUENA VISTA RECORDS

Star Trek: The Motion Picture read-along record and book, album.

$15 $20

CASABLANCA RECORDS, 1979

Disco-style music from Star Trek and other movies, MECO, Casablanca Records.

MECO's *Music From Star Trek and Music From the Black Hole*, disco-style renditions of music from *Star Trek: The Motion Picture* and other movies.

$20 $25

COLUMBIA RECORDS, 1976

"*Star Trek* Theme" 45 single by The Inside Star Trek Orchestra, Columbia Records.

"*Star Trek* Theme," 45 single by The Inside Star Trek Orchestra.

$15 $20

COLUMBIA RECORDS, 1976

Inside Star Trek, Columbia Records.

Inside Star Trek: This is a unique look into some of what it takes to develop a television phenomenon. Gene Roddenberry narrates and discusses his dreams and the difficulties he faced. Roddenberry, William Shatner, DeForest Kelley, Mark Lenard (who played Spock's father, Sarek), and science fiction author Ray Bradbury all met at the United Western Studios in Los Angeles in July 1976 to record the album. Mark Lenard gives you a few insights into the character of Spock. The album includes segments recorded in front of a live studio audience. The live segments include anecdotal stories including what it took to make *Star Trek* by Roddenberry himself. Unfortunately, due to contractual difficulties, Roddenberry could not use Ray Bradbury's part of the interview on the album. To get the Isaac Asimov interview, Roddenberry traveled to New York earlier that same year.

$20 $45

COLUMBIA RECORDS, 1979-96

Star Trek: The Motion Picture soundtrack on LP.

"Star Trek: The Motion Picture" theme on 45.

Star Trek II: The Wrath of Khan soundtrack on LP.

Star Trek III: The Search for Spock soundtrack on LP.

The soundtrack from each movie was released on vinyl.

Star Trek: The Motion Picture.
$5   **$25**

"Star Trek: The Motion Picture" theme, 45 rpm.
$10   **$25**

Star Trek II: The Wrath of Khan, *Star Trek III: The Search for Spock*, *Star Trek IV: The Voyage Home*, *Star Trek V: The Final Frontier*, *Star Trek VI: The Undiscovered Country*.
$5   **$25 each**

DECCA RECORDS, 1968

DOT RECORDS, 1968

The Transformed Man on LP.

First cover variation of *Mr. Spock's Music From Outer Space*.

Second cover variation of *Mr. Spock's Music From Outer Space*.

The Transformed Man: William Shatner's debut album was recorded and released while the original *Star Trek* series was still on the air. This album is best known for showcasing Shatner's now famous vocal style where he uses dramatic pauses and flourishes while he talks or sings.

$65   **$85**

Rare advance release 7-inch 45 single, "How Insensitive."

$45   **$65**

Leonard Nimoy Presents Mr. Spock's Music From Outer Space: This is the album that launched Nimoy's musical career in the late 1960s and 1970s. Desilu Studios executive Herbert F. Solow thought *Star Trek* could be huge in licensing potential, so he sent a memo to the cast and crew stating, "Push any record company that wants to do an outer space or Vulcan or any other single record or album, be it straight dramatic music, weird music, Nichelle Nichols singing, Bill Shatner doing bird calls or even the sound of Gene Roddenberry polishing a semi-precious stone on his grinder." Looking at the back of both covers, it appears that the second cover is a British released reprint of the album, complete with a BBC copyrighted cover image. The text on the back of the first printing discusses Mr. Nimoy portraying Mr. Spock, and then goes on to mention some of his other previous work. On the back of this second cover variation, however, the text is quite different: "Leonard Nimoy may not thank anyone for perpetuating the image of Mr. Spock, second-in-command of the Star Ship Enterprise. After all, his alter ego was created back in the mid-'60s, and although the popular '*Star Trek*' is still the subject of numerous re-runs Leonard Nimoy has long ago shed his Vulcan ears." This is an interesting look at Mr. Nimoy's trepidation regarding his role as Spock sometime after the show had been cancelled. We also experience this "feeling" in 1975 when Mr. Nimoy wrote his autobiography, *I Am Not Spock*, published by Celestial Arts.

Cover with Spock holding Enterprise model.
$55   **$65**

Cover with close-up of Spock on the bridge.
$45   **$55**

DOT RECORDS, 1969

Touch of Leonard Nimoy. Nimoy collaborated with George Tipton, the man responsible for many television theme songs including *The Courtship of Eddie's Father*, *The Love Boat*, *Soap*, and many other well known television themes. Many fans will quickly recognize that one of the songs on this album, "Maiden Wine" was used in the third season episode, "Plato's Stepchildren."

$10 $40

Two Sides of Leonard Nimoy, Dot Records.

The Way I Feel, Leonard Nimoy, Dot Records.

Two Sides of Leonard Nimoy album, features the Mr. Spock persona on one side and Nimoy's "human" persona on the flip side.

$40 $50

The Way I Feel, album.

$40 $55

DOT RECORDS, 1970

Dot Records, 1970, *The New World of Leonard Nimoy*, Dot Records.

"The New World of Leonard Nimoy," 45 single.

The New World of Leonard Nimoy LP. The song "The Sun Will Rise" is the only track Nimoy composed himself.

$20 $40

"The New World of Leonard Nimoy" 45 rpm Single.

$10 $20

The Transformed Man 12-inch Album (Shatner).

$50 $70

EPIC RECORDS

Down To Earth by Nichelle Nichols; contains eight songs including the *Star Trek* Theme.

$45 $65

FAMOUS TWINSET, 1974-1976

Outer Space/Inner Mind with Leonard Nimoy, Famous Twinset, 1974-1976.

Outer Space/Inner Mind with Leonard Nimoy. Released late in 1974 as part of Paramount's "Famous Twinset" series, it became a two-album set compilation of greatest hits from a variety of earlier Nimoy albums including "Mr. Spock's Music from Outer Space." Cover artwork is the same cover art used for the AMT Enterprise model kit released in 1968.

$10 $30

FIFTH CONTINENT MUSIC, CORP. LABEL X

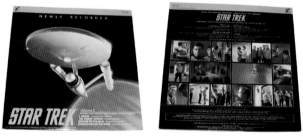

Star Trek Episodes Volume Two, Tony Bremner and the Royal Philharmonic Orchestra.

Star Trek Episodes Volume One: "Is There In Truth No Beauty," and "The Paradise Syndrome" by Tony Bremner and the Royal Philharmonic Orchestra.

$25 $35

Star Trek Episodes Volume Two: "I, Mudd," "The Enemy Within," "Spectre of the Gun," and "Conscience of the King" by Tony Bremner and the Royal Philharmonic Orchestra.

$25 $35

GNP CRESCENDO, 1985

"The Cage/Where No Man Has Gone Before," GNP Crescendo, 1985.

Original Soundtrack television Series, "The Cage/Where No Man Has Gone Before."

$12   **$15**

Limited-edition framed gold record plaque of "The Cage/Where No Man Has Gone Before" soundtrack.

Original Soundtrack television Series, "The Cage/Where No Man Has Gone Before," limited-edition framed Gold record plaque.

$42   **$65**

Original Soundtrack TV Series Volume Three, GNP Crescendo, 1985.

Original Soundtrack Television Series Volume Three, "Shore Leave/The Naked Time."

$12   **$15**

IMPERIAL MUSIC, 1978

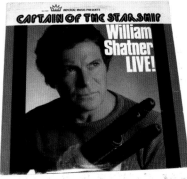

Captain of the Starship, William Shatner Live!, Imperial Music, 1978.

Captain of the Starship, William Shatner Live! Notice Mr. Shatner is holding a tripod backwards, possibly as an attempt by the record label to give him a futuristic "captain" look?

$25   **$50**

GNP CRESCENDO, 1989

Star Trek Sound Effects from the original television series soundtrack; sound effects include the communicator chirp, bridge and console sounds and more.

$15   **$25**

MCA RECORDS

"Deodato," theme from *Star Trek* 45, MCA Records.

"Deodato," theme from *Star Trek*, 45 rpm.

$25   **$30**

PRECISION RECORDS AND TAPES, LTD., 1986

Picture Disc Record, "The Cage/Where No Man Has Gone Before," Precision Records & Tapes, Ltd., 1986.

Picture Disc Record, Original Soundtrack Television Series. Two-sided picture disc: Kirk and Spock on one side and crew transporting down on the other; "The Cage/Where No Man Has Gone Before."

$12   **$20**

PETER PAN RECORDS, 1979

To Starve a Fleaver, an example of one of the re-releases of earlier records now with *Star Trek: The Motion Picture* images.

$10   **$15**

PETER PAN RECORDS, 1975

Since the 1940s, Peter Pan Industries has produced quite a few children's albums either under its Peter Pan or Power records labels. In 1975, it produced eight different Star Trek Story Records showcasing seven different "new" adventures.

Though the records were marketed to children, these records contained realistic adult action stories, some penned by veteran comic book writers Neal Adams and Cary Bates. A few other stories were written by well-known Star Trek author Alan Dean Foster, who would later write the story for *Star Trek: The Motion Picture.* With the release of the Star Trek motion picture, Peter Pan Industries jumped on the merchandising bandwagon and produced four new Star Trek stories.

Peter Pan then re-released the first seven Star Trek stories using images from *Star Trek: The Motion Picture* on the new packaging. Peter Pan Industries released a total of twenty-three various records and packaging combinations that contained eleven different original Star Trek adventure stories between 1975 and 1979. Ten of these record sets contained unique read-along comic books on the inside front cover. Ten records were 7-inch 45 rpm versions, three records were 7-inch 33-1/3 RPM, and the remaining eight records were 12" 33-1/3 LP versions.

POWER RECORDS (A DIVISION OF PETER PAN INDUSTRIES), 1975

Three new exciting episodes: "Passage To Moauv," "In Vino Veritas," and "The Crier In Emptiness." Note the two different back cover variations.

$15   **$20**

Three new exciting *Star Trek* episodes, Power Records, 1975.

Back cover variation #1, showing just the Enterprise crew on the bridge.

Back cover variation #2, showing added word balloons.

7-inch 45 rpm book and record set, *Passage to Moauv.*

To Starve a Fleaver re-release with TMP images, Peter Pan Records, 1979.

7-inch 45 rpm book and record set: "A Mirror for Futility" and "The Time Sealer," "Dinosaur Planet," "Passage to Moauv," "The Crier in Emptiness," and "The Robot Masters."

$10   **$15 each**

POWER RECORDS, 1975

Four exciting all new *Star Trek* adventures, Power Records, 1975.

Star Trek four episodes: "The Time Stealer," "To Starve A Fleaver," "The Logistics Of Stampede," and "A Mirror For Futility."

$15 $20

RECORD BOWL, 1975

Record chip bowl using a *Star Trek* Peter Pan record, 1975.

Chip bowl created from a Peter Pan *Star Trek* episodes record.

$10 $15

POWER RECORDS, 1975

Star Trek Book n' Record Set "Crier in Emptiness."

$5 $10

Book n' Record Little LP 7-inch, "In Vino Veritas."

Star Trek Little LP 7-inch "In Vino Veritas."

$5 $10

SEARS RADIO THEATER, 1971

"Leonard Nimoy's Radio Adventures": The Sears Radio Theater broadcast a weekly radio adventure series. The programs were hosted by popular stars of the late 1960s and early 1970s including Lorne Greene, Andy Griffith, Vincent Price, Cicely Tyson, and Leonard Nimoy.

$25 $50

THE THEME SCENE, 1978

Henry Mancini, The Theme Scene, featuring *Star Trek* and other themes by Mancini and his Orchestra.

$10 $15

Book n' Record Little LP 7-inch, "To Starve A Fleaver."

"To Starve A Fleaver." Inside contains the record and a comic book-style story.

$5 $10

SEARS STEREO, 1972

Reissues of earlier Dot recordings by Leonard Nimoy.

$10 $20

STAR TREK TAPES

A compilation of official press recordings from the 1970s with interviews of the cast of *The Original Series*. Produced by Jack M. Sell.

$5 $10

Henry Mancini The Theme Scene, by Mancini and his Orchestra, 1978.

PRECISION RECORDS AND TAPES

Star Trekkin' by The Firm. Album includes Star Trekkin and Dub Trek.

$15 $20

RANWOOD RECORDS, THEME SONG, 1975

"*Star Trek*" theme song, Charles Randolph Grean Sounde, Ranwood Records, 1975.

Charles Randolph Grean Sounde.

$10 $15

SYNTHETIC PLASTICS, INC., 1981

Star Trek and other space themes, Synthetic Plastics, Inc, 1981.

Star Trek and other space themes, The Now Sound Orchestra, Music By "Bugs" Bowers.

$10 $20

VARESE SARABAND RECORDS

ZYX RECORDS

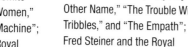
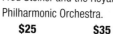

Star Trek Episodes Volume One, Varese Saraband Records.

Star Trek Episodes Volume Two, Fred Steiner and the Royal Philharmonic Orchestra.

Theme from Star Trek, Wonderland Records, 1976.

Star Trek Episodes Volume One: "Charlie X," "The Corbomite Maneuver," "Mudd's Women," and "The Doomsday Machine"; Fred Steiner and the Royal Philharmonic Orchestra.

$25   **$35**

Star Trek Episodes Volume Two: "Mirror Mirror," "By Any Other Name," "The Trouble With Tribbles," and "The Empath"; Fred Steiner and the Royal Philharmonic Orchestra.

$25   **$35**

Theme from Star Trek, Wonderland Records, 1976: Performed by Jeff Wayne Space Shuttle, produced by Ralph Stein. Shows a drawing of a soldier ape from "Planet of the Apes."

$10   **$15**

Star Trek Tekkno Mix, Orion.

Star Trek Tekkno Mix, Orion.

$25   **$35**

LASER-ETCHED DISC PLAQUES

There were two limited-edition laser-etched disc plaques that were produced for the 25th anniversary of *Star Trek* in 1991.

These are very similar to the limited-edition framed gold record plaque of "The Cage/Where No Man Has Gone Before" soundtrack album and many collectors feel that they all go together as a set.

Star Trek Silver Anniversary laser-etched disc, 1991.

Star Trek VI: The Undiscovered Country 24k gold-plated laser-etched disc, 1991.

Star Trek limited-edition Silver Anniversary laser-etched disc, 1991. Limited to only 1,000. The framed plaque features the disc with images of Captain Kirk and the original U.S.S. Enterprise with Captain Picard and the U.S.S. Enterprise-D.

$200   **$275**

Star Trek VI: The Undiscovered Country limited-edition 24k gold-plated laser-etched disc, 1991. Limited to only 2,500. The framed plaque features the disc with images of the cast and ships from the movie.

$150   **$200**

COMPACT DISC

Since most of the record titles mentioned here have since been re-released onto CD, the following list, in no particular order, is a partial selection of some of the more unique CDs that have been released in the past few years with a few notable re-releases thrown in as well.

Down To Earth, Nichelle Nichols.

Nichelle Nichols, *Down To Earth*, album re-issue on CD.
$15   **$20**

Out of this World, Nichelle Nichols.

Nichelle Nichols, *Out of this World*, album re-issue on CD.
$15   **$20**

The Transformed Man, William Shatner.

William Shatner, *The Transformed Man*, album re-issue on CD.
$15   **$20**

William Shatner's *Common People* promo CD.

William Shatner, *Common People*, promotional single release for William Shatner's latest album, arranged by Ben Folds.
$15   **$20**

Mr. Spock's Music From Outerspace, Leonard Nimoy.

Leonard Nimoy's *Mr. Spock's Music From Outerspace*, album re-issue on CD.
$15   **$20**

Spaced Out with Leonard Nimoy and William Shatner.

Leonard Nimoy and William Shatner, *Spaced Out*: "A collection of curiously compelling recordings brought together for the first time, summarizing the talents of two artists who hold cult status in the worlds of both TV and music." Made in England.
$15   **$20**

Star Trek Epics on Audio. Three Classic *Star Trek* Adventures.

Star Trek Epics on Audio. Three Classic *Star Trek* Adventures on four compact discs.
$10   **$25**

Star Trek 25th Anniversary Audio Collection.

Star Trek 25th Anniversary Audio Collection (same content as Epics on Audio).
$10   **$25**

Star Trek: The Motion Picture 25th Anniversary edition soundtrack.

Star Trek: The Motion Picture 25th Anniversary edition soundtrack; deluxe anniversary CD.
$15   **$35**

The Astral Symphony. Compilation of tracks from some of the various *Star Trek* films.

The Astral Symphony. Compilation of tracks from some of the various *Star Trek* films.
$10   **$20**

Fantastic Journey by Erich Kunzel and the Cincinnati Pops Orchestra.

Fantastic Journey, Erich Kunzel and the Cincinnati Pops Orchestra. Various themes from fantasy, sci-fi, and action movies including *Star Trek*.

$10   **$20**

Space-Taculars by John Williams and the Boston Pops.

Space-Taculars, John Williams and the Boston Pops. From the man who created the famous *Star Wars* movie, music takes on various themes from some of the biggest sci-fi movies, including the theme from both the original *Star Trek* series and the motion picture.

$10   **$20**

Star Tracks by Erich Kunzel and the Cincinnati Pops Orchestra.

Star Tracks, Erich Kunzel and the Cincinnati Pops Orchestra. Features a special synthesizer intro and closing.

$10   **$25**

Star Tracks played by the Silver Screen Orchestra.

Star Tracks, original Star Tracks played by the Silver Screen Orchestra.

$10   **$20**

Symphonic Star Trek by Erich Kunzel and the Cincinnati Pops Orchestra.

Symphonic Star Trek, performed by Erich Kunzel and the Cincinnati Pops Orchestra. A collection of tracks from some of the various TV series and movies.

$10   **$25**

Sound Effects from *The Original Series.*

Sound Effects, by producer and editor Neil Norman. A massive compilation of the many sound effects, most lasting mere seconds, that made up the unique sound effects created and used for *The Original Series.* One of my favorites is the first track, "Enterprise Bridge Sequence," that runs for almost six minutes.

$10   **$15**

The Star Trek Album. A two-CD set of music from the motion pictures and TV shows.

Star Trek Album. Tracks from the various television series and movies including a few sound effects' tracks tossed in for fun. One unique sound effect track included is called "Dogfight in Space" and runs for about a minute and a half.

$15   **$25**

The World of Star Trek, a two-CD set of music from *The Original Series.*

The World of Star Trek, a two-CD set. Includes a very nice selection of tracks from "The Cage," "Where No Man Has Gone Before," "The Doomsday Machine," and "Amok Time."

$20   **$35**

The Ultimate Star Trek by Fred Steiner and the Royal Philharmonic Orchestra.

The Ultimate Star Trek. Tracks from some of the various television series and movies.

$20   **$25**

The Music of Star Trek: The First 30 Years.

The Music of Star Trek: The First 30 Years, performed by The London Pops Orchestra. Features themes from some of the various television series and movies.

$15   **$20**

Star Trek 20th Anniversary Special CD.

Best of Star Trek, German.

The Best of Star Trek: The Original Film Scores.

Star Trek Encounters, Neil Norman and His Cosmic Orchestra.

Star Trek 20th Anniversary Special. A small selection of various tracks from some of the series and movies.

$20   **$25**

Best of Star Trek. A nice selection of tracks and sound effects from many of *The Original Series* episodes. Made in Germany.

$25   **$35**

The Best of Star Trek: The Original Film Scores. A small selection of themes and tracks from the first six movies.

$15   **$25**

Star Trek Encounters, Neil Norman. Features a couple of very unique track compilations of *Star Trek*-themed songs put to a rock beat.

$20   **$25**

Cult TV Themes including Star Trek, performed by The London Theatre Orchestra.

Star Trek VI: The Undiscovered Country, read by James Doohan.

Star Trek Generations Soundtrack.

CD compilation of a mix of Star Trek party music.

Cult TV Themes, performed by The London Theatre Orchestra. Features sixteen weird and wonderful favorites, includes the theme from *Star Trek*.

$20   **$30**

Star Trek VI: The Undiscovered Country, read by James Doohan. A unique CD featuring a dramatic reading by James Doohan and enhanced with sound effects and an original score. A must-have.

$25   **$35**

Star Trek Generations Soundtrack. Music composed and conducted by Dennis McCarthy.

$15   **$20**

Star Trek Party Music Mix. Fan-made compilation features theme songs, musical parodies, funny sound bites, songs sung by stars, and more.

$5   **$25**

Star Trek at the National Aeronautics & Space Museum images on CD.

Star Trek at the National Aeronautics and Space Museum. A large compilation of images from the 1992 Star Trek exhibit at NASM.

$5   **$25**

Sleeping Bags, Chairs, and Rugs

When I really started to get serious with collecting, one of the items I considered to be a "holy grail" piece was Mego's Mission to Gamma VI playset. I have since obtained that rare piece, but as of this writing, one piece that I consider an even harder-to-find item is the 1976 Decorion bean bag chair. It just goes to prove that no matter how many pieces you collect and no matter how many hard-to-find items you cross off your "want" list, there will always be that one next piece that seems to stay just out of reach.

BEAN BAGS

DECORION, 1976

Blue and white plastic with color artwork of spaceships.

  $250 $300

DECORION, 1979

Star Trek: The Motion Picture:

Yellow plastic with color artwork of crew and logo.

  $150 $200

Red plastic with color artwork of Kirk, Spock, McCoy, and Enterprise.

  $200 $250

Star Trek: The Motion Picture sleeping bag ad, Decorion, 1979.

INFLATABLE CHAIR

KMART, 1979

Star Trek: The Motion Picture. Color artwork of Spock on back/arms, logo on seat, child's size inflatable chair.

Boxed.

  $175 $200

Loose.

  $75 $100

THROW RUGS

THROW RUGS, 1976

Standard-size plush fur rugs feature color artwork from scenes from *The Original Series* and from poster artwork: Bridge scene; crew; Enterprise; episode photo collage (same collage used in the 1976 Langley Associates collage poster).

  $150 $200 each

SLEEPING BAGS
ALP INDUSTRIES, 1976

Star Trek sleeping bag, Alp Industries, 1976.

Artwork features original animated TV Series images. Also included a vinyl tote.

$150   **$200**

SPORTLINE-KIDNAPPER, 1977

Sleeping bag, U.S.S. Enterprise and other ships with landing party artwork, Sportline-Kidnapper, 1977.

Features U.S.S. Enterprise and other ships. Artwork appears to be taken from the Gold Key comics. The backpacks and field equipment belts are an obvious clue.

$125   **$175**

ALP INDUSTRIES, 1979

Sleeping bag, U.S.S. Enterprise and crew, Alp Industries, 1979.

Artwork features original TV series U.S.S. Enterprise and crew.

$175   **$225**

HENDERSON CAMP PRODUCTS, 1979

Artwork features *Star Trek: The Motion Picture* scenes and crew.

$125   **$175**

Stamps, Decals, and Stickers

In 1973, the Leonard Nimoy Fan Club created special-issue cancelled postage stamps. Stamp collectors would still have to wait a while for anything official from the U.S. Postal Service, though. In 1991, with *Star Trek* celebrating its 25th anniversary, the United States Postal Service released its Space Exploration Commemorative Stamp Set displaying on individual stamps images of Kirk, Spock, McCoy, Sulu, Chekov, Uhura, and Scotty, as well as the Enterprise and a Klingon ship. In 1995, St. Vincent & The Grenadines released their *Star Trek* postage stamp set commemorating 30 years.

On Sept. 6, 1999, the United States Postal Service officially announced a new 33-cent stamp displaying an image of the Enterprise orbiting a planet. The stamp was issued on the 1960s sheet from the "Celebrate the Century" stamp set.

STAMPS

LINCOLN ENTERPRISES, 1974

*S*logan stamp sheets:

#1 Star Trek Lives.

#2 Support Star Trek.

$5   **$10 each**

LINCOLN ENTERPRISES, 1976

Star Trek: The Original Series gummed stamps, 40 stamps per sheet.

$5   **$10**

LINCOLN ENTERPRISES, 1976

Star Trek Portrait Miniatures. Sheet of 100 portrait miniatures including: Enterprise, Kirk, Spock, McCoy, Scotty, Uhura, Sulu, Chapel, Chekov.

$20   **$35 per sheet**

STAR TREK FAN CLUB, 1970

Fan Club-issued slogan stamps: Happiness Is A Warm Gorn, It May Be Logical But Is It Fun, Mr. Spock For President, NBC Is a Klingon Conspiracy.

$10   **$25 per set**

LEONARD NIMOY NATIONAL ASSOCIATION OF FANS (LNNAF)

Special Issue postage stamps with first cancels:

William Shatner as Kirk, Aug. 19, 1973.

$25   **$50**

Leonard Nimoy as Spock, Aug. 20, 1973.

$25   **$50**

MICRO COMPANY, 1972

Photo stamps sold in packs of 50: Portrait of Kirk in black and white; portrait of Kirk in sepia-toned brown; portrait of Spock in sepia tone; photo of Spock in black and white; photo of Leonard Nimoy in black and white.

$5   **$10 each**

MONSTER TIMES, 1975

Star Trek Lives! 144-stamp sheet of Kirk, Spock, McCoy, Scotty, Uhura, and Chekov.

$25   **$55 complete set**

PEPSI, 1977

Perforated 4" x 8" sheets, seven photo stamps with Pepsi logo, set of four.

$35   **$45**

PRIMROSE CONFECTIONARY CO. LTD., 1970

British stamp set of 12 different colored stamps:

Individual stamps.

$10   **$25**

Set of 12.

$125   **$175**

RUSSIAN POSTAL UNION

Adigey First Day cancelled issue, Russian Postal Union.

Adigey First Day cancelled issue.

$20   **$45**

CELEBRITY STAMPS, 1977

Official Star Trek Stamp Album, Celebrity Stamps, 1977.

Official Star Trek Stamp Album, 24-page stamp album.
   $15   **$25**

Stamp sets: Set #1 U.S.S. Enterprise; Set #2 Captain Kirk; Set #3 Mr. Spock; Set #4 Klingons and Romulans; Set #5 Aliens of the Galaxy; Set #6 Creatures of the Galaxy.

Individual set.
   $20   **$30**

All six sets.
   $125   **$150**

SUPPORT STAR TREK STAMPS

Star Trek Lives.
   $15   **$25**

SCI-FI BOOK CLUB, 1977

U.S.S. Enterprise stamp wall plaque, Sci-Fi Book Club, 1977.

U.S.S. Enterprise stamp wall plaque. This was only available to book club members.
   $25   **$45**

ST. VINCENT & THE GRENADINES

Limited-edition foldout display of Star Trek stamp set, St. Vincent & The Grenadines.

$1 set of nine stamps.
   $25   **$35**

Limited-edition foldout display with stamp set.
   $45   **$55**

Star Trek Lives, Support Star Trek Stamps.

U.S. POSTAL SERVICE, 1991

Space Exploration Commemorative Collection, U.S. Postal service, 1991.

Space Exploration Commemorative Stamps Collection.

$25 $35

U.S. Postal Service display, 1991.

U.S. Postal Service display.

$20 $30

U.S. POSTAL SERVICE, 1999

Celebrate the Century, 1960s set, U.S. Postal service, 1999.

Celebrate the Century, 1960s stamp set.

$10 $25

RUBBER STAMPS

AVIVA, 1979

Star Trek: The Motion Picture, Enterprise, Kirk, Spock, Vulcan Salute

$10 $15 each

STAMP OASIS, 1991-93

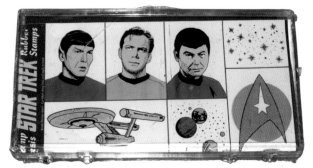

Spock, Kirk, McCoy, and Enterprise, Stamp Oasis, 1991-93.

Spock, Kirk, McCoy, Enterprise & Insignia; Chekov; Enterprise; Kirk; McCoy; Scotty; Spock; Sulu; Uhura; Starfleet Communique Stardate; Twenty-Fifth Anniversary Logo.

$20 $25

T-K GRAPHICS, 1984

Wooden Base Stamps: Approved: Starfleet Command; Beam Me Up, Scotty; Dispatched Stardate___; Live Long and Prosper; Space: The Final Frontier; Starfleet Computer Division; Starfleet Headquarters Classified; Starfleet Headquarters Official Mail; Starfleet Spacegram; UFP Janus Head Emblem; U.S.S. Enterprise Schematic.

$5 $10

STICKERS

LANGLEY & ASSOCIATES, 1976

40 different circular color photo stickers of characters, scenes, and ships.

$5 $10

MORRIS, 1975

Peel-off stickers and story album book, Morris, 1975.

Canadian set of peel off stickers, 12-page story album booklet: Individual packets.

$5 $10

Complete set.

$550 $750

Three different albums/artwork.

$150 $250 each

PANINI, 1979

Italian color photo sticker/album set of 400; 48-page album with color artwork of Kirk, Spock, McCoy, and Enterprise.

$400 $500 complete set with album

POCKET BOOKS, 1986

Star Trek 20th anniversary promotional stickers that read, "The only logical books to read."

$5 $10

DECALS

A.H. PRISMATIC, 1992

Set of nine hologram stickers: bridge scene and McCoy, Spock, Sulu & Uhura; bridge scene with Kirk, Scotty and Chekov; Enterprise; Enterprise and logo; Klingon and ship; Kirk on planet; Kirk in Transporter room; Spock on planet.

$5   **$10**

Uncut sheet.

$15   **$25**

AVIVA, 1979

Star Trek: The Motion Picture instant stained-glass reusable decals: Kirk; Enterprise; Spock; Spock with Vulcan salute; Spock with science symbol; the Vulcan shuttle.

$5   **$10**

Star Trek: The Motion Picture Puffy Sticker set. Six stickers per set with color artwork decals of characters, logos, and ships.

$20   **$25**

Star Trek: The Motion Picture vending capsule color photo stickers packaged in clear plastic vending capsules:

Individually.

$5   **$10**

Kirk, Spock, and Enterprise packaged together.

$5   **$10**

Toys

There has been such a great selection of unique and wonderful toys over the 40-plus years that you can imagine how easily it would be to fill three or more books just of fond memories and special stories on each and every one of them. Instead, this section includes a sampling of some of the most popular releases.

AZRAK-HAMWAY, 1975

Bop Bag: Inflatable punching bag of Mr. Spock.

$150   **$200**

Sky Diving Parachutist. Action figure-type toy connected to a parachute; Kirk and Spock.

$45   **$75 each**

Water pistol.

$40   **$75**

Bop Bag, Azrak-Hamway, 1975.

AZRAK-HAMWAY, 1976

Kirk pinball game, Azrak-Hamway, 1976.

Spock pinball game, Azrak-Hamway, 1976.

Kirk pinball game.

$75   **$100**

Spock pinball game.

$75   **$100**

Phaser with *Star Trek* logo.

$30   **$40**

Mini Phaser space flashlight, Azrak-Hamway, 1976.

Mini Phaser flashlight with click-action sound.

$55   **$75**

Saucer Gun, Azrak-Hamway, 1976.

Saucer Gun.

$25   **$45**

Water pistol U.S.S. Enterprise.

$75   **$100**

AVIVA, 1979

Star Trek: The Motion Picture kite; Enterprise or Spock.

$20   **$30 each**

Motion Picture Phaser water pistol.

$25   **$35**

Star Trek The Motion Picture Water Pistol, Aviva, 1979.

AZRAK-HAMWAY, 1977

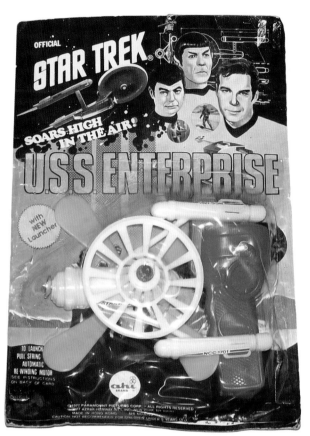

U.S.S. Enterprise with launcher, Azrak-Hamway, 1977.

U.S.S. Enterprise with launcher.

$40   **$60**

CHEMTOY, 1967

Movie Viewer, Chemtoy, 1967.

Movie Viewer. A mini viewer that allows you to view micro film cartridges containing a selection of scenes from the television series.

$40   **$55**

COLORFORMS, 1975

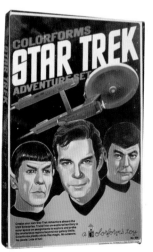

Colorforms Adventure Set; features cardboard bridge layout board with removable stick on character pieces.

$30   **$40**

Star Trek Adventure Set, Colorforms, 1975.

CORGI, 1982

Star Trek II: The Wrath of Khan U.S.S. Enterprise and Klingon Warship die-cast, Corgi, 1982.

Star Trek II:The Wrath of Khan die-cast ship: U.S.S. Enterprise, No. 148.

$25   **$35**

Star Trek II: The Wrath of Khan die-cast ship: Klingon Warship, No. 149.

$25   **$35**

DINKY, 1977

Enterprise, Dinky, 1977.

U.S.S. Enterprise die-cast.

$100   **$125**

Enterprise, Klingon Cruiser with mini catalog, Dinky, 1977.

Klingon Cruiser, Dinky, 1977.

Klingon Cruiser die-cast.

$100   **$125**

Enterprise and Klingon set. Both individually boxed ships sold together as set.

$200   **$250**

DINKY, 1978

Enterprise and Klingon Gift Set die-cast. Both ships packed together in a large window box.

$275   **$325**

DINKY, 1979

Enterprise *Star Trek: The Motion Picture* die-cast.

$20   **$30**

Klingon Cruiser *Star Trek: The Motion Picture* die-cast.

$20   **$30**

ENESCO, 1992

The Original Series Enterprise on command insignia base.

$25   **$45**

ENCO, 1976

Space Fun Helmet, Enco, 1976.

Space Fun Helmet. Most collectors agree that this is certainly one of the stranger toys ever released. Though the bug-eyed Astro helmet was pretty strange as well, at least it had something of a fantasy/sci-fi look to it and didn't resemble part of a fire truck stuck on a scooter helmet.

$200   **$225**

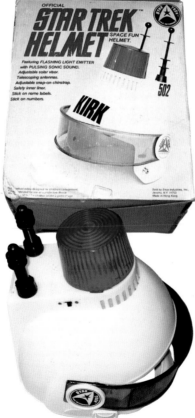

ERNST, 1988

Porcelain Doll Collection. The head, upper body, hands, and feet on these large 14" figures are porcelain.

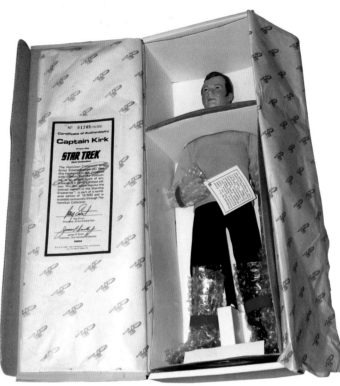

Kirk, Porcelain Doll Collection, Ernst, 1988.

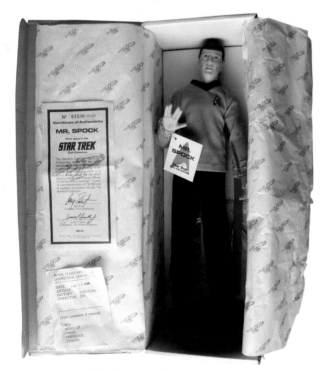

Spock, Porcelain Doll Collection, Ernst, 1988.

Captain Kirk. Accessories: Phaser and Communicator.
    $100   **$150**
Mr. Spock. Accessories: Phaser and Communicator.
    $100   **$150**
Doctor McCoy. Accessories: Clear plastic beaker.
    $200   **$250**
Scotty. Accessories: Phaser and Communicator.
    $200   **$250**
Lt. Uhura. Accessories: Earrings.
    $225   **$265**
Chekov. Accessories: Phaser and Communicator.
    $200   **$250**

ERTL, 1989

Star Trek V: The Final Frontier die-cast miniature ships:

U.S.S. Enterprise, No. 1372.
> **$15**   **$25**

Klingon Bird of Prey, No. 1374.
> **$15**   **$25**

U.S.S. Enterprise and Klingon Bird of Prey die-casts, from *Star Trek V: The Final Frontier*, Ertl, 1989.

FRANKLIN MINT, 1990

Franklin Mint specializes in highly detailed pewter and other unique specialized display pieces. All pieces included a certificate of authenticity.

U.S.S. Enterprise, Franklin Mint.

PEWTER SHIPS

These ships are somewhat fragile due to the inherent softness of pewter. The engine nacelle supports on the Enterprise, for example, are notorious for bending down over time. The gold radar dish can easily be snapped off. The Klingon Battle Cruiser is known for the head as well as the ends of its engines bending or breaking. The other ships suffer from the same or similar problems. These are, however, spectacularly detailed, and feature crystal embellishments and gold-plated trim that makes for an impressive display in any collection.

U.S.S. Enterprise NCC-1701; pewter ship featuring red crystal engine on a command insignia base.
> **$100**   **$250**

Klingon Battle Cruiser; pewter ship featuring on a command insignia base.
> **$100**   **$250**

Romulan Bird of Prey; pewter ship featuring on a command insignia base.
> **$100**   **$250**

Galileo II Shuttlecraft; pewter ship featuring on a command insignia base.
> **$95**   **$175**

Klingon Bird of Prey; pewter ship featuring on a command insignia base.
> **$100**   **$250**

U.S.S. Excelsior; pewter ship featuring on a command insignia base.
> **$250**   **$350**

WEAPONS

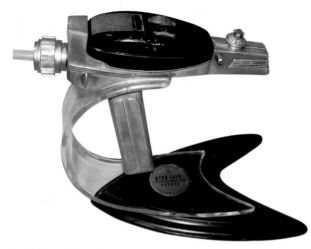

The Original Series Type 2 Phaser. Features removable Type 1 Phaser, working dials and unique plastic display stand on *Star Trek* symbol base.

$150   **$350**

The Original Series Klingon Disruptor. Highly detailed with unique plastic display stand on Klingon symbol base.

$150   **$350**

Detailed pewter Phaser, Franklin Mint.

OTHER DISPLAYS/DIORAMAS

Insignia Collection, 1995 (first set). This set features 12 insignia pieces in .925 sterling silver with gold plating that were authenticated by Paramount Pictures. Each insignia comes with its own certificate of authenticity and a complete description and history of the insignia. Each individual *Star Trek* insignia was shipped in its own velvet-lined box every two months and originally cost around $75 to $80 each. The blue velvet lined glass front display case was also sold separately.

Insignia Collection, Franklin Mint, 1995.

Large 21-1/2" x 16" display case.

$50   **$75**

Insignia Collection, Franklin Mint, 1995.

U.S.S. Enterprise Command Insignia.

Captains Bar.

Starfleet flag Admiral.

Vulcan IDIC—Infinite Diversity in Infinite Combinations.

United Federation of Planets Pennant.

Commander Pin.

Romulan Bird of Prey Symbol.

Ferengi Insignia.

United Federation of Planets Seal.

Starfleet Officers Bar.

Klingon Empire Insignia.

Star Trek:The Next Generation Communicator.

Each individually boxed Insignia.

$50   **$100**

Beyond The Final Frontier. Three-ship pewter display of the Enterprise, Klingon, and Romulan ships on black display base.

$100   **$150**

City on The Edge Forever Diorama. Highly detailed diorama of the scene where McCoy leaps through the Guardian of Forever.

$150   **$200**

30th Anniversary Crystal Sculpture. Spectacular display of the Enterprise made out of shimmering crystal "flying" through an outline of the *Star Trek* command insignia symbol.

$200   **$275**

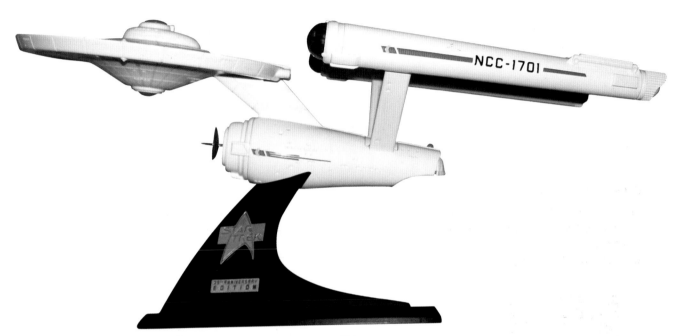

Removable section reveals detailed bridge, U.S.S. Enterprise Die-Cast Franklin Mint, 1991.

U.S.S. Enterprise Die-Cast, Franklin Mint, 1991.

U.S.S. Enterprise Die-Cast, 25th Anniversary, 1991

Large bright white heavy die-cast model of the Starship Enterprise features a pullout "shuttle bay" in the rear revealing a hidden Galileo Shuttlecraft and on the top of the main saucer a removable hull section displaying a small yet detailed bridge.

$250   **$400**

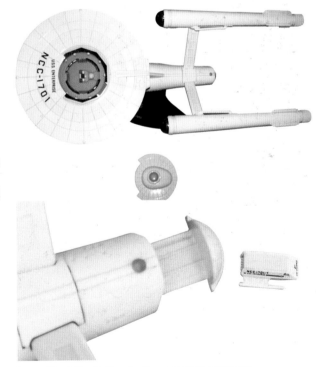

Image of the Galileo Shuttlecraft with opened shuttle bay on ship.

GAF, 1968

View-Master Reel "Omega Glory," GAF, 1968.

View-Master "Omega Glory."
$20   **$25**

GAF, 1974

Talking View-Master Reel, Mr. Spock's Time Trek, GAF, 1974.

Talking View-Master, Mr. Spock's Time Trek.
$15   **$30**

View-Master Reel, Mr. Spock's Time Trek, GAF, 1974.

View-Master, Mr. Spock's Time Trek.
$15   **$20**

GAF, 1978

View-Master set: Spacemen Theatre in the Round, GAF, 1978.

View-Master: Spacemen Theatre in the Round.
$75   **$95**

GAF, 1979

View-Master *Star Trek: The Motion Picture.*
$20   **$25**
View-Master Gift Pack *Star Trek: The Motion Picture.*
$100   **$150**

GALOOB, 1993-97

Star Trek MicroMachines, Galoob, 1993-97.

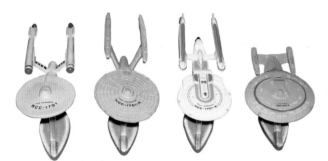

Star Trek MicroMachines, Galoob, 1993-97.

MicroMachines. Set of three Star Trek ships per "Collection" package. Larger sets were made available as more collections were created. I have seen loose ships sell for much more than a MIB Collection set of the same ships:

First edition:

Collection One: S.S. Botany Bay; Klingon Battlecruiser; Romulan Bird of Prey.

$45   **$65**

Collection Two: Shuttlecraft Galileo II; Deep Space K-7; U.S.S. Enterprise.

$45   **$65**

Collection Three: Earth Spacedock; Klingon Bird of Prey; U.S.S. Reliant.

$35   **$45**

Collection Four: Vulcan warp sled Surak; U.S.S. Grissom; U.S.S. Excelsior NX-2000 (rare variant).

$75   **$125**

Vulcan warp sled Surak; U.S.S. Grissom; U.S.S. Excelsior NCC-2000 (common variant).

$55   **$75**

Limited Edition Collector's Set: U.S.S. Enterprise-A.

$25   **$45**

Star Trek MicroMachines, Galoob, 1993-97.

Second edition, Collection One: Enterprise (NCC-1701); Klingon Battlecruiser; Romulan Bird of Prey.

$25   **$45**

Star Trek MicroMachines, Galoob, 1993-97.

Collection Two: Klingon Bird of Prey; Excelsior; Reliant.

$25   **$45**

$1.29

Enterprise Kite, High-Flyer, 1975.

HIGH-FLYER, 1975

Delta Wing Kite: Enterprise; Enterprise and Klingon; Spock.

$20   **$30**

IDEAL, 1978

Pocket Flix Movie Viewer, Ideal, 1978.

Pocket Flix Movie Viewer.

$40   **$75**

Pocket Flix Movie Reel, Ideal, 1978.

Pocket Flix Movie Reel.

$25   **$35**

JETCO, 1976

Metal detector. A working metal detector with *Star Trek*-themed design on the base and handle.

$225   **$400**

LARAMI, 1968

Binoculars.

$50   **$75**

Flashlite Ray Gun, Larami, 1968.

Flashlite Ray Gun.

$50   **$75**

LARAMI, 1979

I.D. Set, *Star Trek: The Motion Picture*, Larami, 1979.

I.D. Set *Star Trek: The Motion Picture*.

$15   **$20**

Space Viewer *Star Trek: The Motion Picture*.

$20   **$30**

The Motion Picture Magic Putty, two variants, Aviva, 1979.

Star Trek: The Motion Picture Magic Putty. Two Variants.

$15   **$25 each**

Flashlite Ray Gun, Larami, 1968.

LONE STAR, 1974

Star Trek Inter-Space Communicator, Lone Star, 1974.

Phaser Rocket Gun.
$100   **$150**
Star Trek Inter-Space Communicator.
$30   **$45**

Phaser Rocket Gun, Lone Star, 1974.

MAKOTO, 1978

Enterprise mobile, Makoto, 1978.

Six silver triple-nacelled Enterprise ships make up this unique mobile.
$50   **$65**

MARBLES

Star Trek marbles.

Unique marbles: Kirk marble; Spock marble; *Star Trek: The Motion Picture* marble.
$5   **$10 each**

MANON, 1990

2" *The Original Series* Enterprise made out of clear cut crystal mounted on a mirror base.
$150   **$200**

MARS, 1980

Star Trek: The Motion Picture Action Mobile, Mars, 1980.

Star Trek: The Motion Picture Action Mobile. This mobile features ship cut-outs from thick cardstock. Includes five ships: The Enterprise, Klingon Cruiser, Vulcan Shuttle, Worker Bee, and Travel Pod. Special mail-away promotion required five wrappers from one or more of the following candy companies: M&M's, Milky Way, Snickers, Summit, or Twix.
$35   **$45**

MCDONALD'S, 1979

Star Trek: The Motion Picture Happy Meals, McDonald's, 1979.

Star Trek Happy Meal Toys, McDonald's, 1979.

Star Trek: The Motion Picture Happy Meals. Each box included a comic printed on the box and a toy inside. Also see "food" and "comics" sections.

$10 $20

MEGO, 1974

Communicators. Two Communicators per package. These work with the Command Communication Console allowing you to talk between the communicators and the base unit. You can also use the Morse Code beeper to send "coded" messages between the Communicators and base unit. Three different package designs:

Window box Communicators, Mego, 1974.

Rare window box.

$225 $350

Solid box Communicators, Mego, 1974.

Solid box.

$175 $250

Carded Communicators, Mego, 1974.

Backer card.

$175 $250

MEGO, 1975

U.S.S. Enterprise Bridge Action Playset features a built-in Transporter mechanism and is sort of a toy within a toy—a very unique and innovative design for the time. Place your Mego figure in the transporter and spin the dial. Pushing down on one of the two top buttons determines whether the figure appears or disappears. Though the playset is far from accurate to the actual bridge from the show, it was a well-designed toy. It also includes a handle on top, making it a carrying case as well. Accessories include captain's chair, navigational/helm console, two stools, label sheets for captain's chair, navigational/helm console and Transporter, three double-sided "view screen" cards, and instruction sheet.

A few variations of this set are known to exist including the captain's chair and navigational/helm console in either blue or yellow, and the stools in either blue or black. Some foreign versions also have unique variations.

U.S.S. Enterprise Action Playset, Mego, 1975.

U.S.S. Enterprise Bridge Action Playset.

$150   **$250**

U.S.S. Enterprise Playset display with some of the crew and alien figures, Mego, 1975.

U.S.S. Enterprise Bridge Action Gift Set. Extremely rare set. Gift set also included the first five action figures in clear bags.

$1,000   **$2,000**

MEGO, 1976

Command Communications Console, Mego, 1976.

Command Communications Console. Designed to replicate the communications console on the Enterprise bridge, this command base also works with the Communicators either by voice or "code," allowing the users to communicate between the Communicator handsets and the base.

$150   **$200**

Phaser Battle Game, Mego, 1976.

Phaser Battle Game. Similar to the smaller "Telescreen Console" this larger tabletop game unit allows you to attack alien ships. Playing is more complex than the Telescreen Console, with more controls including dual action buttons for port and starboard shields featuring a large 16" view screen and a digital-style scoreboard. The Phaser Battle Game is considered one of the original home game systems. For its time it was a pretty cool and unique piece.

$600 $900

Mission to Gamma VI, Mego, 1976.

Mission to Gamma VI. Considered by many collectors to be one of the more obtainable of the rarer "holy grail" vintage pieces in the Star Trek collectors' universe. The playset is based on the large godlike idol seen in the classic episode, "The Apple." The large playset features glowing eyes, movable jaws, a hidden trap door, and a glove-style puppet creature to capture figures. It also includes four colorful aliens, and may look somewhat familiar to those who remember the old Barrel of Monkeys toy because they can link together.

$700 $1,500

Star Trekulator Calculator, Mego, 1976.

Star Trekulator Calculator. An actual working calculator featuring large numbers and nice artwork of Kirk in his casual green uniform.

$150 $200

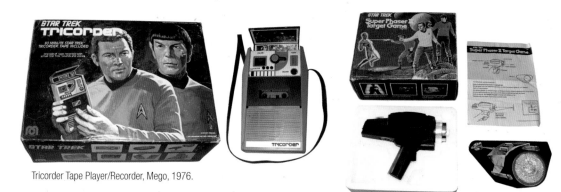

Tricorder Tape Player/Recorder, Mego, 1976.

Tricorder Tape Player/Recorder. This Tricorder toy is an actual working cassette tape player and recorder that also comes with a cassette. Early models featured a cassette tape with about 30 minutes of "The Menagerie" recorded on side A and space sounds recorded on side B. The cassette tape on later models featured again the prerecording of about 30 minutes of the Menagerie on side A but was blank on side B to allow the user to record their own Star Trek adventures.

$150 $225

Super Phaser II Target Game, Mego, 1976.

Super Phaser II Target Game. This role-playing toy features a light emitting a type 2-shaped Phaser beam with a sonic buzzer device that when fired at the included red-badged target reflector would activate the buzzer when hit. The target badge also displays the image of a Klingon D7 Battle Cruiser. This was a unique precursor to the 1980s Laser Tag craze.

$25 $35

MEGO, 1977

Star Trek Intergalactic Planetarium, Mego, 1977.

Intergalactic Planetarium. This is considered extremely rare and has rarely (if ever) been seen. Planetarium included light show projector, Enterprise light pointer, 14 constellation cards that show sections of the galaxy, a standard 20-minute cassette tape with pre-recorded Star Trek information.

$2,000   **$2,500**

Telescreen Console, Mego, 1977.

Telescreen Console. This toy is part game, part playset that allows you to place an 8" Mego action figure in the captain's chair. The console design is reminiscent of the tabletop computers seen in the Enterprise briefing room. Once you power up the unit, you line up the enemy ship in your sites and fire. You get to keep your own score for any hits you register by turning the manual scoring dial. The ability to place an action figure in the captain's chair was a brilliant move by Mego as it added extra play value and encouraged action figure sales.

$200   **$300**

MEGO, 1979

Star Trek The Motion Picture Enterprise Bridge Playset, Mego, 1979.

Star Trek: The Motion Picture Enterprise Bridge Playset. Not one of Mego's better creations. The 12" x 24" long Vacuform plastic playset is scaled for use with Mego's 3-3/4" Star Trek action figures. The toy has been criticized for its thin and easily breakable Vacuformed plastic bridge piece. The playset features a working docking port, helm control center, navigational station, captain's chair, science center, communications console, and authentic decal sheet.

$200   **$250**

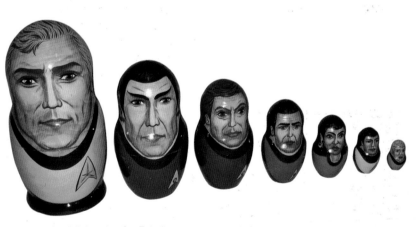

Russian nesting dolls in various Star Trek characters.

Russian Nesting Dolls, date unknown. Russian wooden dolls, also known as nesting dolls, are colorfully painted wooden dolls that continually break down to reveal smaller dolls within the larger one before it. In Russia these are called Matryoshka. In old Russian the name Matryona or Matriosha is a very popular female name. It is believed that this name has a Latin origin of "Mater," which means "mother," and was used to associate the image of a mother of a big peasant family in Russia. It became a symbolic name used to describe the brightly painted wooden figurines.

$50   **$75**

PALITOY, 1976

Transporter. This toy accessory was sold by Palitoy (Bradgate Division) in the United Kingdom. Palitoy is the foreign division of Mego, therefore the Mego logo does not appear on the packaging. You can, however, find "MEGO 1975" molded on the top of the unit. This is a pretty rare toy, and difficult to find complete in the box. It features some of the same artwork found on the Mego 8" action figure packaging. The Transporter toy is basically the Transporter mechanism from Mego's Enterprise Bridge Playset with slight differences like the yellow plastic roof. There is also no instruction sheet, as the operating instructions are printed on the outside of the box.

Transporter, Palitoy, 1976.

$150 $200

PLAYCO (UK), 1977

Star Trek Space Glider: Carded white styrofoam glider features yellow command insignia-type decal on wing and red plastic pistol-style launcher.

$55 $75

PLAYMATES, 1992

U.S.S. Enterprise, Playmates.

Classic Starship Enterprise, No. 6116. As seen in *The Original Series.* Features four ship sounds: photon torpedoes, phasers, warp drive, and bridge effects with light-up nacelles and display stand.

$100 $150

Starship Excelsior NCC-2000 in the box and loose, Playmates.

Classic Starship Excelsior NCC-2000, No. 6127. As seen in *Star Trek III: The Search for Spock.* Features four ship sounds: Energy ribbon, tractor beam, phasers, warning signal with light up deflector and display stand. Includes decals to create an Enterprise-B, which explains why the ship has the energy ribbon effect from the movie, *Star Trek: Generations.*

$125 $250

Starship Enterprise NCC-1701-B, Playmates.

Klingon Bird of Prey, K'Vort class cruiser, Playmates.

Starship Enterprise NCC-1701-B, No. 6172. Excelsior class vessel as seen in *Star Trek: Generations* features four ship sounds: energy ribbon, tractor beam, phasers, and warning signal with light-up deflector, display stand, and exclusive mini movie poster. Included decals to create Excelsior 2000 since this is really just a repackaging of that earlier Playmates toy.

$125 $250

Klingon Bird of Prey, No. 6174. K'Vort class cruiser as seen in the movie *Star Trek: Generations* features three ship sounds: torpedo launch, engine cruise, and disruptor with light-up engine exhaust and torpedo launcher. Includes deluxe movie stand, mini poster, and technical blueprint.

$55 $75

Star Trek Tricorder, Playmates.

Classic Tricorder, No. 6125. Features three Tricorder sounds, light-up viewscreen display, flashing indicators, and technical blueprint.

$75 $125

Classic Communicator, No. 6117. Features three Communicator sounds, working signal lights, flip-up grill and technical blueprint.

$100 $150

Romulan Bird-Of-Prey, Playmates.

Classic Romulan Bird of Prey, No. 16126. Features four ship sounds: Photon torpedoes, phasers, cloaking effect, and bridge effects with light up nacelles and display stand.

$65 $95

Classic Shuttlecraft Galileo, No. 16087. As seen in *The Original Series* episode, "Where No Man Has Gone Before." Features spring powered laser and exclusive 5" Captain Kirk figure.

$55 $75

Star Trek Phaser, Playmates.

Classic Phaser, No. 6118. Features two phaser sounds, light-up adjustable beam emitter, and technical blueprint.

$95 $150

Talk Back Communicator, Playmates.

Classic Talk Back Communicator, No. 16065. Record and play back your own voice. Also features status lights, flip-up grill, and technical blueprint.

$100 $150

Dr. McCoy's Medical Kit, Playmates.

Classic Dr. McCoy's Medical Kit,
No. 16088. Includes Protolaser with light-up
laser tip, medical scanner with digital sound,
and Starfleet diploma.
$75   **$125**

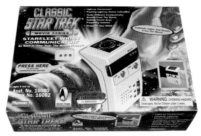

Wrist Communicator, Playmates.

Classic Wrist Communicator, No. 16082.
As seen in *Star Trek: The Motion Picture*.
Features three Communicator sounds, light
up viewscreen, flashing indicators, and
blueprint.
$45   **$65**

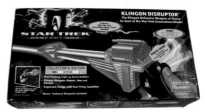

Klingon Disruptor, Playmates.

Klingon Disruptor, No. 6146. As seen in the
movie *Star Trek: Generations*. Features two
sounds, light-up flashing beam emitter,
exclusive mini movie poster, and technical
blueprint.
$25   **$45**

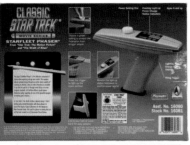

Starfleet Movie Phaser, Playmates.

Classic Starfleet Movie Phaser,
No. 16081. As first seen in the movie,
Star Trek II: The Wrath of Khan. Features
two phaser sounds, light-up energy beam
emitter, power indicator, and blueprint.
$65   **$95**

Captain Pike's laser Pistol, Playmates.

Captain Pike's Laser Pistol, No. 16127.
As seen in the pilot episode "The Cage."
Features two phaser sounds, light-up energy
beam emitter, and technical blueprint.
$75   **$100**
Classic Starfleet Phaser, No. 16144. As seen
in the movies, *Star Trek V: The Final Frontier*
and *Star Trek VI: The Undiscovered Country*.
Features two Phaser sounds, light-up beam
emitter, and blueprint.
$125   **$200**

Playmates complete toy line catalog, 1997.

Playmates Toy Catalog, 1997. Catalog binder
displaying full color pages of the current full
line of Playmates toys for 1997, including the
Star Trek toy line.
$20   **$30**

Playmates complete toy line catalog, 1998.

Playmates Toy Catalog, 1998. Catalog binder
displaying full-color pages of the current full
line of Playmates toys for 1998, including the
Star Trek toy line.
$20   **$30**

PROCTOR AND GAMBLE, 1989

Star Trek V: The Final Frontier promotional Communicators, Proctor and Gamble, 1989.

Star Trek V: The Final Frontier promotional Communicators for Proctor and Gamble. Working walkie talkies with flip-up grids and retractable antennae. Sold in pairs and shipped in plain brown box.

$75   **$100**

PYRA, 1991

4" *The Original Series* Enterprise mounted on a dome in clear cut crystal.

$250   **$300**

RAYLINE, 1968

Tracer Scope Rifle. Same as the Tracer gun and uses the same Jet Disc ammo. The Tracer Scope Rifle is much rarer than the Tracer Gun and is very difficult to find. This rarity is reflected in its estimated value.

$600   **$800**

RAYLINE, 1966

Tracer Gun front and back, Rayline, 1966.

Tracer Gun. The Tracer gun shoots lightweight plastic discs the size of a small coin. The discs used as ammunition are usually called Jet Discs. The Canadian version of the Star Trek Tracer Gun packaging is printed in both French and English. The Tracer gun was sold both as a Star Trek license as well as a plain packaged Tracer Gun with no television tie-in.

$75   **$150**

REMCO, 1967

Along with the Flying Rocket Plane, the Astro series of toys by Remco are among the rarest of all the Star Trek toys. It was a common practice for toy manufacturers in the 1960s and '70s to use molds from an existing toy line to create toys for a new line. The Star Trek Astrotank, Astrocruiser, and Astrotrain are actually Remco's Mighty Mike Astrotank and Astrotrain sets repackaged with Star Trek images on the boxes and Star Trek logo decals on the toys.

The Star Trek Astro Helmet and Rocket Pistol were repackaged from Remco's short-lived Hamilton Invaders playset toys.

Astro Helmet.
    $2,000   **$8,000**

Astrotrain.
    $3,000   **$6,000**

Rocket Pistol.
    $2,000   **$3,000**

Tracer Gun Ammo Discs, Rayline, 1966.

Tracer Gun Ammo Discs in package.
    $15   **$25**

Astrotank, top and side of box, Remco, 1967.

Astrotank.
    $3,000   **$9,000**

Astrocruiser, Remco, 1967.

Astrocruiser.
    $3,000   **$6,000**

Astro Buzz-Ray Gun.
    $450   **$750**

Astro Walkie-Talkie.
    $250   **$300**

REMCO, 1968

Flying Rocket Plane. This is another of the extremely rare Remco toys. This repackaged Remco toy was relabeled with Star Trek-themed decals and box art. Airplane toy has a battery unit connected to the plane by a cable to supply the power. Collectors still debate as to whether the Flying Rocket Plane or one of the Astro toys is rarest.

$5,000   **$12,000**

REMCO, 1975

Did you know that Superman and the Incredible Hulk both used Star Trek communicators? Well, maybe not in the comic books, but in the toy world they did. In another cost saving move, Remco reused some of the molds from its Star Trek Utility Belt toy to help create the Superman and Hulk Utility Belts. Surprisingly, the Remco Wonder Woman and Batman Utility Belts didn't reuse the communicator. The Star Trek Utility Belt came in three different box/artwork variations.

Superman utility belt, Remco.

Incredible Hulk utility belt, Remco.

Utility Belt box version #1, Remco, 1975.

Utility Belt box version #2, Remco, 1975.

Utility Belt box version #3, Remco, 1975.

Utility Belt box version #1.
$100   **$200**

Utility Belt box version #2.
$125   **$250**

Utility Belt box version #3.
$350   **$500**

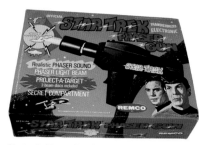

Electronic Phaser Gun, Remco, 1975.

Electronic Phaser Gun. When you pulled the trigger on Remco's Electronic Phaser Gun you got both a flashlight and a high pitch chirping sound.

$100   **$150**

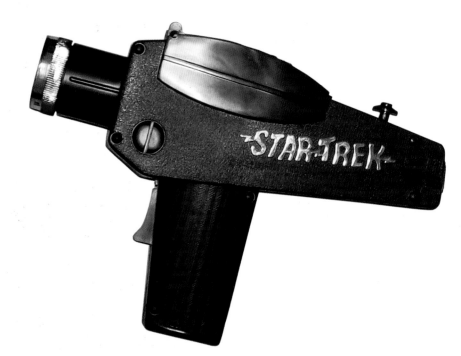

REMCO, 1976

U.S.S. Enterprise CSF, Remco, 1976.

CSF Canadian, Remco, 1976.

U.S.S. Enterprise CSF (Controlled Space Flight). This was Remco's version of Mattel's Vertibird toy. The Enterprise section features an electric motor in the saucer section of the ship. To make it fly there is a counterweight on the other end of the rod that is connected to the Enterprise section allowing it to fly forward and reverse, hover, and pick up the three included accessories with its attached hook. As with many of the early Star Trek toys, a few box artwork variations exist for the Enterprise CSF, as can be seen in the Canadian/foreign versions. There are two variations in the flying controls as well, with one using a turning controller knob, and the other using two control levers. Remco repackaged the Star-Trek CSF U.S.S. Enterprise (item #602) in 1979 to create the BatMan CSF Copter (item #605), Spider-Man CSF Copter (item #614), and Hulk CSF Copter (item #649).

$150   **$250**

Canadian/foreign.

$250   **$350**

SILVER DEER, 1990

3-3/4" original series Enterprise made out of clear cut crystal. Individually numbered and a limited edition of only 1,200.

$350   **$400**

SOUTH BEND, 1979

Electronic dueling Phasers game, South Bend, 1979.

Star Trek: The Motion Picture Duel Phaser II set. South Bend took the idea of Laser Tag to an interesting level when it released its Duel Phaser II gun toy set. These battery-powered electronic phasers were designed to target each other instead of a reflector as in the Mego Super Phaser II toy.

$125   **$200**

Belt Buckle and Insignia, South Bend, 1979.

Star Trek U.S.S. Enterprise, South Bend, 1979.

Electronic U.S.S. Enterprise. South Bend created what many collectors feel is one of the coolest Enterprise toys ever made. The ship is modular, allowing it to be taken apart and reassembled in 15 different configurations. Interestingly, the modular examples shown on the side of the box are movie versions of some of Franz Joseph's Star Fleet Technical Manual starship designs.

$200   **$225**

Belt Buckle and Insignia.

$35   **$45**

TOLTOYS, LTD (AUSTRALIA)

Battery Operated Space Complex, Toltoys, LTD.

Battery Operated Space Complex. This hard-to-find and unique vintage playset features space security modules, space crawler, lunar personnel carrier, computer motivator MK. II, mobile solar generator, and an astro prime mover. Just like many of the early Remco toys, this playset by the Australian toy company Toltoys does not depict anything actually seen on *Star Trek*.

$25   **$50**

WHITMAN, 1979
MAGIC SLATES

Magic Slates have a clear outer sheet layer that is written on with the included "pen." Pulling the outer film up and away erases your work.

Kirk, Spock, and Enterprise artwork on top.
$50   **$65**

Spock artwork on top.
$40   **$55**

Magic Slate with Enterprise artwork, Whitman, 1979.

Magic Slate with Kirk artwork, Whitman, 1979.

Enterprise artwork on top.
$30   **$45**

Kirk artwork on top.
$40   **$55**

CUSTOM TOYS/PLAYSETS:

As with action figures, quite a few fan-made custom playsets were produced over the years. Shown here is just one example of the kind of custom work that can be found that can add a unique look to any collection.

Scotty action figure with Engineering Playset.

Other action figures with Engineering Playset.

Custom-made Mego-style Engineering Playset. Scotty action figure included, and other action figures sold separately. This custom playset is made in the style of the Mego Enterprise Playset. Some of the many features include: Jefferies Tube, Decontamination Chamber, Hallways, Shuttle Bay, Sliding door, and Medical Sick Bay.

$350   **$450**

Jefferies Tube, Engineering Playset.

Decontamination Chamber, Engineering Playset.

Hallways, Engineering Playset.

MISCELLANEOUS

Working Communicator with metal grid and spinning Morei',
Star Trek The Experience.

Talosian Maquette Bust.

Star Trek The Experience Communicator. Features metal grid, working lights, sounds and spinning Morei'. Sold at the Star Trek Experience in Las Vegas, Nev. Considered one of the most accurate Communicators currently available.

$125   **$200**

Talosian Maquette Bust by Illusive Concepts. Large detailed bust of the Talosian Keeper from the pilot episode, "The Cage," and the later two-part episode, "The Menagerie." Features lifelike "skin," fabric outfit, and jeweled necklace. Each bust includes a plaque displaying the number sequence on its base. Includes certificate of authenticity. Limited edition of only 7,500.

$100   **$150**

STUFFED/PLUSH

Plush stuffed bears in various characters.

NORTH AMERICAN BEAR COMPANY, 1979
VIB (VERY IMPORTANT BEAR)

Mr. Spock VIB Bear, North American Bear Company, 1979.

Large well-made bear features Communicator and Tricorder props.

$65   **$85**

Large Mr. Spock Bear.

Mr. Spock Bear, large.

$35   **$45**

Small Mr. Spock Bear.

Mr. Spock Bear, small.

$25   **$35**

Captain Kirk Bear.

Captain Kirk Bear.

$35   **$45**

Lt. Uhura Bear.

Lt. Uhura Bear. Features red cloth dress and black boots.

$35   **$45**

Kirk Bear in red movie uniform.

Kirk Bear in red movie uniform.

$45   **$55**

TRIBBLES

Since "The Trouble with Tribbles" first aired, Tribbles have been a very popular collectible.
As Lt. Uhura says in the episode, "They give us love. A Tribble is the only love money can buy."

Tribbles, light brown, white and dark brown, Starstruck, 1991.

"From the far regions of the galaxy…Only the sweetest creature known to man—Tribbles." Available in three colors.
Sold in open-style packaging. The white Tribble is the most desirable followed by the light brown, then the dark brown.

$25 $45 each

STAR TREK THE EXPERIENCE

Small Tribbles sold loose with hangtag. Available individually and in assorted colors including white, gray, and brown.

$25   **$30**

Small Electronic Tribble, Star Trek The Experience.

Small Tribbles sold loose with hangtag. Electronic version. Tap or pat the Tribble and it shakes and "purrs." Available individually and in assorted colors including white, gray, and brown.

$45   **$55**

Large Electronic Tribble, Star Trek The Experience.

Large electronic Tribble is well over twice the size of small versions.

$65   **$85**

STAR TREK THE EXPERIENCE

Live Tribble, Do Not Feed, Star Trek The Experience.

Tribble in a live specimen type container "Handle With Care-Do Not Feed." Available in assorted colors; white is the most desirable.

$25   **$45**

PLUSH/STUFFED STARSHIPS

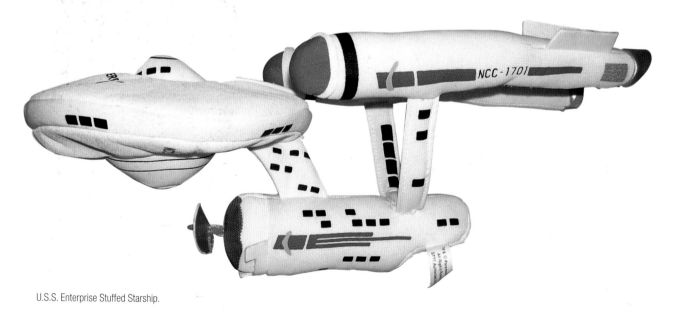

U.S.S. Enterprise Stuffed Starship.

U.S.S. Enterprise Starship.

$25   **$45**

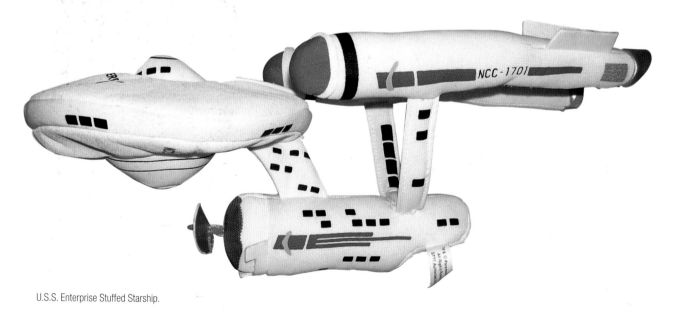

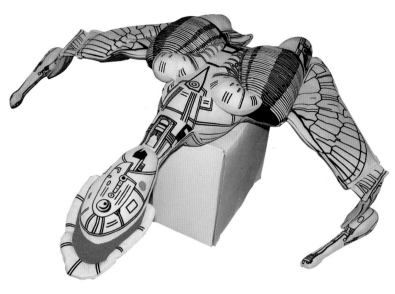

Klingon Bird of Prey Plush Starship.

Klingon Bird of Prey Starship.
$25   **$45**

G4 promotional foam hand.

Foam Hand, Star Trek G4, "Tune in and prosper." Foam hand Vulcan salute advertisement for *Star Trek: The Original Series* on the G4 channel.
$15   **$25**

OTHER TOYS

SMITHSONIAN MUSEUM SHOPS, 1987

U.S.S. Enterprise die-cast, Smithsonian Museum Shops, 1987.

U.S.S. Enterprise die-cast metal miniature ship.
$25   **$35**

UNIVERSAL STUDIOS TOUR, 1988

Star Trek Adventure Carrying Case and contents, Universal Studios Tour, 1988.

Adventure Carrying Case. Features detailed MS-1 Landing Party System graphics inside, including a lenticular motion card.
$25   **$45**

Trading/Collector Cards

A&BC, BRITISH, 1969

Front and back views of several cards color set, A & BC, 1969.

Color set of 55 cards:

Complete set.	Display box.	Wrapper.
$1,000 **$2,000**	**$750** **$1,000**	**$250** **$500**
Single cards.	Unopened box.	Unopened pack.
$10 **$25**	**Value unknown-extremely rare.**	**Value unknown-extremely rare.**

LEAF, 1967

Selection of loose cards, LEAF, 1967.

Set includes 72 black and white cards:

Complete set.
    $1,000   **$2,500**
Display box.
    $600   **$1,000**
Single cards.
    $15   **$45**

Unopened box complete set, LEAF, 1967.

Unopened box.
    Value unknown-extremely rare
Unopened pack.
    $300   **$500**
Wrapper.
    $200   **$400**
#1, #72.
    $20   **$50**

LEAF, 1967

Complete set of European reprints, LEAF, 1967.

European reprint set of 72 black and white cards:

Complete set.
    $25   **$75**
Single cards.
    $.50   **$1**
Uncut sheet.
    $50   **$100**

TOPPS, 1976

Store display box and Star Trek gum card wrapper,
TOPPS, 1976.

Star Trek gum cards, TOPPS, 1976.

Star Trek gum card stickers, TOPPS, 1976.

Set of 88 color cards and 22 stickers:

Complete set.		Sticker set.	
$200	**$400**	**$100**	**$175**
Store display box.		Unopened box.	
$25	**$50**	**$500**	**$1000**
Single cards: #1, #88.		Wrapper.	
$5	**$10**	**$5**	**$15**
Single stickers.			
$5	**$8**		

TOPPS, 1979

Gum cards, *Star Trek: The Motion Picture*, TOPPS, 1979.

Gum card stickers, *Star Trek: The Motion Picture*, TOPPS, 1979.

Star Trek: The Motion Picture set of 88 cards and 22 stickers.

Complete set.	
$50	**$75**
Display box (empty).	
$10	**$20**
Single cards.	
$1	**$2**
Single stickers.	
$1	**$2**
Sticker set.	
$15	**$20**
Unopened box.	
$125	**$175**
Wrapper.	
$1	**$2**

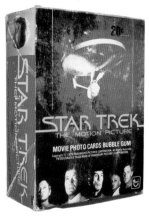

Unopened box set, *Star Trek: The Motion Picture*, TOPPS, 1979.

BREAD COLLECTOR CARDS, 1979

Each set includes 33 cards:

Colonial Bread set.		
	$20	**$30**
Kilpatrick Bread set.		
	$20	**$30**
Manor Bread set.		
	$30	**$40**
Rainbo Bread set.		
	$15	**$20**
Single cards.		
	$1	**$2**

Rainbo Bread cards, BREAD Collector cards, 1979.

STAR TREK II: THE WRATH OF KHAN MOVIE TRADING CARDS, DUTCH, 1982

Star Trek II The Wrath of Khan Movie Trading Cards, Dutch 1982.

Fairly rare Holland-issued 100-card set. Cards are slightly smaller than standard trading cards.

Unopened box and uncut sheets are rare.

Each card.		
	$1	**$2**
Card wrapper.		
	$10	**$15**
Complete set.		
	$100	**$250**
Uncut sheet.		
	$75	**$100**
Display box.		
	$50	**$75**
Unopened box.		
	$250	**$400**

MODERN RELEASES

A wide variety of different collector cards have been released in recent years. Many appear to contain similar looking designs and images to previously released card sets. Here are some examples of the trading and collector cards available.

Star Trek Master Series Trading Cards.   Star Trek Official Trading Cards Series I.

Master Series 1993-1994 Trading Cards.

$20   **$25 per box**

Official Trading Cards Series I.

$20   **$25 per box**

Star Trek Official Trading Cards Series II.

Star Trek Edition Collector Cards, SkyBox.

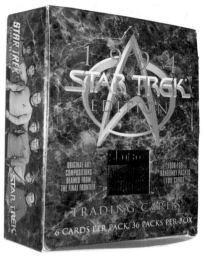

Star Trek Edition Collector cards, SkyBox.

Official Trading Cards Series II.

$20　　　　　**$25 per box**

Star Trek Edition Collector Cards
by SkyBox.

$25　　　　　**$35 per box**

Star Trek Edition Collector cards
by SkyBox, 1994.

$25　　　　　**$30 per box**

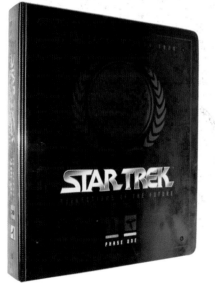

Star Trek Reflections of the Future card binder.

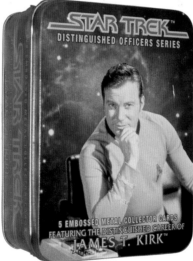

Star Trek Distinguished Officers Series cards in tin.

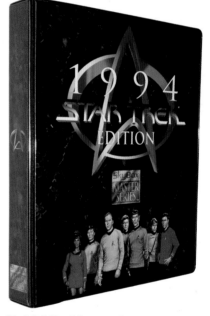

Star Trek Edition Collector card binder.

Star Trek Reflections of the Future card
binder.

$20　　　　　**$25**

Star Trek Distinguished Officers Series
collector cards. Packaged in a limited edition
metal tin card holder.

$15　　　　　**$20**

Star Trek Edition Collector card binder.

$20　　　　　**$25**

Star Trek Reflections of the Future collector
cards.

$25　　　　　**$35 per box**

Star Trek :The Original Series lenticular "In Motion" collector cards.

Star Trek Art & Images card set.

Star Trek: The Original Series

"In Motion" collector cards. Three Lenticular cards per pack.

$25   **$45 per box**

Star Trek Art & Images card set. Images taken from the original series and given an "artistic" flare. This is a very unusual set and has become popular in both the collector card circles as well as with Star Trek collectors. The cards feature pictures from the original series and have gone through what looks to be a computer enhancement to give each card a unique painted/artist effect.

$25   **$35**

Star Trek: The Animated Series card set.

Star Trek: The Animated Series card set;
180-plus card set featuring images from the Animated Series.

$20   **$25 per set**

Star Trek: The Animated Series advertisement cards.

Star Trek: The Animated Series
advertisement cards.

$25   **$45 per set**

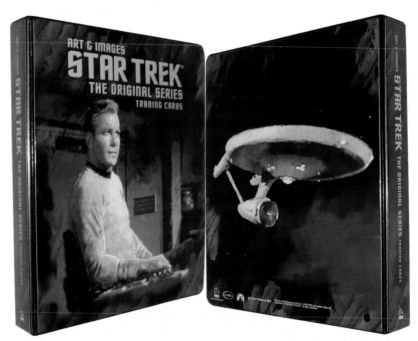

Star Trek Art & Images card binder.

Art & Images card binder.

$35   **$45**

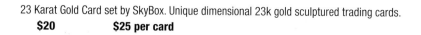

Star Trek 23 Karat Gold Cards, SkyBox.

Kirk, Spock, and McCoy in the Transporter, SkyBox Gold card.

"City on the Edge of Forever," SkyBox Gold card.

23 Karat Gold Card set by SkyBox. Unique dimensional 23k gold sculptured trading cards.

$20   **$25 per card**

Star Trek Generations, SkyBox Gold card.

Star Trek II: The Wrath of Khan Photo Collector Cards.

Star Trek II: The Wrath of Khan Photo Collector Cards. Photo cards were 5" x 7" and were packaged 2 giant cards to a "bag." Includes Kirk, Spock, Khan, Enterprise.

$10   **$15 per bag**

Collector Card store poster advertisement.

Collector Card store poster advertisement.

$5   **$15**

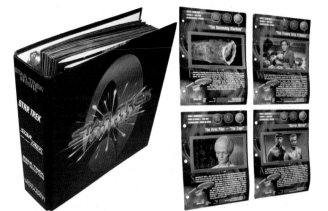

Star Trek Universe Fact and Photo cards. Licensed by Paramount Pictures, each 8" x 10" glossy card highlights many of the facts and trivia from just about every aspect of Star Trek. After sending away for the introductory offer for the first 30 cards, each additional set of cards would then be sent. Each packet of cards shipped would contain a series of random cards covering different series. It would take a lot of these packs to try and complete a full set/series:

Starter binder with starter a set of 30 cards.

$5   **$10**

Additional card packets.

$1   **$5**

Star Trek Universe Fact and Photo collector card set.

CARD PLAQUES

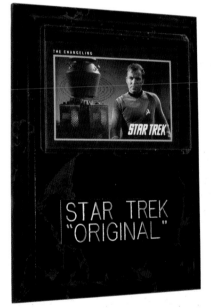

Star Trek wooden collector card plaque.

Small wooden plaques featuring a collector card from a set released based on the original series.

$5   **$10**

PRE-PAID PHONE CARDS

Pre-Paid phone cards.

Pre-paid phone cards with artwork of the various Star Trek movie posters:

Phone cards.

$5   **$10 each**

Uncut sheet.

$45   **$55**

STAR TREK ID COLLECTOR CARDS

Star Trek ID collector cards.

Individually themed ID wallet cards include: Command Insignia ID card; Sciences Insignia ID card; Engineering Insignia ID card; Vulcan IDIC ID card; Klingon Symbol ID card.

$1   **$5 each**

Video and Laser Discs

Paramount Home Video made history in the early 1980s when it released *Star Trek II: The Wrath of Khan* on Beta and VHS formats at the "bargain" price of $24.99 during the height of the "Format Wars." The low price and high interest in the popular film attracted consumers to video in record-breaking numbers, and Paramount quickly reduced prices on other titles to capitalize on the frenzy.

VIDEO DISCS

RCA SELECTRA VISION VIDEO DISCS, 1979

The Menagerie, RCA Selectra Vision Video Discs, 1979.

Amok Time/Journey to Babel, RCA Selectra Vision Video Discs, 1979.

City On the Edge of Forever/Let That Be Your Last Battlefield, RCA Selectra Vision Video Discs, 1979.

Balance of Terror/Mirror, Mirror, RCA Selectra Vision Video Discs, 1979.

Star Trek: The Original Series. Two episodes per disc made up the 79 episodes.

$5 $15

RCA SELECTRA VISION VIDEO DISCS, 1981

Star Trek: The Motion Picture.
$25 $35

LASER DISCS

PIONEER LASER DISCS, 1982

The Wrath of Khan Laser Disc.

The Search for Spock Laser Disc.

The Final Frontier Laser Disc.

The Undiscovered Country Laser Disc.

The Original Series on Laser Disc Collection. Two episodes per disc make up the 79 episodes.
$25   **$35 per disc**

The Animated Series on Laser Disc Collection. Two episodes per disc make up the 22 episodes
$25   **$35 per disc**

The Motion Pictures on Laser Disc Collection:

Star Trek: The Motion Picture.

Star Trek II: The Wrath of Khan.

Star Trek III: The Search for Spock.

Star Trek IV: The Voyage Home.

Star Trek V: The Final Frontier.

Star Trek VI: The Undiscovered Country.
$25   **$35 each**

BETA, SONY
PARAMOUNT HOME VIDEO

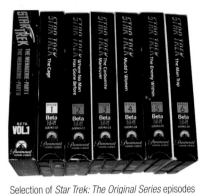

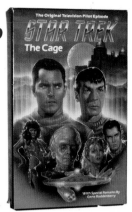

Selection of *Star Trek: The Original Series* episodes on Beta, Paramount Home Video.

"The Cage" on Beta, Paramount Home Video.

"Where No Man Has Gone Before" on Beta, Paramount Home Video.

Two episodes per tape of *The Original Series* on Beta, Paramount Home Video.

Star Trek: The Original Series on Beta. One episode per tape made up the 79 episodes available.

$5   **$10 per tape**

Paramount Home Video. *Star Trek: The Original Series* on Beta, two episodes per tape.

$5   **$10 per tape**

SUPER-8

Star Trek IV: The Voyage Home on Super-8.

It is unknown how many different *Star Trek* tapes were produced in the Super-8 format. They are rare finds on today's collector market.

Star Trek IV: The Voyage Home.

$15   **$25**

VHS
COLUMBIA HOUSE HOME VIDEO, 1990

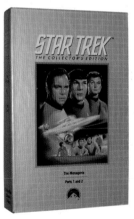

The Menagerie Parts I & II on VHS, Columbia House Home Video, 1990.

Star Trek: The Original Series. Two episodes per tape made up the 79 episodes available.

$5   **$10**

MOUNTAIN VIDEO, BRITISH, 1990S

Star Trek: The Original Series on VHS, Mountain Video.

Star Trek: The Original Series. One episode per tape made up the 79 episodes available.

$10   **$15 per tape**

PARAMOUNT HOME VIDEO, 1986-93

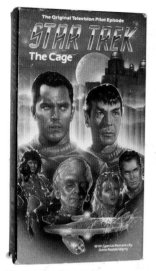 

Star Trek: The Original Series on VHS, Paramount Home Video.

Re-issued Star Trek: The Original Series with new artwork, VHS, Paramount Home Video.

Star Trek: The Original Series on VHS. One episode per tape made up the 79 episodes available.

$5 $10 per tape

Re-issued with new artwork.

$5 $10 per tape

PARAMOUNT HOME VIDEO, 1992-94

Star Trek: The Animated Series on VHS. Two episodes per tape made up the 22 episodes available.

$5 $15 per tape

Number 000001 of a Limited Edition Movie Collection on VHS, Paramount Home Video (UK).

PARAMOUNT HOME VIDEO, 1992-98

The Motion Picture on VHS, Paramount Home Video.

The Motion Pictures Collection on VHS. The movies were first released individually on VHS, then released together as boxed sets. Due to the release of new movies in theaters and then later on home video, each older boxed set was updated and re-released with the "latest" movie added. Since VHS is all but dead with DVD and now Blue-Ray, VHS tapes usually have little to no value unless rare, unique, or in a deluxe numbered set.

Star Trek: The Motion Picture.

Star Trek II: The Wrath of Khan.

Star Trek III: The Search for Spock.

Star Trek IV: The Voyage Home.

Star Trek V: The Final Frontier.

Star Trek VI: The Undiscovered Country.

$5 $10 each

Paramount Home Video Poster.

Paramount Home Video Poster.

$20 $25

PARAMOUNT HOME VIDEO, BRITISH (UK), 1996

Limited Edition 30th Anniversary Boxed Set. The Movie Collection on VHS. Each deluxe boxed set was individually numbered and included a special 26-page booklet. The boxed set pictured in this book is extremely rare as it is the very first set released and contains a Starfleet Registry No. 000001. The higher of the two values stated here is based on obtaining a very low numbered set, like the one seen here. Each movie was digitally re-mastered and came in a special sleeve.

$50 $150

STAR TREK BLOOPERS

Viewing the blooper reel is one of the most popular events at any Star Trek convention. Compilations of the cast's on-set bloopers and flubs sometimes include small movie-style clips originally assembled by the film/edit crew as humorous versions of "dailies." These clips eventually made their way to VHS. Quality varies from somewhat "watchable" to pretty grainy footage, but fans appreciate these unique slices of the filming process.

Star Trek Bloopers on VHS.

$5   **$25**

TELSTAR VIDEO, BRITISH, EARLY 1990S

The Sci-Fi Master game, Star Trek Edition, TELSTAR Video.

Trivial Pursuit on VHS-PAL. The Sci-Fi Master Game. *Star Trek* Edition.

$25   **$45**

DVD

PARAMOUNT HOME VIDEO, 1999-PRESENT

 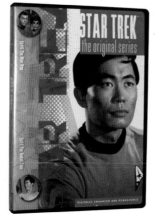  

"Where No Man Has Gone Before" and "The Corbomite Maneuver" on DVD.

"The Man Trap" and "The Naked Time" on DVD.

"Charlie X" and "Balance of Terror" on DVD.

Seasons one, two and three in boxed DVD sets.

The Original Series released on DVD. Episodes were first released two episodes per DVD. This is the same dual episode format Paramount used on the VHS versions.

Star Trek: The Original Series DVD Collection. 40 discs made up the entire set and were sold individually with two episodes per DVD.

$15   **$25 per disc**

Star Trek: The Original Series boxed DVD set. Each boxed set was sold either in a display box or shrink wrapped around the plastic case.

Season one (yellow); season two (blue); season three (red).

$45   **$75 per boxed set**

Star Trek remastered on HD-DVD.

Trekkies and Trekkies 2 on DVD.

Star Trek: The Original Series HD-DVD. CBS-Paramount released on HD-DVD the re-mastered first season of The Original Series. These newly remastered HD-DVD versions feature updated special effects given a slightly "grainy" effect to seamlessly match the original 1960s footage. Some re-mastered episodes now feature additional scenes. As of this writing, the HD-DVD format was discontinued in favor of Blue-Ray. This means that prices for HD-DVD releases will begin to drop as sellers begin to clear out current inventory. When and if the second or third seasons might be released in HD-DVD format remains unknown.

Season One.

$150   **$250**

Trekkies. A documentary about the fans. Hosted by Denise Crosby, Lt. Natasha Yar from *Star Trek: The Next Generation,* the documentary interviews and follows a variety of fans through mostly everyday life.

$15   **$20**

Trekkies 2. Sequel to the popular Trekkies documentary. The continuing adventures and everyday life of what some would consider fanatical fans.

$15   **$20**

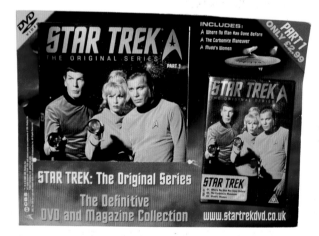

UK British release of *The Original Series* on DVD with bonus magazine.

Complete set of all three seasons in one boxed set.

UK British release of *Star Trek: The Original Series* on DVD. Each DVD featured three episodes per disc and included a magazine.

$25   **$35**

Complete set of all three seasons in one boxed set. Interesting looking well produced short run DVD boxed set containing all three seasons. Rare. Possibly fan made.

$75   **$95**

Special Director's Edition, *Star Trek: The Motion Picture* on DVD.

Special Director's Edition, *Star Trek II: The Wrath of Khan* on DVD.

Special Collector's Edition, *Star Trek III: The Search for Spock* on DVD.

Special Collector's Edition, *Star Trek IV: The Voyage Home* on DVD.

Special Edition The Final Frontier on DVD.

Special Edition The Undiscovered Country on DVD.

THE MOTION PICTURES COLLECTION

Each movie was first released individually, and then reissued individually as a special collector edition with added bonus features. The films have also been released as a complete set.

Star Trek: The Motion Picture was completely updated and re-mastered for its re-released DVD. Director Robert Wise worked with Industrial Light & Magic (ILM) to update the special effects, and finally made the movie what he had wanted it to be back in 1979. Those fans yet to see this remastered version are in for a treat.

Star Trek: The Motion Picture.

Star Trek II: The Wrath of Khan.

Star Trek III: The Search for Spock.

Star Trek IV: The Voyage Home.

Star Trek V: The Final Frontier.

Star Trek VI: The Undiscovered Country.

$10   **$25**

STAR TREK: THE ANIMATED SERIES

The animated series on DVD has existed for a while now, thanks to some very impressive fan-made creations:

Unknown manufacturer.

$25   **$45**

Paramount Pictures.

$65   **$95**

The Animated Series on DVD. Possibly fan made.

The "Official" Animated Series on DVD.

STAR TREK BLOOPERS ON DVD

Star Trek Bloopers on DVD. Fan produced.

Convention or fan-made compilations of on-set bloopers and flubs by the cast or small movies originally made by the crew as humorous type film "dailies" that have since found their way onto video and now DVD. Quality averages from somewhat watchable to pretty grainy footage.

$5   **$20**

STAR TREK PERSONAL MEMORABILIA COLLECTIONS DVD

My personal Star Trek collection on DVD, CATV Channel 8.

In the fall of 2007, Steve Giroux at CATV-8 in White River Junction, Vermont interviewed me and shot extensive footage of my collection. The roughly one-hour interview was then aired locally and is now available on DVD.

$10 shipped

ADDITIONAL ITEMS OF INTEREST

STAR TREK ORIGINAL FILM CEL DISPLAYS

Star Trek II: The Wrath of Khan film cel display.

Star Trek IV: he Voyage Home film cel display.

Star Trek: Generations film cel display.

Unique displays made up of sections from a reel of movie film.

Star Trek: The Motion Picture.

Star Trek II: The Wrath of Khan.

Star Trek III: The Search for Spock.

Star Trek IV: The Voyage Home.

Star Trek V: The Final Frontier.

Star Trek VI: The Undiscovered Country.

Star Trek: Generations.

$25   **$45**

STAR TREK ORIGINAL FILM CELS FROM STAR TREK: THE MOTION PICTURE

Star Trek: The Motion Picture original film cels.

One-of-a-kind original film cels encased in an acrylic see-through display.

Film cel, single.

$5   **$15**

Film cel, boxed set.

$25   **$45**

STAR TREK FILM CELS IN FRAMED DISPLAY

The Motion Picture film cells in framed display.

Cels from *Star Trek: The Motion Picture*, limited edition of only 100.

$25   **$45**

STAR TREK SLIDES

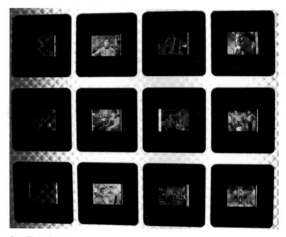

Star Trek slides.

Slides featuring scenes from *The Original Series:*

Individual slides.

$1   **$5**

Sheet of slides.

$10   **$25**

STORE PROMOTIONAL ITEMS

Star Trek V: The Final Frontier video tabletop displays.

Paramount Home Video, 1989. *The Final Frontier* tabletop video displays of Kirk and Spock.

$10   **$20 for the set**

Star Trek Video Collection vinyl store banner.

*Star Trek Video Collectio*n large vinyl banner.

$35   **$55**

Plastic *Star Trek Video Collection* hanging store sign.

Star Trek: The Star Trek Video Collection plastic hanging store display sign. Display was shipped in a plain brown box stamped on the bottom, Paramount.

$25   **$45**

More to Help You Prosper in Your Collecting

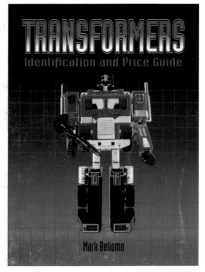

TRANSFORMERS
Identification and Price Guide
by Mark Bellomo

Explore the value and true identity of your favorite "robots in disguise" collectible toys using the pricing, listings and 1,000+ color photos in this definitive Transformers guide.

Determine the true identity of each robot, their role, motto, alternate mode, and a ranking of key traits they possess, including strength, intelligence, speed, endurance, and firepower.

Softcover • 8¼" x 10⅞" • 256 pages
1,000 color photos
Item# Z0516 • $24.99

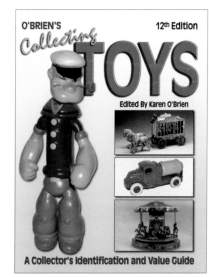

O'BRIEN'S COLLECTING TOYS
12th Edition
Edited by Karen O'Brien

More than 17,000 listings with 50,000 values for toys from the 1880s to 1950s include history, current values, manufacturer information and more.

Categories of collectible toys include:
- Aircraft
- Premiums
- Guns
- Wooden Toys
- Battery Operated
- Tin Wind-Up

Softcover • 8¼" x 10⅞" • 768 pages
3,000 b&w photos
16-page color section
Item# CTY12 • $29.99

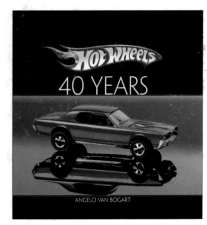

HOT WHEELS: FORTY YEARS
by Angelo Van Bogart, with photography by Doug Mitchel

Forty years of Hot Wheels history is celebrated in 600 superb color photos, company history, interviews with Mattel designers, and innovation insight about Redlines, Blackwalls, Prototypes and more.

Hardcover w/jacket • 10¾" x 10¾" • 256 pages
600+ color photos
Item# Z1047 • $30.00

WARMAN'S® LUNCH BOXES FIELD GUIDE
Values and Identification
by Karen O'Brien and Joe Soucy

This compact and affordable identification guide features fantastic photos and current collector prices for 600 metal lunch boxes, many with bottles, made in the early 1950s and during the lunch box revival of the 1980s.

Softcover • 4³⁄₁₆" x 5³⁄₁₆" • 512 pages
700 color photos
Item# Z2700 • $12.99

Order directly from the publisher at **www.krausebooks.com**

Krause Publications, Offer **ACB8**
P.O. Box 5009
Iola, WI 54945-5009
www.krausebooks.com

Call **800-258-0929** 8 a.m. - 5 p.m. to order direct from the publisher, or visit booksellers nationwide or antiques and hobby shops.

Please reference offer **ACB8** with all direct-to-publisher orders